Bret Harte

Idyls of the foothills. In prose and verse

Bret Harte

Idyls of the foothills. In prose and verse

ISBN/EAN: 9783742823236

Manufactured in Europe, USA, Canada, Australia, Japa

Cover: Foto ©Andreas Hilbeck / pixelio.de

Manufactured and distributed by brebook publishing software (www.brebook.com)

Bret Harte

Idyls of the foothills. In prose and verse

"THE TAUCHNITZ COLLECTION"

is allowed to circulate among the University officers, professors, and students, only on condition that the Librarian shall permanently withdraw from circulation any volume which is out of print, and that all volumes lost or unfit for use shall be promptly replaced by the Librarian at the University's expense.

EACH VOLUME SOLD SEPARATELY.

Stanton.

COLLECTION
OF
BRITISH AUTHORS

TAUCHNITZ EDITION.

VOL. 1450.

IDYLS OF THE FOOTHILLS BY BRET HARTE.

IN ONE VOLUME.

LEIPZIG: BERNHARD TAUCHNITZ.

PARIS: C. REINWALD & CIE, 15, RUE DES SAINTS-PÈRES.

PARIS: THE GALIGNANI LIBRARY, 224, RUE DE RIVOLI, AND AT NICE, 16, QUAI MASSENA.

This Collection is published with copyright for Continental circulation, but all purchasers are earnestly requested not to introduce the volumes into England or into any British Colony.

COLLECTION
OF
BRITISH AUTHORS

TAUCHNITZ EDITION.

VOL. 1450.

IDYLS OF THE FOOTHILLS BY BRET HARTE.

IN ONE VOLUME.

TAUCHNITZ EDITION.

By the same Author,

PROSE AND POETRY (TALES OF THE ARGONAUTS; SPANISH AND AMERICAN LEGENDS; CONDENSED NOVELS; CIVIC AND CHARACTER SKETCHES; POEMS)	2 vols.
GABRIEL CONROY	2 vols.
TWO MEN OF SANDY BAR	1 vol.
THANKFUL BLOSSOM AND OTHER TALES . .	1 vol.
THE STORY OF A MINE	1 vol.
DRIFT FROM TWO SHORES	1 vol.
AN HEIRESS OF RED DOG & OTHER SKETCHES	1 vol.
THE TWINS OF TABLE MOUNTAIN, ETC. . .	1 vol.
JEFF BRIGGS'S LOVE STORY	1 vol.
FLIP AND OTHER STORIES	1 vol.

IDYLS

OF THE FOOTHILLS.

IN PROSE AND VERSE.

BY

BRET HARTE.

AUTHORIZED EDITION.

LEIPZIG
BERNHARD TAUCHNITZ
1874.

CONTENTS.

PROSE.

	Page
Bret Harte, a Sketch	9
Author's Preface (to Continental Edition)	17
A Passage in the Life of Mr. John Oakhurst	21
The Rose of Tuolumne	53
An Episode of Fiddletown	88
A Monte Flat Pastoral	152
Baby Sylvester	177
Wan Lee, the Pagan	199

IN VERSE.

	Page
Luke	225
"The Babes in the Woods"	231
Guild's Signal	235
Truthful James to the Editor	238
Don Diego of the South	241
"For the King"	246
Friar Pedro's Ride	255
Miss Blanche Says	262
Dolly Varden	267

CONTENTS.

	Page
Caldwell of Springfield	270
Poem	273
At the Hacienda	277
What the Chimney Sang	278

PROSE.

BRET HARTE.

Some ten years ago, Thomas Starr King, then unknowingly near the end of his short but noble and glowing life, was guiding an acquaintance through the dingy, gold-strewn recesses of the Government Mint building in San Francisco. Pausing before entering the secretary's little office, he said: "Now I want you to meet a young man who will be heard of far and wide some of these days." The visitor went in and was introduced to Francis Bret Harte, then secretary of the Branch Mint. We all know how the later career of the young writer has more than justified the affectionate prediction of Starr King; for, since that day, Bret Harte's fame has, to borrow the language of his admiring German translator, "extended from the coasts of the Pacific Ocean to the English coast of the North Sea." "His works have drawn hearts to him wherever the language of Shakespeare, of Milton, and Byron is spoken."

A man who has so many readers must needs inspire a kindly curiosity to know something of the antecedents in a life which has given such generous promise of nobler works to come. Mr. Harte was born at Albany, New York, in 1839. He was christened Francis Bret Harte; but the second name, —an old family one,—was that by which he was familiarly known among home friends and acquaintances. Later in life, the initial of his Christian name was dropped altogether, and the world learned to know and love him by the somewhat crisp title of "Bret Harte."

Young Harte grew up surrounded by refining influences; his father was a teacher of girls, and a ripe and cultured student withal. Left fatherless, Harte wandered off to California in 1854, dazzled with the golden visions which then transfigured that distant land; and, won by the fantastic romance with which stories of the early Spanish occupation, sudden wealth, surprising adventure, and novel life and scenery invested the country, he cast himself into the changeful stream of humanity which ebbed and flowed among the young cities by the sea, the pine-clad ridges of the Sierra, and the rude camps of the gold-hunters which were then breaking the stillness of long unvexed solitudes. No age nor condition, no quality of manhood, nor grade of moral or mental culture was unrepresented in that motley tide of migration. The dreamy young student, the future poet of the Argonauts of 1849, drifted on with the rest.

For two or three years, he, like all the restless wanderers of those days, pursued a various calling and had no fixed abode. An unsatisfied desire for change, a half-confessed impatience with long tarrying in any spot, seemed to possess every soul.

Mining camps and even thrifty towns were depopulated in a single day, the unnoted casualties of their rough life emptying a few places, the rest being eagerly left behind by men who drifted far and wide; their lately coveted "claims" were quickly occupied by other rovers from other fields. Harte mined a little, taught school a little, tried his hand at type-setting and frontier journalism, climbed mountains and threaded ravines as the mounted messenger of an express company, or acted as agent for that company in some of the mountain towns which we have learned to know so well as Sandy Bar, Poker Flat, and Wingdam. But all the while the lithe, agile, and alert young artist was absorbing impressions of the picturesque life, scenery, manners, and talk which surrounded him as an atmosphere.

In 1857, or thereabouts, he drifted back to San Francisco—"The Bay," as the pleasant city by the sea was fondly called by the wandering sons of adventure. The Bay was the little heaven where were cool sea-winds, good cheer, and glimpses of that sensuous life which was then thought of as a far-off, faintly-remembered good found only in "the States." Here Harte speedily developed into a clever young *littérateur*. Working in the composing-room of a weekly literary journal, he put into type some of his own graceful little sketches by way of experiment. These were noticed and appreciated by the editor, and he was translated from "the case" to the editorial room of *The Golden Era*, where some of the pleasant papers which find place in his later published works were written. These were chiefly local sketches, like "A Boy's Dog," "Sidewalkings" and "From a Balcony." Meantime marriage and the cares of a growing household had changed the vagrant fancy of the young writer, and he roved no more. He wrote a great deal which has not been gathered up, and in the columns of daily papers, as well as in *The Californian*, a literary weekly which he some time edited, appeared innumerable papers which enriched the current literature of those times, and swelled the volume of that higher quality of California journalism which seems now to have passed quite away.

In 1864 he was appointed Secretary of the United States Branch Mint in San Francisco, a position which, during the six years he held it, gave him time and opportunity for more careful work than any which he had heretofore accomplished. During this time some of the most famous of his poems and sketches were written. "John Burns of Gettysburg," "The Pliocene Skull," "The Society upon the Stanislow," "How are you, Sanitary?" and other little unique gems of verse were written about this time and first appeared (for the most part) anonymously in the San Francisco newspapers. In July, 1868, the publication of *The Overland Monthly* was begun, with Bret Harte as its organizer and editor. The success of the magazine was immediate and decided. We cannot tell how much of its renown was owing to the series of remarkable stories which immediately began to flow from the pen of its accomplished editor, nor how much to the rare talent which he seems to have had in awaking the dormant energies of those who constituted his loyal staff of contributors. *The Overland* became at once a unique, piquant and highly-desired element in the current literature of the Republic; and it found a multitude of readers on both sides of the Atlantic. In its pages, August, 1868, appeared "The Luck of Roaring Camp," a story which, whatever may be the merits of those which have succeeded it, gave Harte the first of his great fame as a prose-writer. But it was not until January of the next year that the stimulated appetite of the impatient public was appeased by the production of "The Outcasts of Poker Flat," a dramatic tale which probably contains more firmly-drawn and distinct characters than have appeared in any one of Harte's stories or sketches. "Miggles" came next, and, marshaled in their long array, the inimitable personages who figure in still later stories emerged from their shadowy realm and passed into the language and familiar acquaintance of the English-speaking world. Col. Starbottle, John Oakhurst, Stumpy, Tennessee's Partner and Miggles—with laughter and with tears we remember them all; we shall know them as long as we know Sam Weller, Micawber, Little Nell and the goodly company called into being by that other magician who has, at last, laid down his wand forever.

Harte's poems are more thickly scattered through his later work in California than elsewhere. Some of the best-known were written between 1865 and

1870; "Plain Language from Truthful James," popularly quoted as the "Heathen Chinee," appeared in *The Overland* of September, 1870. A more ambitious work, "The Lost Galleon," was an earlier production, and gave title to a thin volume of fugitive bits of verse published in San Francisco a year or two before. Harte's first book was the *Condensed Novels*, a collection of wonderful imitations, too real to be called parodies, first printed in *The Californian*, published in a poorly executed volume in New York, called in and republished and reinforced in 1871. Four new volumes have issued from the pen of the poet-storyteller, and a great constituency hungrily waits for more.

In the Spring of 1871, Harte, resigning the editorial position which he held, as well as the Professorship of Recent Literature in the University of California, to which he had lately been called, returned to his native State with the ripened powers and generous fame which he had gathered during his seventeen years of absence. When his life shall have been adjusted to the new conditions which meet here any long-absent wanderer, we shall, no doubt, see the somewhat wavering panorama of his genius move on more steadily, glowing with more vivid colors and crowded with more life-like shapes than any which his magical touch has yet placed on canvas.

What Harte's repute and standing are in his own land need not now be told. Few writers of modern times have been more discussed; it were better if his critics had always been generous as well as just. But it would not be fair to close this little sketch without noting the fact that most of his works have found eager readers in other lands. English editions of his stories are popular and widely circulated. In Germany, the genial old poet, Ferdinand Freiligrath, has translated a volume of Harte's prose tales, to which is prefixed a charming preface by the translator. We cannot forbear making this extract, so full of the simple-hearted Freiligrath's goodness:—

"Nevertheless he remains what he is—the Californian and the gold-digger. But the gold for which he has dug, and which he found, is not the gold in the bed of rivers,—not the gold in the veins of mountains; it is the gold of love, of goodness, of fidelity, of humanity, which even in rude and wild hearts,—even under the rubbish of vices and sins,—remains forever uneradicated from the human heart. That he there searched for this gold, —that he found it there and triumphantly exhibited it to the world,—that is his greatness and his merit. That it is which drew hearts to him wherever the language of Shakespeare, of Milton and Byron is spoken. And that it is which has made me, the old German poet, the translator of the young American colleague; and which has led me to-day to reach to him warmly and cordially my hand across the sea. Good luck, Bret Harte! Good luck, my gold-digger!"

Th. Dentzon has charmingly introduced some of Harte's California sketches to the French world of readers, and, in an article in the *Revue des Deux*

Mondes, he has given at great length a critical analysis of the powers and genius of our favorite story-teller. Our French and German friends alike wrestle with the difficulties of the untranslatable; but, *malgré* their failure to master the dialect of the gold-digger, they reproduce admirably the delicate finish and felicitous manipulation of the author. Thus his genius has found expression in many languages, and the gentle, loving spirit which animates his works lives and walks in other lands beyond the sea.

AUTHOR'S PREFACE.

A PREFACE to these little stories, of which the present edition, published by Baron Tauchnitz, is the only authorized one on the Continent of Europe, may seem somewhat gratuitous to that English reading audience who have good humoredly accepted my previous performances without special introduction from their author. But as I am partly responsible for this present publication on the Continent, I am emboldened to address myself more confidently to those English readers with whom I am thus brought into closer relation.

Otherwise there would be little to add to the few words with which "The Luck of Roaring Camp" was first introduced to the American public. Since the publication of that work California has become better known and more accessible. The completion of the Pacific Railway, and the increased facilities for speedy transit have placed that hitherto isolated community within easy reach of the ordinary tourist. The Sierra Nevada—that Chinese wall of California exclusiveness—has been pierced to let in the foreigner. Already there are ominously shaven faces and Poole's coats to be seen on Montgomery

Street, tweed suits on railways, and the obvious print of an English walking shoe in the red dust of the mountains.

It may be well imagined that these conditions are disastrous to the writer of dramatic romance, who would fain keep his little stage from the invasion of the critic in the stalls, or the enthusiast in the boxes. It is very possible that this scenery, so effective from the gallery, is mean in detail; these flats, so striking at a little distance, viewed closely are but broad splatches of color. Even the performers may suffer. This hero, lounging at the wings, is unmistakably loud and unpleasant, this little lady, whose Magdalen virtues made us weep only a moment ago, is certainly no better than she should be.

To this hypothetical criticism I fear I must add the more practical view of a patriotic local press, namely, that no idea consistent with material progress, conducive to immigration or appreciative of real estate, is to be gathered from these pages, and that the "Luck of Roaring Camp" is not to be accepted by the casual visitor with the same profit and security that obtains with recent works upon the resources of California. Let me briefly add for the benefit of those who have a pecuniary or business interest in that country, that the characters and elements herein described belong to an era long past, and now no longer found except in localities remote from the populous centres; that life and property are, in the larger cities, as safe as they are in Broadway or the Strand; that Vigilance

Committees no longer patrol the streets; and that the tourist of to-day will meet nothing more dangerous than the native wine, or more aggressive than the native hospitality.

An explanation of this change—a change that leaves behind it so little of the past even in debris or ruin—may be necessary to those who are more familiar with the results than the peculiar processes of American civilization. The real pioneer or adventurer, like his prototype, the Indian, retires before improvement and progress, and seldom remains to be civilized or merged into the commonalty. He lives to form the nucleus of another settlement, perhaps one or two more, with precisely the same result. The conditions of San Francisco life in 1849, were repeated in Sacramento in '50, in the Southern Mines in '54, in Virginia City in '60, and in every one of the later discovered mining districts —by the same actors. The *dramatis personæ* were the same; the incidents were monotonously alike. The climaxes were identical. Judge Lynch rode a circuit in California. But it was most remarkable that the actors left no trace nor impress on the after civilization. Their footprints vanished utterly and were swallowed up. They left no memorial even in the shape of a ruin; their very vices were not the vices of to-day. It is to be even feared that they did not meet that fate which was the logical conclusion of their lives and deeds; that, pointing no moral whatever, they flourished and still flourish in remoter regions in abiding and efflorescent impropriety, without reform and without punishment. A very small proportion only have been elected to legislative functions, or appointed to office.

I like to think, however, that there may be some kindlier readers who, even at the risk of being thought sentimental, will still love to linger with me over those scenes that suffering, weakness, and sin have made human.

I believe that it will not be necessary for them to draw any moral that shall be inconsistent with their experience or knowledge of a higher plane of life than it has been my lot to study and transcribe. It is only three years ago that I stood upon that spot of which my readers have learned something in its fictitious title of "Roaring Camp." The sun shone as vividly, the hillsides looked as green, and the outlying pines as sedate and reticent as on the first day I saw it. But a new and thriving settlement stood upon the river bank, and of the settlers but one remembered the past history of the camp. At the head of the gulch a few children were playing under a large pine tree. I knew that at its roots lay the dust of one who had walked these pages under another name than that which had been obliterated from the bark of the tree, and was now forgotten. It was the name of a man of desperate deeds, of many sins, and baleful example. But looking at the children I could only tell them, in reply to their artless questioning, how long ago he had been singularly kind to a truant school-boy.

BRET HARTE.

A PASSAGE IN THE LIFE OF MR. JOHN OAKHURST.

HE always thought it must have been Fate. Certainly nothing could have been more inconsistent with his habits than to have been in the Plaza at seven o'clock of that midsummer morning. The sight of his colorless face in Sacramento was rare at that season, and indeed at any season, anywhere, publicly, before two o'clock in the afternoon. Looking back upon it in after years, in the light of a chanceful life, he determined, with the characteristic philosophy of his profession, that it must have been Fate.

Yet it is my duty, as a strict chronicler of facts, to state that Mr. Oakhurst's presence there that morning was due to a very simple cause. At exactly half-past six, the bank being then a winner to the amount of twenty thousand dollars, he had risen from the faro table, relinquished his seat to an accomplished assistant, and withdrawn quietly, without attracting a glance from the silent, anxious faces bowed over the table. But when he entered his luxurious sleeping-room, across the passage-way, he was a little shocked at finding the sun streaming through an inadvertently-opened window. Something in the rare beauty of the morning, perhaps something in the novelty of the idea, struck him as he was about to close the blinds, and he hesitated. Then, taking his hat from the table, he stepped down a private staircase into the street.

The people who were abroad at that early hour were of a class quite unknown to Mr. Oakhurst. There were milkmen and hucksters delivering their wares, small trades-people opening their shops, house-maids sweeping door-steps, and occasionally a child. These Mr. Oakhurst regarded with a certain cold curiosity, perhaps quite free from the cynical disfavor with which he generally looked upon the more pretentious of his race whom he was in the habit of meeting. Indeed, I think he was not altogether displeased with the admiring glances which these humble women threw after his handsome face and figure, conspicuous even in a country of fine-looking men. While it is very probable that this wicked vagabond, in the pride of his social isolation, would have been coldly indifferent to the advances of a fine lady, a little girl who ran admiringly by his side in a ragged dress had the power to call a faint flush into his colorless cheek. He dismissed her at last, but not until she had found out—what sooner or later her large-hearted and discriminating sex inevitably did—that he was exceedingly free and open-handed with his money, and also—what perhaps none other of her sex ever did—that the bold, black eyes of this fine gentleman were in reality of a brownish and even tender gray.

There was a small garden before a white cottage in a side street that attracted Mr. Oakhurst's attention. It was filled with roses, heliotrope and verbena—flowers familiar enough to him in the expensive and more portable form of bouquets, but, as it seemed to him then, never before so notably lovely. Perhaps it was because the dew was yet fresh upon them, perhaps it was because they were unplucked, but Mr. Oakhurst admired them, not as a possible future tribute to the fascinating and accomplished Miss Ethelinda, then performing at the Varieties, for Mr. Oakhurst's especial benefit as she had often assured him—nor yet as a *douceur* to the enthralling Miss Montmorrissy, with whom Mr. Oakhurst expected to sup that evening, but simply for himself, and mayhap for the flowers' sake. Howbeit he passed on and so out into the open plaza, where, finding a bench under a cotton-wood tree, he first dusted the seat with his handkerchief, and then sat down.

It was a fine morning. The air was so still and calm that a sigh from the sycamores seemed like the deep-drawn breath of the just awakening tree, and the faint rustle of its boughs as the outstretching of cramped and reviving limbs. Far away the Sierras stood out against a sky so remote as to be of no positive color; so remote that even the sun despaired of ever reaching it, and so expended its strength recklessly on the whole landscape, until it fairly glittered in a white and vivid contrast. With a very rare impulse, Mr. Oakhurst took off his hat, and half reclined on the bench, with his face to the sky. Certain birds who had taken a critical attitude on a spray above him, apparently began an animated discussion regarding his possible malevolent intentions. One or two, emboldened by the silence, hopped on the ground at his feet, until the sound of wheels on the gravel walk frightened them away.

Looking up, he saw a man coming slowly toward him, wheeling a nondescript vehicle in which a woman was partly sitting, partly reclining. Without knowing why, Mr. Oakhurst instantly conceived that the carriage was the invention and workmanship of the man, partly from its oddity, partly from the strong, mechanical hand that grasped it, and partly from a certain pride and visible consciousness in the manner in which the man handled it. Then Mr. Oakhurst saw something more; the man's face was familiar. With that regal faculty of not forgetting a face that had ever given him professional audience, he instantly classified it under the following mental formula: "At 'Frisco, Polka Saloon. Lost his week's wages. I reckon—seventy dollars—on red. Never came again." There was, however, no trace of this in the calm eyes and unmoved face that he turned upon the stranger, who, on the contrary, blushed, looked embarrassed, hesitated, and then stopped with an involuntary motion that brought the carriage and its fair occupant face to face with Mr. Oakhurst.

I should hardly do justice to the position she will occupy in this veracious chronicle by describing the lady now—if, indeed, I am able to do it at all. Certainly, the popular estimate was conflicting. The late Col. Starbottle—to whose large experience of a charming sex I have before been indebted for many valuable suggestions—had, I regret to say, depreciated her fascinations. "A yellow-faced cripple, by dash—a sick woman, with mahogany eyes. One of your blanked spiritual creatures—with no flesh on her bones." On the other hand, however, she enjoyed later much complimentary disparagement from her own sex. Miss Celestina Howard, second leader in the *ballet* at the Varieties, had, with great alliterative directness, in after years, denominated her as an "aquiline asp." Mlle. Brimborion remembered that she had always warned "Mr. Jack" that this woman would "empoison" him. But Mr. Oakhurst, whose impressions are perhaps the most important, only saw a pale, thin, deep-eyed woman —raised above the level of her companion by the refinement of long suffering and isolation, and a certain shy virginity of manner. There was a suggestion of physical purity in the folds of her fresh-looking robe, and a certain picturesque tastefulness in the details, that, without knowing why, made him think that the robe was her invention and handiwork, even as the carriage she occupied was evidently the work of her companion. Her own hand, a trifle too thin, but well-shaped, subtle-fingered, and gentlewomanly, rested on the side of the carriage, the counterpart of the strong mechanical grasp of her companion's.

There was some obstruction to the progress of the vehicle, and Mr. Oakhurst stepped forward to assist. While the wheel was being lifted over the curbstone, it was necessary that she should hold his arm, and for a moment her thin hand rested there, light and cold as a snow-flake, and then—as it seemed to him—like a snow-flake melted away. Then there was a pause, and then conversation—the lady joining occasionally and shyly.

It appeared that they were man and wife. That for the past two years she had been a great invalid, and had lost the use of her lower limbs from rheumatism. That until lately she had been confined to her bed, until her husband—who was a master carpenter—had bethought himself to make her this carriage. He took her out regularly for an airing before going to work, because it was his only time, and—they attracted less attention. They had tried many doctors, but without avail. They had been advised to go to the Sulphur Springs, but it was expensive. Mr. Decker, the husband, had once saved eighty dollars for that purpose, but while in San Francisco had his pocket picked—Mr. Decker was so senseless. (The intelligent reader need not be told that it is the lady who is speaking.) They had never been able to make up the sum again, and they had given up the idea. It was a dreadful thing to have one's pocket picked. Did he did not think so?

Her husband's face was crimson, but Mr. Oakhurst's countenance was quite calm and unmoved, as he gravely agreed with her, and walked by her side until they passed the little garden that he had admired. Here Mr. Oakhurst commanded a halt, and, going to the door, astounded the proprietor by a preposterously extravagant offer for a choice of the flowers. Presently he returned to the carriage with his arms full of roses, heliotrope, and verbena, and cast them in the lap of the invalid. While she was bending over them with childish delight, Mr. Oakhurst took the opportunity of drawing her husband aside.

"Perhaps," he said, in a low voice, and a manner quite free from any personal annoyance, "perhaps it's just as well that you lied to her as you did. You can say now that the pickpocket was arrested the other day, and you got your money back." Mr. Oakhurst quietly slipped four twenty-dollar gold pieces into the broad hand of the bewildered Mr. Decker. "Say that—or anything you like—but the truth. Promise me you won't say that!"

The man promised. Mr. Oakhurst quietly returned to the front of the little carriage. The sick woman was still eagerly occupied with the flowers, and as she raised her eyes to his her faded cheek seemed to have caught some color from the roses, and her eyes some of their dewy freshness. But at that instant Mr. Oakhurst lifted his hat, and before she could thank him was gone.

I grieve to say that Mr. Decker shamelessly broke his promise. That night, in the very goodness of his heart and uxorious self-abnegation—he, like all devoted husbands, not only offered himself, but his friend and benefactor, as a sacrifice on the family altar. It is only fair, however, to add that he spoke with great fervor of the generosity of Mr.

Oakhurst, and dealt with an enthusiasm quite common with his class on the mysterious fame and prodigal vices of the gambler.

"And now, Elsie dear, say that you'll forgive me," said Mr. Decker, dropping on one knee beside his wife's couch; "I did it for the best. It was for you, dearey, that I put that money on them cards that night in 'Frisco. I thought to win a heap— enough to take you away, and enough left to get you a new dress."

Mrs. Decker smiled and pressed her husband's hand. "I do forgive you, Joe, dear," she said, still smiling, with eyes abstractedly fixed on the ceiling; "and you ought to be whipped for deceiving me so, you bad boy, and making me make such a speech. There, say no more about it. If you'll be very good hereafter, and will just now hand me that cluster of roses, I'll forgive you." She took the branch in her fingers, lifted the roses to her face, and presently said, behind their leaves:

"Joe!"

"What is it, lovey?"

"Do you think that this Mr.—what do you call him?—Jack Oakhurst would have given that money back to you if I hadn't made that speech?"

"Yes."

"If he hadn't seen me at all?"

Mr. Decker looked up. His wife had managed in some way to cover up her whole face with the roses, except her eyes, which were dangerously bright.

"No; it was you, Elsie—it was all along of seeing you that made him do it."

"A poor sick woman like me?"

"A sweet, little, lovely, pooty Elsie—Joe's own little wifey! How could he help it?"

Mrs. Decker fondly cast one arm around her husband's neck, still keeping the roses to her face with the other. From behind them she began to murmur gently and idiotically, "Dear, ole square Joey. Elsie's oney booful big bear." But, really, I do not see that my duty as a chronicler of facts compels me to continue this little lady's speech any further, and out of respect to the unmarried reader I stop.

Nevertheless, the next morning Mrs. Decker betrayed some slight and apparently uncalled-for irritability on reaching the plaza, and presently desired her husband to wheel her back home. Moreover, she was very much astonished at meeting Mr. Oakhurst just as they were returning, and even doubted if it were he, and questioned her husband as to his identity with the stranger of yesterday as he approached. Her manner to Mr. Oakhurst, also, was quite in contrast with her husband's frank welcome. Mr. Oakhurst instantly detected it. "Her husband has told her all, and she dislikes me," he said to himself, with that fatal appreciation of the half truths of a woman's motives that causes the wisest masculine critic to stumble. He lingered only long enough to take the business address of the husband and then lifting his hat gravely, without looking at the lady, went his way. It struck the honest master carpenter as one of the charming anomalies of his wife's character, that, although the meeting was evidently very much constrained and unpleasant, instantly afterward his wife's spirits began to rise. "You was hard on him—a leetle hard, wasn't you, Elsie?" said Mr. Decker deprecatingly —"I'm afraid he may think I've broke my promise." "Ah, indeed," said the lady indifferently. Mr. Decker instantly stepped round to the front of the vehicle. "You look like an A1 first-class lady riding down Broadway in her own carriage, Elsie," said he; "I never seed you lookin' so peart and sassy before."

A few days later the proprietor of the San Isabel Sulphur Springs received the following note in Mr. Oakhurst's well-known dainty hand:

DEAR STEVE: I've been thinking over your proposition to buy Nichols' quarter interest, and have concluded to go in. But I don't see how the thing will pay until you have more accommodation down there, and for the best class—I mean *my* customers. What we want is an extension to the main building, and two or three cottages put up. I send down a builder to take hold of the job at once. He takes his sick wife with him, and you are to look after them as you would for one of us.

I may run down there myself, after the races, just to look after things; but I sha'n't set upon any game this season.
Yours always,
JOHN OAKHURST.

It was only the last sentence of this letter that provoked criticism: "I can understand," said Mr. Hamlin, a professional brother, to whom Mr. Oakhurst's letter was shown, "I can understand why Jack goes in heavy and builds, for it's a sure spec, and is bound to be a mighty soft thing in time, if

he comes here regularly. But why in blank he
don't set up a bank this season and take the chance
of getting some of the money back that he puts
into circulation in building, is what gets me. I
wonder now," he mused deeply, "what *is* his little
game."

The season had been a prosperous one to Mr.
Oakhurst, and proportionally disastrous to several
members of the Legislature, Judges, Colonels, and
others who had enjoyed but briefly the pleasure of
Mr. Oakhurst's midnight society. And yet Sacramento had become very dull to him. He had
lately formed a habit of early-morning walks—so
unusual and startling to his friends, both male and
female, as to occasion the intensest curiosity. Two
or three of the latter set spies upon his track, but
the inquisition resulted only in the discovery that
Mr. Oakhurst walked to the plaza, sat down upon
one particular bench for a few moments, and then
returned without seeing anybody, and the theory
that there was a woman in the case was abandoned.
A few superstitious gentlemen of his own profession
believed that he did it for "luck." Some others,
more practical, declared that he went out to "study
points."

After the races at Marysville, Mr. Oakhurst went
to San Francisco; from that place he returned to
Marysville, but a few days after was seen at San
José, Santa Cruz, and Oakland. Those who met
him declared that his manner was restless and
feverish, and quite unlike his ordinary calmness and
phlegm. Col. Starbottle pointed out the fact that

at San Francisco at the club, Jack had declined to deal. "Hand shaky, Sir; depend upon it; don't stimulate enough—blank him!"

From San José he started to go to Oregon by land with a rather expensive outfit of horses and camp equipage, but on reaching Stockton he suddenly diverged, and four hours later found him with a single horse entering the cañon of the San Isabel Warm Sulphur Springs.

It was a pretty triangular valley lying at the foot of three sloping mountains, dark with pines and fantastic with madroño and manzanita. Nestling against the mountain side, the straggling buildings and long piazza of the hotel glittered through the leaves; and here and there shone a white toy-like cottage. Mr. Oakhurst was not an admirer of nature, but he felt something of the same novel satisfaction in the view that he experienced in his first morning walk in Sacramento. And now carriages began to pass him on the road filled with gayly-dressed women, and the cold, California outlines of the landscape began to take upon themselves somewhat of a human warmth and color. And then the long hotel piazza came in view, efflorescent with the full-toiletted fair. Mr. Oakhurst, a good rider, after the California fashion, did not check his speed as he approached his destination, but charged the hotel at a gallop, threw his horse on his haunches within a foot of the piazza, and then quietly emerged from the cloud of dust that veiled his dismounting.

Whatever feverish excitement might have raged within, all his habitual calm returned as he stepped upon the piazza. With the instinct of long habit he turned and faced the battery of eyes with the same cold indifference with which he had for years encountered the half-hidden sneers of men and the half-frightened admiration of women. Only one person stepped forward to welcome him. Oddly enough, it was Dick Hamilton, perhaps the only one present who, by birth, education, and position might have satisfied the most fastidious social critic. Happily for Mr. Oakhurst's reputation, he was also a very rich banker and social leader. "Do you know who that is you spoke to?" asked young Parker, with an alarmed expression. "Yes;" replied Hamilton, with characteristic effrontery, "the man you lost a thousand dollars to last week. *I* only know him *socially.*" "But isn't he a gambler?" queried the youngest Miss Smith. "He is," replied Hamilton, "but I wish, my dear young lady, that we all played as open and honest a game as our friend yonder, and were as willing as he is to abide by its fortunes."

But Mr. Oakhurst was happily out of hearing of this colloquy, and was even then lounging listlessly, yet watchfully, along the upper hall. Suddenly he heard a light footstep behind him, and then his name called in a familiar voice that drew the blood quickly to his heart. He turned and she stood before him.

But how transformed! If I have hesitated to describe the hollow-eyed cripple — the quaintly-dressed artisan's wife, a few pages ago — what shall I do with this graceful, shapely, elegantly-attired gentlewoman into whom she has been merged within these two months? In good faith she was very pretty. You and I, my dear madame, would have been quick to see that those charming dimples were misplaced for true beauty, and too fixed in their quality for honest mirthfulness, that the delicate lines around these aquiline nostrils were cruel and selfish, that the sweet virginal surprise of these lovely eyes were as apt to be opened on her plate as upon the gallant speeches of her dinner partner, that her sympathetic color came and went more with her own spirits than yours. But you and I are not in love with her, dear madame, and Mr. Oakhurst is. And even in the folds of her Parisian gown I am afraid this poor fellow saw the same subtle strokes of purity that he had seen in her homespun robe. And then there was the delightful revelation that she could walk, and that she had dear little feet of her own in the tiniest slippers of her French shoemaker—with such preposterous blue bows, and Chappell's own stamp, Rue de something or other, Paris, on the narrow sole.

He ran toward her with a heightened color and outstretched hands. But she whipped her own behind her, glanced rapidly up and down the long hall, and stood looking at him with a half audacious, half mischievous admiration in utter contrast to her old reserve.

"I've a great mind not to shake hands with you, at all. You passed me just now on the piazza without speaking, and I ran after you, as I suppose many another poor woman has done."

Mr. Oakhurst stammered that she was so changed.
"The more reason why you should know me. Who changed me? You. You have recreated me. You found a helpless, crippled, sick, poverty-stricken woman, with one dress to her back, and that her own make, and you gave her life, health, strength, and fortune. You did, and you know it, Sir. How do you like your work?" She caught the side seams of her gown in either hand and dropped him a playful courtesy. Then, with a sudden, relenting gesture, she gave him both her hands.

Outrageous as this speech was, and unfeminine, as I trust every fair reader will deem it, I fear it pleased Mr. Oakhurst. Not but that he was accustomed to a certain frank female admiration; but then it was of the *coulisses* and not of the cloister, with which he always persisted in associating Mrs. Decker. To be addressed in this way by an invalid Puritan, a sick saint, with the austerity of suffering still clothing her; a woman who had a Bible on the dressing-table, who went to church three times a day, and was devoted to her husband, completely bowled him over. He still held her hands as she went on:

"Why didn't you come before? What were you doing in Marysville, in San José, in Oakland? You see I have followed you. I saw you as you came down the cañon, and knew you at once. I saw your letter to Joseph, and knew you were coming. Why didn't you write to me? You will some time! Good evening, Mr. Hamilton."

She had withdrawn her hands, but not until

Hamilton, ascending the staircase, was nearly abreast of them. He raised his hat to her with well-bred composure, nodded familiarly to Oakhurst, and passed on. When he had gone Mrs. Decker lifted her eyes to Mr. Oakhurst. "Some day I shall ask a great favor of you!"

Mr. Oakhurst begged that it should be now. "No, not until you know me better. Then, some day, I shall want you to—kill that man!"

She laughed, such a pleasant little ringing laugh, such a display of dimples—albeit a little fixed in the corners of her mouth—such an innocent light in her brown eyes, and such a lovely color in her cheeks, that Mr. Oakhurst—who seldom laughed—was fain to laugh too. It was as if a lamb had proposed to a fox a foray into a neighboring sheep-fold.

A few evenings after this, Mrs. Decker arose from a charmed circle of her admirers on the hotel piazza, excused herself for a few moments, laughingly declined an escort, and ran over to her little cottage—one of her husband's creation—across the road. Perhaps from the sudden and unwonted exercise in her still convalescent state, she breathed hurriedly and feverishly as she entered her boudoir, and once or twice placed her hand upon her breast. She was startled on turning up the light to find her husband lying on the sofa.

"You look hot and excited, Elsie, love," said Mr. Decker; "you ain't took worse—are you?"

Mrs. Decker's face had paled, but now flushed

again. "No," she said, "only a little pain here," as she again placed her hand upon her corsage.

"Can I do anything for you," said Mr. Decker, rising with affectionate concern.

"Run over to the hotel and get me some brandy, quick!"

Mr. Decker ran. Mrs. Decker closed and bolted the door, and then putting her hand to her bosom, drew out the pain. It was folded four square, and was, I grieve to say, in Mr. Oakhurst's handwriting. She devoured it with burning eyes and cheeks until there came a step upon the porch. Then she hurriedly replaced it in her bosom and unbolted the door. Her husband entered; she raised the spirits to her lips and declared herself better.

"Are you going over there again to-night," asked Mr. Decker, submissively.

"No," said Mrs. Decker, with her eyes fixed dreamily on the floor.

"I wouldn't if I was you," said Mr. Decker with a sigh of relief. After a pause he took a seat on the sofa, and drawing his wife to his side, said: "Do you know what I was thinking of when you came in, Elsie?" Mrs. Decker ran her fingers through his stiff black hair, and couldn't imagine.

"I was thinking of old times, Elsie; I was thinking of the days when I built that kerridge for you, Elsie—when I used to take you out to ride, and was both hoss and driver! We was poor then, and you was sick, Elsie, but we was happy. We've got money now, and a house, and you're quite another woman. I may say, dear, that you're a *new* woman.

And that's where the trouble comes in. I could build you a kerridge, Elsie; I could build you a house, Elsie—but there I stopped. I couldn't build up *you*. You're strong and pretty, Elsie, and fresh and new. But somehow, Elsie, you ain't no work of mine!"

He paused. With one hand laid gently on his forehead and the other pressed upon her bosom as if to feel certain of the presence of her pain, she said sweetly and soothingly:

"But it was your work, dear."

Mr. Decker shook his head sorrowfully. "No, Elsie, not mine. I had the chance to do it once and I let it go. It's done now; but not by me."

Mrs. Decker raised her surprised, innocent eyes to his. He kissed her tenderly and then went on in a more cheerful voice.

"That ain't all I was thinking of, Elsie. I was thinking that may be you give too much of your company to that Mr. Hamilton. Not that there's any wrong in it, to you or him. But it might make people talk. You're the only one here, Elsie," said the master carpenter, looking fondly at his wife, "who isn't talked about: whose work ain't inspected or condemned?"

Mrs. Decker was glad he had spoken about it. She had thought so, too, but she could not well be uncivil to Mr. Hamilton, who was a fine gentleman, without making a powerful enemy. "And he's always treated me as if I was a born lady in his own circle," added the little woman, with a certain pride that made her husband fondly smile. "But I have thought of a plan. He will not stay here if I should go away. If, for instance, I went to San Francisco to visit Ma for a few days he would be gone before I should return."

Mr. Decker was delighted. "By all means," he said, "go to-morrow. Jack Oakhurst is going down, and I'll put you in his charge."

Mrs. Decker did not think it was prudent. "Mr. Oakhurst is our friend, Joseph, but you know his reputation." In fact she did not know that she ought to go now, knowing that he was going the same day—but with a kiss Mr. Decker overcame her scruples. She yielded gracefully. Few women, in fact, knew how to give up a point as charmingly as she.

She stayed a week in San Francisco. When she returned she was a trifle thinner and paler than she had been. This she explained as the result of perhaps too active exercise and excitement. "I was out of doors nearly all the time, as Ma will tell you," she said to her husband, "and always alone. I am getting quite independent now," she added, gayly, "I don't want any escort—I believe, Joey dear, I could get along even without you—I'm so brave!"

But her visit, apparently, had not been productive of her impelling design. Mr. Hamilton had not gone, but had remained, and called upon them that very evening. "I've thought of a plan, Joey dear," said Mrs. Decker when he had departed. "Poor Mr. Oakhurst has a miserable room at the hotel—suppose you ask him when he returns from San Francisco to stop with us. He can have our spare room. I don't think," she added archly, "that Mr. Hamilton will call often." Her husband laughed, intimated that she was a little coquette, pinched her cheek, and complied. "The queer thing about a woman," he said afterward confidentially to Mr. Oakhurst, "is, that without having any plan of her own she'll take anybody's and build a house on it entirely different to suit herself. And dern my skin if you'll be able to say whether or not you didn't give the scale and measurements yourself. That's what gets me."

The next week Mr. Oakhurst was installed in the Deckers' cottage. The business relations of her husband and himself were known to all, and her own reputation was above suspicion. Indeed, few women were more popular. She was domestic, she was prudent, she was pious. In a country of great feminine freedom and latitude, she never rode or walked with anybody but her husband; in an epoch of slang and ambiguous expression, she was always precise and formal in her speech; in the midst of a fashion of ostentatious decoration she never wore a diamond, nor a single valuable jewel. She never permitted an indecorum in public; she never countenanced the familiarities of California society. She declaimed against the prevailing tone of infidelity and skepticism in religion. Few people, who were present, will ever forget the dignified yet stately manner with which she rebuked Mr. Hamilton in the public parlor for entering upon the discussion of a work on materialism, lately published,

—and some among them, also will not forget the expression of amused surprise on Mr. Hamilton's face that gradually changed to sardonic gravity as he courteously waived his point. Certainly not Mr. Oakhurst, who, from that moment, began to be uneasily impatient of his friend, and even—if such a term could be applied to any moral quality in Mr. Oakhurst—to fear him.

For, during this time, Mr. Oakhurst had begun to show symptoms of a change in his usual habits. He was seldom, if ever, seen in his old haunts, in a bar-room, or with his old associates. Pink and white notes, in distracted handwriting, accumulated on the dressing-table in his rooms at Sacramento. It was given out in San Francisco that he had some organic disease of the heart for which his physician had prescribed perfect rest. He read more, he took long walks, he sold his fast horses, he went to church.

I have a very vivid recollection of his first appearance there. He did not accompany the Deckers, nor did he go into their pew, but came in as the service commenced, and took a seat quietly in one of the back pews. By some mysterious instinct his presence became presently known to the congregation, some of whom so far forgot themselves, in their curiosity, as to face around and apparently address their responses to him. Before the service was over it was pretty well understood that "miserable sinners" meant Mr. Oakhurst. Nor did this mysterious influence fail to affect the officiating clergyman, who introduced an allusion to

Mr. Oakhurst's calling and habits in a sermon on the architecture of Solomon's Temple, and in a manner so pointed and yet labored as to cause the youngest of us to flame with indignation. Happily, however, it was lost upon Jack—I do not think he even heard it. His handsome, colorless face—albeit a trifle worn and thoughtful—was inscrutable. Only once, during the singing of a hymn, at a certain note in the contralto's voice, there crept into his dark eyes a look of wistful tenderness, so yearning and yet so hopeless that those who were watching him felt their own glisten. Yet I retain a very vivid remembrance of his standing up to receive the benediction, with the suggestion in his manner and tightly-buttoned coat, of taking the fire of his adversary at ten paces. After church he disappeared as quietly as he had entered, and fortunately escaped hearing the comments on his rash act. His appearance was generally considered as an impertinence—attributable only to some wanton fancy—or possibly a bet. One or two thought that the sexton was exceedingly remiss in not turning him out after discovering who he was; and a prominent pew-holder remarked that if he couldn't take his wife and daughters to that church without exposing them to such an influence, he would try to find some church where he could. Another traced Mr. Oakhurst's presence to certain Broad Church radical tendencies, which he regretted to say he had lately noted in their Pastor. Deacon Sawyer, whose delicately organized, sickly wife had already borne him eleven children and died in an ambitious attempt to complete the dozen, avowed that the presence of a person of Mr. Oakhurst's various and indiscriminate gallantries, was an insult to the memory of the deceased, that, as a man, he could not brook.

It was about this time that Mr. Oakhurst, contrasting himself with a conventional world in which he had hitherto rarely mingled, became aware that there was something in his face, figure, and carriage, quite unlike other men—something that if it did not betray his former career, at least showed an individuality and originality that was suspicious. In this belief he shaved off his long, silken mustache, and religiously brushed out his clustering curls every morning. He even went so far as to affect a negligence of dress and hid his small, slim, arched feet in the largest and heaviest walking shoes. There is a story told that he went to his tailor in Sacramento, and asked him to make him a suit of clothes like everybody else. The tailor, familiar with Mr. Oakhurst's fastidiousness, did not know what he meant. "I mean," said Mr. Oakhurst savagely, "something *respectable*—something that doesn't exactly fit me you know." But however Mr. Oakhurst might hide his shapely limbs in homespun and home-made garments, there was something in his carriage, something in the pose of his beautiful head, something in the strong and fine manliness of his presence, something in the perfect and utter discipline and control of his muscles, something in the high repose of his nature—a repose not so much a matter of intellectual ruling as of his very nature—that go where he would and with whom, he was always a notable man in ten thousand. Perhaps this was never so clearly intimated to Mr. Oakhurst as when, emboldened by Mr. Hamilton's advice and assistance and his own predilections, he became a San Francisco broker. Even before objection was made to his presence in the Board—the objection, I remember, was urged very eloquently by Watt Sanders, who was supposed to be the inventor of the "freezing out" system of disposing of poor stock-holders, and who also enjoyed the reputation of having been the impelling cause of Briggs of Tuolumne's ruin and suicide—even before this formal protest of respectability against lawlessness, the aquiline suggestions of Mr. Oakhurst's mien and countenance, not only prematurely fluttered the pigeons, but absolutely occasioned much uneasiness among the fish-hawks, who circled below him with their booty. "Dash me!—but he's as likely to go after us as anybody," said Joe Fielding.

It wanted but a few days before the close of the brief Summer season at San Isabel Warm Springs. Already there had been some migration of the more fashionable, and there was an uncomfortable suggestion of dregs and lees in the social life that remained. Mr. Oakhurst was moody—it was hinted that even the secure reputation of Mrs. Decker could no longer protect her from the gossip which his presence excited. It is but fair to her to say that during the last few weeks of this trying ordeal she looked like a sweet, pale martyr, and conducted herself toward her traducers with the gentle, forgiving manner of one who relied not upon the idle homage of the crowd, but upon the security of a principle that was dearer than popular favor. "They talk about myself and Mr. Oakhurst, my dear," she said to a friend, "but heaven and my husband can best answer their calumny. It never shall be said that my husband ever turned his back upon a friend in the moment of his adversity because the position was changed, because his friend was poor and he was rich." This was the first intimation to the public that Jack had lost money, although it was known generally that the Deckers had lately bought some valuable property in San Francisco.

A few evenings after this an incident occurred which seemed to unpleasantly discord with the general social harmony that had always existed at San Isabel. It was at dinner, and Mr. Oakhurst and Mr. Hamilton, who sat together at a separate table, were observed to rise in some agitation. When they reached the hall, by a common instinct they stepped into a little breakfast-room which was vacant and closed the door. Then Mr. Hamilton turned, with a half-amused, half-serious smile, toward his friend, and said:

"If we are to quarrel, Jack Oakhurst—you and I—in the name of all that is ridiculous, don't let it be about a——!"

I do not know what was the epithet intended. It was either unspoken or lost. For at that very instant Mr. Oakhurst raised a wine-glass and dashed its contents into Hamilton's face.

As they faced each other the men seemed to have changed natures. Mr. Oakhurst was trembling with excitement, and the wine-glass that he returned to the table shivered between his fingers. Mr. Hamilton stood there, grayish white, erect, and dripping. After a pause he said, coldly:

"So be it. But remember!—our quarrel commences here. If I fall by your hand you shall not use it to clear her character; if you fall by mine you shall not be called a martyr. I am sorry it has come to this, but amen!—the sooner now the better."

He turned proudly, dropped his lids over his cold steel-blue eyes as if sheathing a rapier, bowed, and passed coldly out.

They met twelve hours later in a little hollow two miles from the hotel, on the Stockton road. As Mr. Oakhurst received his pistol from Col. Starbottle's hands he said to him, in a low voice: "Whatever turns up or down I shall not return to the hotel. You will find some directions in my room. Go there—" but his voice suddenly faltered, and he turned his glistening eyes away, to his second's intense astonishment. "I've been out a dozen times with Jack Oakhurst," said Col. Starbottle afterward, "and I never saw him anyways cut before. Blank me if I didn't think he was losing his sand, till he walked to position."

The two reports were almost simultaneous. Mr. Oakhurst's right arm dropped suddenly to his side, and his pistol would have fallen from his paralyzed fingers, but the discipline of trained nerve and muscle prevailed, and he kept his grasp until he had shifted it to the other hand, without changing his position. Then there was a silence that seemed interminable, a gathering of two or three dark figures where a smoke curl still lazily floated, and then the hurried, husky, panting voice of Col. Starbottle in his ear: "He's hit hard—through the lungs —you must run for it!"

Jack turned his dark, questioning eyes upon his second, but did not seem to listen—rather seemed to hear some other voice, remoter in the distance. He hesitated, and then made a step forward in the direction of the distant group. Then he paused again as the figures separated, and the surgeon came hastily toward him.

"He would like to speak with you a moment," said the man. "You have little time to lose, I know; but," he added, in a lower voice, "it is my duty to tell you he has still less."

A look of despair, so hopeless in its intensity, swept over Mr. Oakhurst's usually impassive face, that the surgeon started. "You are hit," he said, glancing at Jack's helpless arm.

"Nothing—a mere scratch," said Jack hastily. Then he added, with a bitter laugh, "I'm not in luck to day. But come! We'll see what he wants."

His long, feverish stride outstripped the surgeon's, and in another moment he stood where the dying man lay—like most dying men—the one calm, composed central figure of an anxious group.

Mr. Oakhurst's face was less calm as he dropped on one knee beside him and took his hand. "I want to speak with this gentleman alone," said Hamilton, with something of his old imperious manner, as he turned to those about him. When they drew back, he looked up in Oakhurst's face.

"I've something to tell you, Jack."

His own face was white, but not so white as that which Mr. Oakhurst bent over him—a face so ghastly, with haunting doubts and a hopeless presentiment of coming evil—a face so piteous in its infinite weariness and envy of death that the dying man was touched, even in the languor of dissolution, with a pang of compassion, and the cynical smile faded from his lips.

"Forgive me, Jack," he whispered more feebly, "for what I have to say. I don't say it in anger, but only because it must be said. I could not do my duty to you—I could not die contented until you knew it all. It's a miserable business at best, all around. But it can't be helped now. Only I ought to have fallen by Decker's pistol and not yours."

A flush like fire came into Jack's cheek, and he would have risen, but Hamilton held him fast.

"Listen! in my pocket you will find two letters. Take them—there! You will know the handwriting. But promise you will not read them until you are in a place of safety. Promise me!"

Jack did not speak, but held the letters between his fingers as if they had been burning coals.

"Promise me," said Hamilton, faintly.

"Why?" asked Oakhurst, dropping his friend's hand coldly.

"Because," said the dying man with a bitter smile, "because—when you have read them—you —will—go back—to capture—and death!"

They were his last words. He pressed Jack's hand faintly. Then his grasp relaxed, and he fell back a corpse.

It was nearly ten o'clock at night, and Mrs. Decker reclined languidly upon the sofa with a novel in her hand, while her husband discussed the politics of the country in the bar-room of the hotel. It was a warm night, and the French window looking out upon a little balcony was partly open. Suddenly she heard a foot upon the balcony, and she raised her eyes from the book with a slight start. The next moment the window was hurriedly thrust wide and a man entered.

Mrs. Decker rose to her feet with a little cry of alarm.

"For heaven's sake, Jack, are you mad? He has only gone for a little while—he may return at any moment. Come an hour later—to-morrow— any time when I can get rid of him—but go, now, dear, at once."

Mr. Oakhurst walked toward the door, bolted it, and then faced her without a word. His face was haggard, his coat-sleeve hung loosely over an arm that was bandaged and bloody.

Nevertheless her voice did not falter as she turned again toward him. "What has happened, Jack. Why are you here?"

He opened his coat, and threw two letters in her lap.

"To return your lover's letters—to kill you—and then myself," he said in a voice so low as to be almost inaudible.

Among the many virtues of this admirable woman was invincible courage. She did not faint, she did not cry out. She sat quietly down again, folded her hands in her lap, and said calmly:

"And why should you not?"

Had she recoiled, had she shown any fear or contrition, had she essayed an explanation or apology, Mr. Oakhurst would have looked upon it as an evidence of guilt. But there is no quality that courage recognizes so quickly as courage; there is no condition that desperation bows before but desperation; and Mr. Oakhurst's power of analysis was not so keen as to prevent him from confounding her courage with a moral quality. Even in his fury he could not help admiring this dauntless invalid.

"Why should you not," she repeated with a smile. "You gave me life, health, and happiness, Jack. You gave me your love. Why should you not take what you have given. Go on. I am ready."

She held out her hands with that same infinite grace of yielding with which she had taken his own on the first day of their meeting at the hotel. Jack raised his head, looked at her for one wild moment, dropped upon his knees beside her and raised the folds of her dress to his feverish lips. But she was too clever not to instantly see her victory; she was too much of a woman, with all her cleverness, to refrain from pressing that victory home. At the same moment, as with the impulse of an outraged and wounded woman, she rose and, with an imperious gesture, pointed to the window. Mr. Oakhurst rose in his turn, cast one glance upon her, and without another word passed out of her presence forever.

When he had gone, she closed the window and bolted it, and going to the chimney-piece placed the letters, one by one, in the flame of the candle until they were consumed. I would not have the reader think that during this painful operation she was unmoved. Her hand trembled and — not being a brute — for some minutes, (perhaps longer,) she felt very badly, and the corners of her sensitive mouth were depressed. When her husband arrived it was with a genuine joy that she ran to him and nestled against his broad breast with a feeling of security that thrilled the honest fellow to the core.

"But I've heard dreadful news to night, Elsie," said Mr. Decker, after a few endearments were exchanged.

"Don't tell me anything dreadful, dear, I'm not well to-night," she pleaded sweetly.

"But it's about Mr. Oakhurst and Hamilton."

"Please!" Mr. Decker could not resist the petitionary grace of those white hands and that sensitive mouth, and took her to his arms. Suddenly he said, "What's that?"

He was pointing to the bosom of her white

dress. Where Mr. Oakhurst had touched her there was a spot of blood.

It was nothing; she had slightly cut her hand in closing the window; it shut so hard! If Mr. Decker had remembered to close and bolt the shutter before he went out, he might have saved her this. There was such a genuine irritability and force in this remark that Mr. Decker was quite overcome by remorse. But Mrs. Decker forgave him with that graciousness which I have before pointed out in these pages, and with the halo of that forgiveness and marital confidence still lingering above the pair, with the reader's permission we will leave them and return to Mr. Oakhurst.

But not for two weeks. At the end of that time he walked into his rooms in Sacramento, and in his old manner took his seat at the faro-table.

"How's your arm, Jack?" asked an incautious player.

There was a smile followed the question, which, however, ceased as Jack looked up quietly at the speaker.

"It bothers my dealing a little, but I can shoot as well with my left."

The game was continued in that decorous silence which usually distinguished the table at which Mr. John Oakhurst presided.

THE ROSE OF TUOLUMNE.

CHAPTER I.

It was nearly two o'clock in the morning. The lights were out in Robinson's Hall, where there had been dancing and revelry, and the moon, riding high, painted the black windows with silver. The cavalcade that an hour ago had shocked the sedate pines with song and laughter, were all dispersed; one enamored swain had ridden east, another west, another north, another south, and the object of their adoration, left within her bower at Chemisal Ridge, was calmly going to bed.

I regret that I am not able to indicate the exact stage of that process. Two chairs were already filled with delicate enwrappings and white confusion, and the young lady herself, half hidden in the silky threads of her yellow hair, had at one time borne a faint resemblance to a partly-husked ear of Indian corn. But she was now clothed in that one long, formless garment that makes all women equal, and the round shoulders and neat waist that an hour ago had been so fatal to the peace of mind of Four Forks had utterly disappeared. The face above it was very pretty; the foot below, albeit shapely, was not small. "The flowers, as a general thing, don't raise their heads *much* to look after me," she had said with superb frankness to one of her lovers.

The expression of "The Rose" to-night was contentedly placid. She walked slowly to the window, and, making the smallest possible peep-hole through the curtain, looked out. The motionless figure of a horseman still lingered on the road, with an excess of devotion that only a coquette or a woman very much in love could tolerate. "The Rose" at that moment was neither, and after a reasonable pause turned away, saying, quite audibly, that it was "too ridiculous for anything." As she came back to her dressing-table it was noticeable that she walked steadily and erect, without that slight affectation of lameness common to people with whom bare feet are only an episode. Indeed, it was only four years ago that, without shoes or stockings, a long-limbed, colty girl, in a waistless calico gown, she had leaped from the tail-board of her father's emigrant wagon when it first drew up at Chemisal Ridge. Certain wild habits of the Rose had outlived transplanting and cultivation.

A knock at the door surprised her. In another moment she had leaped into bed, and, with darkly-frowning eyes, from its secure recesses demanded "Who's there?"

An apologetic murmur on the other side of the door was the response.

"Why—father—is that you?"

There were further murmurs, affirmative, deprecatory, and persistent.

"Wait," said the Rose. She got up, unlocked the door, leaped nimbly into bed again, and said, "Come."

The door opened timidly. The broad, stooping shoulders and grizzled head of a man past the middle age appeared; after a moment's hesitation a pair of large diffident feet shod with canvas slippers concluded to follow. When the apparition was complete it closed the door softly, and stood there—a very shy ghost indeed, with apparently more than the usual spiritual indisposition to begin a conversation. The Rose resented this impatiently, though I fear not altogether intelligibly:

"Do, father, I declare!"

"You was abed, Jinny," said Mr. McClosky, slowly, glancing with a singular mixture of masculine awe and paternal pride upon the two chairs and their contents. "You was abed and ondressed."

"I was."

"Surely," said Mr. McClosky, seating himself on the extreme edge of the bed, and painfully tucking his feet away under it, "Surely." After a pause he rubbed a short, thick stumpy beard, that bore a general resemblance to a badly-worn blacking-brush, with the palm of his hand, and went on, "You had a good time, Jinny?"

"Yes, father."

"They was all there?"

"Yes, Rance and York and Ryder and Jack."

"And Jack!" Mr. McClosky endeavored to throw an expression of arch inquiry into his small, tremulous eyes, but meeting the unabashed, widely-opened lid of his daughter, he winked rapidly and blushed to the roots of his hair.

"Yes, Jack was there," said Jenny, without change of color, or the least self-consciousness in her great gray eyes, "and he came home with me." She paused a moment, locking her two hands under her head, and assuming a more comfortable position on the pillow. "He asked me that same question again, father, and I said 'Yes.' It's to be—soon. We're going to live at Four Forks, in his own house, and next Winter we're going to Sacramento. I suppose it's all right, father, eh?" She emphasized the question with a slight kick through the bed-clothes as the parental McClosky had fallen into an abstract reverie.

"Yes, surely," said Mr. McClosky, recovering himself with some confusion. After a pause he looked down at the bed-clothes, and, patting them tenderly, continued. "You couldn't have done better, Jinny. They isn't a girl in Tuolumne ez could strike it ez rich ez you hev—even if they got the chance." He paused again and then said, "Jinny?"

"Yes, father."

"You'se in bed and ondressed?"

"Yes."

"You couldn't," said Mr. McClosky, glancing

hopelessly at the two chairs and slowly rubbing his chin, "you couldn't dress yourself again—could yer—"

"Why, father!"

"—Kinder get yourself into them things again?" he added, hastily. "Not all of 'em, you know, but some of 'em. Not if I helped you?—sorter stood by and lent a hand now and then with a strap or a buckle, or a neck-tie, or a shoe-string," he continued, still looking at the chairs, and evidently trying to boldly familiarize himself with their contents.

"Are you crazy, father?" demanded Jenny, suddenly sitting up with a portentous switch of her yellow mane. Mr. McClosky rubbed one side of his beard, which already had the appearance of having been quite worn away by that process, and faintly dodged the question.

"Jenny," he said, tenderly stroking the bed-clothes as he spoke, "this yer's what's the matter. Thar is a stranger down stairs—a stranger to you, lovey, but a man ez I've knowed a long time. He's been here about an hour, and he'll be here ontil fower o'clock, when the up stage passes. Now I wants ye, Jinny dear, to get up and come down stairs and kinder help me pass the time with him. It's no use, Jinny," he went on, gently raising his hand to deprecate any interruption, "it's no use—he won't go to bed! He won't play keerds; whisky don't take no effect on him. Ever since I knowed him he was the most onsatisfactory critter to hev round—"

"What do you have him round for then?" interrupted Miss Jinny, sharply.

Mr. McClosky's eyes fell. "Ef he hedn't kem out of his way to-night to do me a good turn, I wouldn't ask ye, Jinny. I wouldn't, so help me! But I thought ez I couldn't do anything with him, you might come down and sorter fetch him, Jinny, as you did the others."

Miss Jenny shrugged her pretty shoulders.

"Is he old or young?"

"He's young enough, Jinny, but he knows a power of things."

"What does he do?"

"Not much, I reckon. He's got money in the mill at Four Forks. He travels round a good deal. I've heard, Jinny, that he's a poet — writes them rhymes, you know." Mr. McClosky here appealed submissively, but directly, to his daughter. He remembered that she had frequently been in receipt of printed elegiac couplets known as "mottoes," containing inclosures equally saccharine.

Miss Jenny slightly curled her pretty lip. She had that fine contempt for the illusions of fancy which belongs to the perfectly healthy young animal.

"Not," continued Mr. McClosky, rubbing his head reflectively, "not ez I'd advise ye, Jinny, to say anything to him about poetry. It ain't twenty minutes ago ez *I* did. I set the whisky afore him in the parlor. I wound up the music-box and set it goin'. Then I sez to him, sociable-like and free, 'Jest consider yourself in your own house and repeat what you allow to be your finest production,' and he raged. That man, Jinny, jest raged. Thar's no end of the names he called me. You see, Jinny," continued Mr. McClosky, apologetically, "he's known me a long time."

But his daughter had already dismissed the question with her usual directness. "I'll be down in a few moments, father," she said, after a pause, "but don't say anything to him about it—don't say I was abed."

Mr. McClosky's face beamed. "You was allers a good girl, Jinny," he said, dropping on one knee the better to imprint a respectful kiss on her forehead. But Jenny caught him by the wrists and for a moment held him captive. "Father," said she, trying to fix his shy eyes with the clear, steady glance of her own, "all the girls that were there to-night had some one with them. Mame Robinson had her aunt, Lucy Rance had her mother, Kate Pierson had her sister—all except me had some other woman. Father, dear," her lip trembled just a little, "I wish mother hadn't died when I was so small. I wish there was some other woman in the family besides me. I ain't lonely with you, father dear; but if there was only some one, you know, when the time comes for John and me—"

Her voice here suddenly gave out, but not her brave eyes, that were still fixed earnestly upon his face. Mr. McClosky, apparently tracing out a pattern on the bed-quilt, essayed words of comfort:

"There ain't one of them gals ez you've named, Jinny, ez could do what you've done with a whole

Noah's ark of relations at their backs! Thar ain't one ez wouldn't sacrifice her nearest relation to make the strike that you hev. Ez to mothers, may be, my dear, you're doin' better without one." He rose suddenly, and walked toward the door. When he reached it he turned, and, in his old deprecating manner, said: "Don't be long, Jinny," smiled, and vanished from the head downward, his canvas slippers asserting themselves resolutely to the last.

When Mr. McClosky reached his parlor again his troublesome guest was not there. The decanter stood on the table untouched, three or four books lay upon the floor, a number of photographic views of the Sierras were scattered over the sofa; two sofa pillows, a newspaper, and a Mexican blanket lay on the carpet, as if the late occupant of the room had tried to read in a recumbent position. A French window, opening upon a veranda, which never before in the history of the house had been unfastened, now betrayed by its waving lace curtain the way that the fugitive had escaped. Mr. McClosky heaved a sigh of despair; he looked at the gorgeous carpet purchased in Sacramento at a fabulous price, at the crimson satin and rosewood furniture unparalleled in the history of Tuolumne, at the massively-framed pictures on the walls, and looked beyond it, through the open window, to the reckless man who, fleeing these sybaritic allurements, was smoking a cigar upon the moonlit road. This room, which had so often awed the youth of Tuolumne into filial respect, was evidently a failure. It remained to be seen if the Rose herself had lost her fragrance. "I reckon Jinny will fetch him yet," said Mr. McClosky, with parental faith.

He stepped from the window upon the veranda. But he had scarcely done this before his figure was detected by the stranger, who at once crossed the road. When within a few feet of McClosky he stopped. "You persistent old plantigrade," he said, in a low voice, audible only to the person addressed, and a face full of affected anxiety, "why don't you go to bed? Didn't I tell you to go and leave me here alone? In the name of all that's idiotic and imbecile, why do you continue to shuffle about here? Or are you trying to drive me crazy with your presence, as you have with that wretched music box that I've just dropped under yonder tree? It's an hour and a half yet before the stage passes; do you think, do you imagine for a single moment, that I can tolerate you until then—eh? Why don't you speak? Are you asleep? You don't mean to say that you have the audacity to add somnambulism to your other weaknesses; you're not low enough to repeat yourself under any such weak pretext as that—eh?"

A fit of nervous coughing ended this extraordinary exordium, and half sitting, half leaning against the veranda, Mr. McClosky's guest turned his face and part of a slight elegant figure toward his host. The lower portion of this upturned face wore an habitual expression of fastidious discontent, with an occasional line of physical suffering. But the brow above was frank and critical, and a pair of dark mirthful eyes sat in playful judgment over the super-sensitive mouth and its suggestion.

"I allowed to go to bed, Ridgeway," said Mr. McClosky, meekly, "but my girl Jinny's jist got back from a little tear up at Robinson's, and ain't inclined to turn in yet. You know what girls is. So I thought we three would jist have a social chat together to pass away the time."

"You mendacious old hypocrite, she got back an hour ago," said Ridgeway, "as that savage-looking escort of hers, who has been haunting the house ever since, can testify. My belief is, that, like an enterprising idiot, as you are, you've dragged that girl out of her bed that we might mutually bore each other."

Mr. McClosky was too much stunned by this evidence of Ridgeway's apparently superhuman penetration to reply. After enjoying his host's confusion for a moment with his eyes, Ridgeway's mouth asked grimly:

"And who is this girl, anyway?"

"Nancy's."

"Your wife's?"

"Yes. But look yar, Ridgeway," said McClosky, laying one hand imploringly on Ridgeway's sleeve, "not a word about her to Jinny. She thinks her mother's dead—died in Missouri. Eh!"

Ridgeway nearly rolled from the veranda in an excess of rage. "Good God! Do you mean to say that you have been concealing from her a fact that any day, any moment, may come to her ears? That you've been letting her grow up in ignorance of something that by this time she might have outgrown and forgotten? That you have been, like a besotted old ass, all these years slowly forging a thunderbolt that any one may crush her with? That"——but here Ridgeway's cough took possession of his voice, and even put a moisture into his dark eyes, as he looked at McClosky's aimless hand feebly employed upon his beard.

"But," said McClosky, "look how she's done. She's held her head as high as any of 'em. She's to be married in a month to the richest man in the county, and," he added, cunningly, "Jack Ashe ain't the kind o' man to sit by and hear anything said of his wife or her relations, you bet. But hush—that's her foot on the stairs. She's cummin'."

She came. I don't think the French window ever held a finer view than when she put aside the curtains and stepped out. She had dressed herself simply and hurriedly, but with a woman's knowledge of her best points, so that you get the long curves of her shapely limbs, the shorter curves of her round waist and shoulders, the long sweep of her yellow braids, the light of her gray eyes, and even the delicate rose of her complexion, without knowing how it was delivered to you.

The introduction by Mr. McClosky was brief. When Ridgeway had got over the fact that it was two o'clock in the morning, and that the cheek of this Tuolumne goddess nearest him was as dewy and fresh as an infant's—that she looked like Marguerite, without probably ever having heard of Goethe's heroine, he talked, I dare say, very sensibly. When

Miss Jenny, who from her childhood had been brought up among the sons of Anak, and who was accustomed to have the supremacy of our noble sex presented to her as a physical fact, found herself in the presence of a new and strange power in the slight and elegant figure beside her, she was at first frightened and cold. But finding that this power, against which the weapons of her own physical charms were of no avail, was a kindly one, albeit general, she fell to worshiping it, after the fashion of woman, and casting before it the fetiches and other idols of her youth. She even confessed to it. So that in half an hour Ridgeway was in possession of all the facts connected with her life, and a great many, I fear, of her fancies—except one. When Mr. McClosky found the young people thus amicably disposed, he calmly went to sleep.

It was a pleasant time to each. To Miss Jenny it had the charm of novelty, and she abandoned herself to it for that reason much more freely and innocently than her companion, who knew something more of the inevitable logic of the position. I do not think, however, he had any intention of love-making. I do not think he was at all conscious of being in the attitude. I am quite positive he would have shrunk from the suggestion of disloyalty to the one woman whom he admitted to himself he loved. But, like most poets, he was much more true to an idea than a fact, and, having a very lofty conception of womanhood, with a very sanguine nature, he saw in each new face the possibilities of a realization of his ideal. It was, perhaps, an unfortunate thing for the women, particularly as he brought to each trial a surprising freshness which was very deceptive, and quite distinct from the *blasé* familiarity of the man of gallantry. It was this perennial virginity of the affections that most endeared him to the best women, who were prone to exercise toward him a chivalrous protection—as of one likely to go astray unless looked after—and indulged in the dangerous combination of sentiment with the highest maternal instincts. It was this quality which caused Jenny to recognize in him a certain boyishness that required her womanly care, and even induced her to offer to accompany him to the cross-roads when the time of his departure arrived. With her superior knowledge of woodcraft and the locality, she would have kept him from being lost. I wot not but that she would have protected him from bears or wolves, but chiefly, I think, from the feline fascinations of Mame Robinson and Lucy Rance, who might be lying in wait for this tender young poet. Nor did she cease to be thankful that Providence had, so to speak, delivered him as a trust into her hands.

It was a lovely night. The moon swung low and languished softly on the snowy ridge beyond. There were quaint odors in the still air, and a strange incense from the woods perfumed their young blood and seemed to swoon in their pulses. Small wonder that they lingered on the white road, that their feet climbed unwillingly the little hill where they were to part, and that when they at last reached it, even the saving grace of speech seemed to have forsaken them.

For there they stood, alone. There was no sound nor motion in earth, or woods, or heaven. They might have been the one man and woman for whom this goodly earth that lay at their feet, rimmed with the deepest azure, was created. And seeing this, they turned toward each other with a sudden instinct, and their hands met, and then their lips in one long kiss.

And then out of the mysterious distance came the sound of voices and the sharp clatter of hoofs and wheels, and Jenny slid away—a white moonbeam —from the hill. For a moment she glimmered through the trees, and then, reaching the house, passed her sleeping father on the veranda, and, darting into her bedroom, locked the door, threw open the window, and, falling on her knees beside it, leaned her hot cheeks upon her hands and listened. In a few moments she was rewarded by the sharp clatter of hoofs on the stony road, but it was only a horseman, whose dark figure was swiftly lost in the shadows of the lower road. At another time she might have recognized the man, but her eyes and ears were now all intent on something else. It came presently, with dancing lights, a musical rattle of harness, a cadence of hoof-beats, that set her heart to beating in unison, and was gone. A sudden sense of loneliness came over her, and tears gathered in her sweet eyes.

She arose and looked around her. There was

the little bed, the dressing-table, the roses that she had worn last night, still fresh and blooming in the little vase. Everything was there, but everything looked strange; the roses should have been withered, for the party seemed so long ago; she could hardly remember when she had worn this dress that lay upon the chair. So she came back to the window and sank down beside it, with her cheek, a trifle paler, leaning on her hand, and her long braids reaching to the floor. The stars paled slowly, like her cheek; yet with eyes that saw not, she still looked from her window for the coming dawn.

It came, with violet deepening into purple, with purple flushing into rose, with rose shining into silver and glowing into gold. The straggling line of black picket-fence below, that had faded away with the stars, came back with the sun. What was that object moving by the fence? Jenny raised her head, and looked intently. It was a man endeavoring to climb the pickets, and falling backward with each attempt. Suddenly she started to her feet, as if the rosy flushes of the dawn had crimsoned her from forehead to shoulders; then she stood, white as the wall, with her hands clasped upon her bosom. Then, with a single bound she reached the door, and with flying braids and fluttering skirt, sprang down the stairs and out in the garden walk. When within a few feet of the fence she uttered a cry— the first she had given—the cry of a mother over her stricken babe, of a tigress over her mangled cub, and in another moment she had leaped the fence and knelt beside Ridgeway, with his fainting head upon her breast.

"My boy—my poor, poor boy! who has done this?"

Who, indeed? His clothes were covered with dust, his waistcoat was torn open; and his handkerchief, wet with the blood it could not stanch, fell from a cruel stab beneath his shoulder.

"Ridgeway!—my poor boy—tell me what has happened."

Ridgeway slowly opened his heavy blue-veined lids, and gazed upon her. Presently a gleam of mischief came into his dark eyes, a smile stole over his lips as he whispered slowly:

"It—was—your kiss—did it—Jenny, dear! I had forgotten—how high priced—the article was here. Never mind, Jenny!"—he feebly raised her hand to his white lips—"it was—worth it," and fainted away.

Jenny started to her feet and looked wildly around her. Then, with a sudden resolution, she stooped over the insensible man, and, with one strong effort, lifted him in her arms as if he had been a child. When her father, a moment later, rubbed his eyes and awoke from his sleep upon the veranda, it was to see a goddess erect and triumphant, striding toward the house, with the helpless body of a man lying across that breast where man had never lain before—a goddess at whose imperious mandate he arose and cast open the doors before her. And then when she had laid her unconscious burden on the sofa, the goddess fled, and a woman, helpless and trembling, stood before him. A woman that cried out that she had "killed him"—that she was "wicked! wicked!" and that, even saying so, staggered and fell beside her late burden. And all that Mr. McClosky could do was to feebly rub his beard, and say to himself, vaguely and incoherently, that "Jinny had fetched him."

CHAPTER II.

BEFORE noon the next day it was generally believed throughout Four Forks that Ridgeway Dent had been attacked and wounded at Chemisal Ridge by a highwayman, who fled on the approach of the Wingdam coach. It is to be presumed that this statement met with Ridgeway's approval, as he did not contradict it, nor supplement it with any details. His wound was severe, but not dangerous. After the first excitement had subsided, there was, I think, a prevailing impression, common to the provincial mind, that his misfortune was the result of the defective moral quality of his being a stranger, and was in a vague sort of a way a warning to others and a lesson to him. "Did you hear how that San Francisco feller was took down the other night," was the average tone of introductory remark. Indeed, there was a general suggestion that Ridgeway's presence was one that no self-respecting, high-minded highwayman, honorably conservative of the best interests of Tuolumne County, could for a moment tolerate.

Except for the few words spoken on that eventful morning, Ridgeway was reticent of the past. When Jenny strove to gather some details of the affray that might offer a clue to his unknown assailant, a subtle twinkle in his brown eyes was the only response. When Mr. McClosky attempted the same process the young gentleman threw abusive epithets, and eventually slippers, teaspoons, and other lighter articles within the reach of an invalid, at the head of his questioner. "I think he's coming round, Jinny," said Mr. McClosky, "he laid for me this morning with a candlestick."

It was about this time that Miss Jenny, having sworn her father to secrecy regarding the manner in which Ridgeway had been carried into the house, conceived the idea of addressing the young man as "Mr. Dent," and of apologizing for intruding whenever she entered the room in the discharge of her household duties. It was about this time that she became more rigidly conscientious to those duties, and less general in her attentions; it was at this time that the quality of the invalid's diet improved, and that she consulted him less frequently about it. It was about this time that she began to see more company, that the house was greatly frequented by her former admirers, with whom she rode, walked, and danced. It was at about this time, also, and when Ridgeway was able to be brought out on the veranda in a chair, that, with great archness of manner, she introduced to him Miss Lucy Ashe, the sister of her betrothed—a flashing brunette and terrible heart-breaker of Four Forks. And in the midst of this gayety she concluded that she would spend a week with the Robinsons—to whom she owed a visit. She enjoyed herself greatly there, so much indeed that she became quite hollow-eyed, the result, as she explained to her father, of a too frequent indulgence in festivity. "You see, father, I won't have many chances after John and I are married—you know how queer he is—and I must make the most of my time," and she laughed an odd little laugh, which had lately become habitual to her. "And how is Mr. Dent getting on?" Her father replied that he was getting on very well indeed, so well, in fact, that he was able to leave for San Francisco two days ago. "He wanted to be remembered to you, Jinny—'remembered kindly,'— yes, they is the very words he used," said Mr. McClosky, looking down and consulting one of his large shoes for corroboration. Miss Jenny was glad to hear that he was so much better. Miss Jenny could not imagine anything that pleased her more than to know that he was so strong as to be able to rejoin his friends again, who must love him so much and be so anxious about him. Her father thought she would be pleased, and now that he was gone there was really no necessity for her to hurry back. Miss Jenny, in a high metallic voice, did not know that she had expressed any desire to stay— still if her presence had become distasteful at home —if her own father was desirous of getting rid of her—if, when she was so soon to leave his roof forever, he still begrudged her those few days remaining—if—"My God, Jinny, so help me!" said Mr. McClosky, clutching despairingly at his beard, "I didn't go for to say anything of the kind. I thought that you—" "Never mind, father," interrupted Jenny, magnanimously, "you misunderstood me; of course you did, you couldn't help it—you're a MAN!" Mr. McClosky, sorely crushed, would have vaguely protested, but his daughter, having relieved herself, after the manner of her sex, with a mental personal application of an abstract statement, forgave him with a kiss.

Nevertheless, for two or three days after her return, Mr. McClosky followed his daughter about the house with yearning eyes, and occasionally with timid, diffident feet. Sometimes he came upon her suddenly at her household tasks with an excuse so palpably false, and a careless manner so outrageously studied, that she was fain to be embarrassed for him. Later he took to rambling about the house at night, and was often seen noiselessly passing and repassing through the hall after she had retired. On one occasion he was surprised first by sleep and then by the early-rising Jenny as he lay on the rug outside her chamber door. "You treat me like a child, father," said Jenny. "I thought, Jinny," said the father, apologetically, "I thought I heard sounds as if you was takin' on inside, and listenin' I fell asleep." "You dear old simple-minded baby," said Jenny, looking past her father's eyes, and lifting his grizzled locks one by one with meditative fingers, "what should I be takin' on for? Look how much taller I am than you," she said, suddenly lifting herself up to the extreme of her superb figure. Then rubbing his head rapidly with both hands, as if she were anointing his hair with some rare unguent, she patted him on the back and returned to her room. The result of this and one or two other equally sympathetic interviews was to produce a change in Mr. McClosky's manner, which was, if possible, still more discomposing. He grew unjustifiably hilarious, cracked jokes with the servants, and repeated to Jenny humorous stories, with the attitude of facetiousness carefully preserved throughout the entire narration, and the point utterly ignored and forgotten. Certain incidents reminded him of funny things, which invariably turned out to have not the slightest relevancy or application. He occasionally brought home with him practical humorists, with a sanguine hope of setting them going, like the music-box, for his daughter's edification. He essayed the singing of melodies with great freedom of style and singular limitation of note. He sang "Come, Haste to the Wedding, Ye Lasses and Maidens," of which he knew a single line, and that incorrectly, as being peculiarly apt and appropriate. Yet away from the house and his daughter's presence he was silent and distraught. His absence of mind was particularly noted by his workmen at the "Empire Quartz Mill." "Ef the old man don't look out and wake up," said his foreman, "he'll hev them feet of his yet under the stamps. When he ain't givin' his mind to 'em, they is altogether too promiskuss."

A few nights later, Miss Jenny recognized her father's hand in a timid tap at the door. She opened it, and he stood before her, with a valise in his hand, equipped as for a journey. "I takes the stage to night, Jinny dear, from Four Forks to 'Frisco. Maybe I may drop in on Jack afore I go. I'll be back in a week. Good-by."

"Good-by." He still held her hand. Presently he drew her back into the room, closing the door carefully, and glancing around. There was a look of profound cunning in his eye as he said slowly:

"Bear up and keep dark, Jinny dear, and trust to the old man. Various men has various ways. Thar is ways as is common and ways as is uncommon, ways as is easy and ways as is oneasy. Bear up and keep dark." With this Delphic utterance he put his finger to his lips and vanished.

It was ten o'clock when he reached Four Forks. A few minutes later he stood on the threshold of that dwelling described by the Four Forks *Sentinel* as "the palatial residence of John Ashe," and known to the local satirist as the "ash-box." "Hevin' to lay by two hours, John," he said to his prospective son-in-law, as he took his hand at the door, "a few words of social converse, not on business, but strictly private, seems to be about as nat'ral a thing as a man can do." This introduction, evidently the result of some study and plainly committed to memory, seemed so satisfactory to Mr. McClosky that he repeated it again, after John Ashe had led him into his private office, where, depositing his valise in the middle of the floor and sitting down before it, he began carefully to avoid the eye of his host. John Ashe, a tall, dark, handsome Kentuckian—with whom even the trifles of life were evidently full of serious import—waited with a kind of chivalrous respect the further speech of his guest. Being utterly devoid of any sense of the ridiculous, he always accepted Mr. McClosky as a grave fact, singular only from his own want of experience of the class.

"Ores is running light now," said Mr. McClosky, with easy indifference.

John Ashe returned that he had noticed the same fact in the receipts of the mill at Four Forks.

Mr. McClosky rubbed his beard and looked at his valise, as if for sympathy and suggestion.

"You don't reckon on having any trouble with any of them chaps ez you cut out with Jinny?"

John Ashe, rather haughtily, had never thought of that. "I saw Rance hanging round your house the other night when I took your daughter home, but he gave me a wide berth," he added, carelessly.

"Surely," said Mr. McClosky, with a peculiar winking of the eye. After a pause, he took a fresh departure from his valise.

"A few words, John, ez between man and man, ez between my daughter's father and her husband who expects to be, is about the thing, I take it, as is fair and square. I kem here to say them. They're about Jinny, my gal."

Ashe's grave face brightened, to Mr. McClosky's evident discomposure.

"Maybe I should have said, about her mother; but the same bein' a stranger to you, I says, naterally, 'Jinny.'"

Ashe nodded courteously. Mr. McClosky, with his eyes on his valise, went on:

"It is sixteen year ago as I married Mrs. McClosky in the State of Missouri. She let on, at the time, to be a widder—a widder with one child.

When I say let on, I mean to imply that I subsekently found out that she was not a widder, nor a wife, and the father of the child was, so to speak —onbeknowst. Thet child was Jinny—my gal."

With his eyes on his valise, and quietly ignoring the wholly-crimsoned face and swiftly-darkening brow of his host, he continued:

"Many little things sorter tended to make our home in Missouri onpleasant. A disposition to smash furniture and heave knives around, an inclination to howl when drunk, and that frequent; a habitooal use of vulgar language, and a tendency to cuss the casooal visitor, seemed to pint," added Mr. McClosky with submissive hesitation—"thet—she—was—so to speak—quite onsuited to the marriage relation in its holiest aspeck."

"Damnation! Why didn't—" burst out John Ashe, erect and furious.

"At the end of two year," continued Mr. McClosky, still intent on the valise, "I allowed I'd get a diworce. Et about thet time, however, Providence sends a circus into thet town and a feller ez rode three hosses to onct. Hevin' allez a taste for athletic sports, she left town with this feller, leavin' me and Jinny behind. I sent word to her thet if she would give Jinny to me we'd call it quits. And she did."

"Tell me," gasped Ashe, "did you ask your daughter to keep this from me, or did she do it of her own accord?"

"She doesn't know it," said Mr. McClosky: "she thinks I'm her father, and that her mother's dead."

"Then, Sir, this is your——"

"I don't know," said Mr. McClosky, slowly, "ez I've asked any one to marry my Jinny. I don't know ez I've persood that ez a biziness, or even taken it up as a healthful recreation."

John Ashe paced the room furiously. Mr. McClosky's eyes left the valise and followed him curiously. "Where is this woman?" demanded Ashe, suddenly. McClosky's eyes sought the valise again.

"She went to Kansas; from Kansas she went into Texas. From Texas she eventooally came to Californy. Being here, I've purvided her with money—when her business was slack—through a friend."

John Ashe groaned. "She's gettin' rather old and shaky for hosses, and now does the tight-rope business and flying trapeze. Never hevin' seen her perform," continued Mr. McClosky, with conscientious caution, "I can't say how she gets on. On the bills she looks well. Thar is a poster—" said Mr. McClosky glancing at Ashe, and opening his valise, "thar is a poster givin' her performance at Marysville next month." Mr. McClosky slowly unfolded a large yellow and blue printed poster, profusely illustrated. "She calls herself 'Mam'selle J. Miglawski—the great Russian Trapeziste.'"

John Ashe tore it from his hand. "Of course," he said, suddenly facing Mr. McClosky, "you don't expect me to go on with this?"

Mr. McClosky picked up the poster, carefully refolded it and returned it to his valise. "When you break off with Jenny," he said quietly, I don't want anything said 'bout this. She doesn't know it. She's a woman and I reckon you're a white man."

"But what am I to say? How am I to go back of my word?"

"Write her a note. Say something hez come to your knowledge—don't say what—that makes you break it off. You needn't be afeard Jinny'll ever ask you what."

John Ashe hesitated. He felt he had been cruelly wronged. No gentleman—no Ashe—could go on further in this affair. It was preposterous to think of it. But somehow he felt at the moment very unlike a gentleman or an Ashe, and was quite sure he should break down under Jenny's steady eyes. But then—he could write to her.

"So ores is about as light here as on the Ridge. Well, I reckon they'll come up before the rains. Good night." Mr. McClosky took the hand that his host mechanically extended, shook it gravely, and was gone.

When Mr. McClosky, a week later, stepped again upon his own veranda, he saw through the French window the figure of a man in his parlor. Under his hospitable roof the sight was not unusual, but for an instant a subtle sense of disappointment thrilled him. When he saw it was not the face of Ashe turned toward him he was relieved, but when he saw the tawny beard and quick, passionate eyes of Henry Rance he felt a new sense of apprehension, so that he fell to rubbing his beard almost upon his very threshold.

Jenny ran into the hall, and seized her father with a little cry of joy. "Father," said Jenny, in a hurried whisper, "don't mind *him*"—indicating Rance with a toss of her yellow braids—"he's going soon, and I think, father, I've done him wrong. But it's all over with John and me now; read that note, and see how he's insulted me." Her lip quivered, but she went on: "It's Ridgeway that he means, father, and I believe it was *his* hand struck Ridgeway down, or that he knows who did. But hush now; not a word."

She gave him a feverish kiss, and glided back into the parlor, leaving Mr. McClosky perplexed and irresolute with the note in his hand. He glanced at it hurriedly and saw that it was couched in almost the very words he had suggested. But a sudden apprehensive recollection came over him; he listened, and with an exclamation of dismay he seized his hat and ran out of the house. But too late; at the same moment a quick, nervous footstep was heard upon the veranda, the French window flew open, and with a light laugh of greeting Ridgeway stepped into the room.

Jenny's finer ear first caught the step, Jenny's swifter feelings had sounded the depths of hope, of joy, of despair, before he entered the room. Jenny's pale face was the only one that met his, self-possessed and self-reliant, when he stood before them. An angry flush suffused even the pink roots of Rance's beard as he rose to his feet; an ominous fire sprang into Ridgeway's eyes, and a spasm of hate and scorn passed over the lower part of his face and left the mouth and jaw immobile and rigid.

Yet he was the first to speak. "I owe you an apology," he said to Jenny, with a suave scorn that brought the indignant blood back to her cheek, "for this intrusion, but I ask no pardon for withdrawing from the only spot where that man dare confront me with safety."

With an exclamation of rage, Rance sprang toward him. But as quickly Jenny stood between them, erect and menacing. "There must be no quarrel here," she said to Rance. "While I protect your right as my guest, don't oblige me to remind you of mine as your hostess." She turned with a half-deprecatory air to Ridgeway, but he was gone. So was her father. Only Rance remained, with a look of ill-concealed triumph on his face.

Without looking at him she passed toward the door. When she reached it she turned. "You asked me a question an hour ago. Come to me in the garden at nine o'clock to-night and I will answer you. But promise me first to keep away from Mr. Dent; give me your word not to seek him—to avoid him if he seeks you. Do you promise? It is well."

He would have taken her hand, but she waved him away. In another moment he heard the swift rustle of her dress in the hall, the sound of her feet upon the stair, the sharp closing of her bedroom door, and all was quiet.

And even thus quietly the day wore away, and the night rose slowly from the valley and overshadowed the mountains with purple wings that fanned the still air into a breeze, until the moon followed it and lulled everything to rest as with the laying on of white and benedictory hands. It was a lovely night, but Henry Rance, waiting impatiently beneath a sycamore at the foot of the garden, saw no beauty in earth or air or sky. A thousand suspicions common to a jealous nature, a vague superstition of the spot, filled his mind with distrust and doubt. "If this should be a trick to keep my hands off that insolent pup!" he muttered, but even as the thought passed his tongue, a white figure slid from the shrubbery near the house, glided along the line of picket fence, and then stopped, midway, motionless in the moonlight.

It was she. But he scarcely recognized her in the white drapery that covered her head, and shoulders, and breast. He approached her with a hurried whisper. "Let us withdraw from the moonlight. Everybody can see us here."

"We have nothing to say that cannot be said in the moonlight, Henry Rance," she replied, coldly receding from his proffered hand. She trembled for a moment, as if with a chill, and then suddenly turned upon him: "Hold up your head and let me look at you! I've known only what men are; let me see what a traitor looks like!"

He recoiled more from her wild face than her words. He saw for the first that her hollow cheeks and hollow eyes were blazing with fever. He was no coward, but he would have fled.

"You are ill, Jenny," he said; "you had best return to the house. Another time—"

"Stop!" she cried, hoarsely; "move from this spot and I'll call for help! Attempt to leave me now and I'll proclaim you the assassin that you are!"

"It was a fair fight," he said, doggedly.

"Was it a fair fight to creep behind an unarmed and unsuspecting man? Was it a fair fight to try to throw suspicion on some one else? Was it a fair fight to deceive me? Liar and coward that you are!"

He made a stealthy step toward her with evil eyes, and a wickeder hand that crept within his breast. She saw the motion, but it only stung her to newer fury.

"Strike!" she said, with blazing eyes, throwing her hands open before him. "Strike? Are you afraid of the woman who dares you?—or do you keep your knife for the backs of unsuspecting men? Strike! I tell you! No? Look, then!" With a sudden movement she tore from her head and shoulders the thick lace shawl that had concealed her figure and stood before him. "Look!" she cried, passionately, pointing to the bosom and shoulders of her white dress, darkly streaked with faded stains and ominous discoloration. "Look! This is the dress I wore that morning when I found him lying here—*here*—bleeding from your cowardly knife. Look! Do you see? This is his blood—my darling boy's blood!—

one drop of which, dead and faded as it is, is more precious to me than the whole living pulse of any other man! Look! I come to you to-night christened with his blood and dare you to strike—dare you to strike him again through me and mingle my blood with his! Strike! I implore you! Strike! if you have any pity on me—for God's sake! Strike! if you are a man! Look! Here lay his head on my shoulder; here I held him to my breast, where never—so help me my God!—another man——Ah!——"

She reeled against the fence, and something that had flashed in Rance's hand dropped at her feet; for another flash and report rolled him over in the dust, and across his writhing body two men strode and caught her ere she fell.

"She has only fainted," said Mr. McClosky. "Jinny dear, my girl, speak to me!"

"What is this on her dress?" said Ridgeway, kneeling beside her, and lifting his set and colorless face. At the sound of his voice the color came faintly back to her cheek; she opened her eyes and smiled.

"It's only your blood, dear boy," she said, "but look a little deeper and you'll find my own."

She put up her two yearning hands and drew his face and lips down to her own. When Ridgeway raised his head again her eyes were closed, but her mouth still smiled as with the memory of a kiss.

They bore her to the house still breathing but unconscious. That night the road was filled with clattering horsemen, and the summoned skill of the country side for leagues away gathered at her couch. The wound, they said, was not essentially dangerous, but they had grave fears of the shock to a system that already seemed suffering from some strange and unaccountable nervous exhaustion. The best medical skill of Tuolumne happened to be young and observing, and waited patiently an opportunity to account for it. He was presently rewarded.

For toward morning she rallied and looked feebly around. Then she beckoned her father toward her, and whispered, "Where is he?"

"They took him away, Jinny dear, in a cart. He wont trouble you agin." He stopped, for Miss Jenny had raised herself on her elbow, and was leveling her black brows at him. But two kicks from the young surgeon, and a significant motion toward the door, sent Mr. McClosky away muttering, "How should I know that '*he*' meant Ridgeway," he said apologetically, as he went and returned with the young gentleman. The surgeon, who was still holding her pulse, smiled, and thought that with—a little care—and attention—the stimulants—might be—diminished—and—he—might leave—the patient for some hours, with perfect safety. He would give further directions to Mr. McClosky—down stairs.

It was with great archness of manner that half an hour later Mr. McClosky entered the room, with a preparatory cough, and it was with some disappointment that he found Ridgeway standing quietly by the window, and his daughter apparently fallen

into a light doze. He was still more concerned
when, after Ridgeway had retired, noticing a pleasant
smile playing about her lips, he said softly:
"You was thinking of some one, Jinny?"
"Yes, father"—the gray eyes met his steadily—
"of poor John Ashe!"
Her recovery was swift. Nature, that had seemed
to stand jealously aloof from her in her mental
anguish, was kind to the physical hurt of her favorite
child. The superb physique which had been her
charm and her trial, now stood her in good stead.
The healing balsam of the pine, the balm of resinous
gums and the rare medicaments of Sierran
altitudes touched her as it might have touched the
wounded doe. So that in two weeks she was able
to walk about, and when at the end of the month
Ridgeway returned from a flying visit to San Francisco
and jumped from the Wingdam coach at four
o'clock in the morning, the Rose of Tuolumne, with
the dewy petals of either cheek fresh as when first
unfolded to his kiss, confronted him on the road.

With a common instinct their young feet both
climbed the little hill now sacred to their thought.
When they reached its summit they were both, I
think, a little disappointed. There is a fragrance in
the unfolding of a passion that escapes the perfect
flower. Jenny thought the night was not as beautiful;
Ridgeway, that the long ride had blunted his
perceptions. But they had the frankness to confess
it to each other, with the rare delight of such a
confession and the comparison of details which they
thought each had forgotten. And with this and an

occasional pitying reference to the blank period when they had not known each other, hand in hand, they reached the house.

Mr. McClosky was awaiting them impatiently upon the veranda. When Miss Jenny had slipped up stairs to replace a collar that stood somewhat suspiciously awry, Mr. McClosky drew Ridgeway solemnly aside. He held a large theatre poster in one hand and an open newspaper in the other.

"I allus said," he remarked slowly, with the air of merely renewing a suspended conversation, "I allus said that riding three horses to onct wasn't exactly in her line. It would seem that it ain't! From remarks in this yer paper it would appear that she tried it on at Marysville last week and broke her neck."

AN EPISODE OF FIDDLETOWN.

In 1858, Fiddletown considered her a very pretty woman. She had a quantity of light chestnut hair, a good figure, a dazzling complexion, and a certain languid grace which passed easily for gentlewomanliness. She always dressed becomingly, and in what Fiddletown accepted as the latest fashion. She had only two blemishes: one of her velvety eyes, when examined closely, had a slight cast, and her left cheek bore a small scar left by a single drop of vitriol—happily the only drop of an entire phial thrown upon her by one of her own jealous sex that reached the pretty face it was intended to mar. But when the observer had studied the eyes sufficiently to notice this defect he was generally incapacitated for criticism, and even the scar on her cheek was thought by some to add piquancy to her smile. The youthful editor of the Fiddletown *Avalanche* had said privately that is was "an exaggerated dimple." Colonel Starbottle was instantly "reminded of the beautifying patches of the days of Queen Anne, but more particularly, sir, of the blankest beautiful women, that, blank you, you ever laid your two blank eyes upon. A creole woman, sir, in New Orleans. And this woman had a scar —a line extending, blank me, from her eye to her blank chin. And this woman, sir, thrilled you, sir, maddened you, sir, absolutely sent your blank soul to perdition with her blank fascination. And one day I said to her, 'Celeste, how in blank did you come by that beautiful scar, blank you?' And she said to me, 'Star, there isn't another white man that I'd confide in but you, but I made that scar myself, purposely, I did, blank me.' These were her very words, sir, and perhaps you think it a blank lie, sir, but I'll put up any blank sum you can name and prove it, blank me."

Indeed, most of the male population of Fiddletown were or had been in love with her. Of this number about one-half believed that their love was returned, with the exception, possibly, of her own husband. He alone had been known to express skepticism.

The name of the gentleman who enjoyed this infelicitous distinction was Tretherick. He had been divorced from an excellent wife to marry this Fiddletown enchantress. She also had been divorced, but it was hinted that some previous experiences of hers in that legal formality had made it perhaps less novel and probably less sacrificial. I would not have it inferred from this that she was deficient in sentiment or devoid of its highest moral expression. Her intimate friend had written (on the occasion of her second divorce), "The cold world does not understand Clara yet," and Col. Starbottle had remarked, blankly, that with the exception of a single woman in Opelousas Parish, Louisiana, she had more soul than the whole caboodle of them put together. Few indeed could read those lines entitled "Infelissimus," commencing. "Why waves no cypress o'er this brow," originally published in the *Avalanche* over the signature of "The Lady Clare," without feeling the tear of sensibility tremble on his eyelids, or the glow of virtuous indignation mantle his cheek at the low brutality and pitiable jocularity of the *Dutch Flat Intelligencer*, which the next week had suggested the exotic character of the cypress and its entire absence from Fiddletown as a reasonable answer to the query.

Indeed it was this tendency to elaborate her feelings in a metrical manner and deliver them to the cold world through the medium of the newspapers that first attracted the attention of Tretherick. Several poems descriptive of the effects of California scenery upon a too sensitive soul, and of the vague yearnings for the infinite which an enforced study of the heartlessness of California society produced in the poetic breast, impressed Mr. Tretherick, who was then driving a six-mule freight wagon between Knight's Ferry and Stockton, to seek out the unknown poetess. Mr. Tretherick was himself dimly conscious of a certain hidden sentiment in his own nature, and it is possible that some reflections on the vanity of his pursuit—he supplied several mining camps with whisky and tobacco—in conjunction with the dreariness of the dusty plain on which he habitually drove, may have touched some chord in sympathy with this sensitive woman. Howbeit, after a brief courtship—as brief as was consistent with some previous legal formalities—they were married, and Mr. Tretherick brought his blushing bride to Fiddletown, or "Fidéletown," as Mrs. T. preferred to call it in her poems.

The union was not a felicitous one. It was not long before Mr. Tretherick discovered that the sentiment he had fostered while freighting between Stockton and Knight's Ferry was different from that which his wife had evolved from the contemplation of California scenery and her own soul. Being a man of imperfect logic, this caused him to beat her, and she, being equally faulty in deduction, was impelled to a certain degree of unfaithfulness on the same premise. Then Mr. Tretherick began to drink, and Mrs. T. to contribute regularly to the columns of the *Avalanche*. It was at this time that Col. Starbottle discovered a similarity in Mrs. T.'s verse to the genius of Sappho, and pointed it out to the citizens of Fiddletown in a two-columned criticism, signed "A. S.," also published in the *Avalanche* and supported by extensive quotation. As the *Avalanche* did not possess a font of Greek type, the editor was obliged to reproduce the Leucadian numbers in the ordinary Roman letter, to the intense disgust of Col. Starbottle, and the vast delight of Fiddletown, who saw fit to accept the text as an excellent imitation of Choctaw—a language with which the Colonel, as a whilom resident of the Indian territories, was supposed to be familiar. Indeed, the next week's *Intelligencer* contained some vile doggerel, supposed to be an answer to Mrs.

T.'s poem, ostensibly written by the wife of a Digger Indian chief, accompanied by a glowing eulogium signed "A. S. S."

The result of this jocularity was briefly given in a later copy of the *Avalanche*. "An unfortunate rencontre took place on Monday last between the Hon. Jackson Flash, of the *Dutch Flat Intelligencer*, and the well-known Col. Starbottle of this place, in front of the Eureka Saloon. Two shots were fired by the parties without injury to either, although is is said that a passing Chinaman received fifteen buck-shot in the calves of his legs from the Colonel's double-barreled shot-gun which were not intended for him. John will learn to keep out of the way of Melican man's fire-arms hereafter. The cause of the affray is not known, although it is hinted that there is a lady in the case. The rumor that points to a well-known and beautiful poetess whose lucubrations have often graced our columns, seems to gain credence from those that are posted."

Meanwhile the passiveness displayed by Tretherick under these trying circumstances was fully appreciated in the gulches. "The old man's head is level," said one long-booted philosopher. "Ef the Colonel kills Flash, Mrs. Tretherick is avenged; if Flash drops the Colonel, Tretherick is all right. Either way he's got a sure thing." During this delicate condition of affairs Mrs. Tretherick one day left her husband's home and took refuge at the Fiddletown Hotel, with only the clothes she had on her back. Here she stayed for several weeks, during which period it is only justice to say that she bore herself with the strictest propriety.

It was a clear morning in early spring that Mrs. Tretherick, unattended, left the hotel and walked down the narrow street toward the fringe of dark pines which indicated the extreme limits of Fiddletown. The few loungers at that early hour were preoccupied with the departure of the Wingdown coach at the other extremity of the street, and Mrs. Tretherick reached the suburbs of the settlement without discomposing observation. Here she took a cross street or road running at right angles with the main thoroughfare of Fiddletown, and passing through a belt of woodland. It was evidently the exclusive and aristocratic avenue of the town; the dwellings were few, ambitious, and uninterrupted by shops. And here she was joined by Col. Starbottle.

The gallant Colonel, notwithstanding that he bore the swelling port which usually distinguished him—that his coat was tightly buttoned and his boots tightly fitting, and that his cane, hooked over his arm, swung jauntily—was not entirely at his ease. Mrs. Tretherick, however, vouchsafed him a gracious smile and a glance of her dangerous eyes, and the Colonel, with an embarrassed cough and a slight strut, took his place at her side.

"The coast is clear," said the Colonel, "and Tretherick is over at Dutch Flat on a spree; there is no one in the house but a Chinaman, and you need fear no trouble from him. *I*," he continued, with a slight inflation of the chest that imperiled the security of his button, "I will see that you are protected in the removal of your property."

"I'm sure it's very kind of you, and so disinterested," simpered the lady as they walked along. "It's so pleasant to meet some one who has soul— some one to sympathize with in a community so hardened and heartless as this." And Mrs. Tretherick cast down her eyes, but not until they had wrought their perfect and accepted work upon her companion.

"Yes, certainly, of course," said the Colonel, glancing nervously up and down the street; "yes, certainly." Perceiving, however, that there was no one in sight or hearing, he proceeded at once to inform Mrs. Tretherick that the great trouble of his life, in fact, had been the possession of too much soul. That many women—as a gentleman she would excuse him, of course, from mentioning names—but many beautiful women had often sought his society, but, being deficient, madam, absolutely deficient in this quality, he could not reciprocate. But when two natures thoroughly in sympathy— despising alike the sordid trammels of a low and vulgar community and the conventional restraints of a hypocritical society—when two souls in perfect accord met and mingled in poetical union, then— but here the Colonel's speech, which had been remarkable for a certain whisky-and-watery fluency, grew husky, almost inaudible, and decidedly incoherent. Possibly Mrs. Tretherick may have heard something like it before, and was enabled to fill the hiatus. Nevertheless, the cheek that was on the side of the Colonel was quite virginal and bashfully conscious until they reached their destination.

It was a pretty little cottage, quite fresh and warm with paint, very pleasantly relieved against a platoon of pines, some of whose foremost files had been displaced to give freedom to the fenced inclosure in which it sat. In the vivid sunlight and perfect silence it had a new, uninhabited look, as if the carpenters and painters had just left it. At the further end of the lot a Chinaman was stolidly digging, but there was no other sign of occupancy. "The coast," as the Colonel had said, was indeed "clear." Mrs. Tretherick paused at the gate. The Colonel would have entered with her, but was stopped by a gesture. "Come for me in a couple of hours, and I shall have everything packed," she said, as she smiled and extended her hand. The Colonel seized and pressed it with great fervor. Perhaps the pressure was slightly returned, for the gallant Colonel was impelled to inflate his chest and trip away as smartly as his stubby-toed high-heeled boots would permit. When he had gone, Mrs. Tretherick opened the door, listened a moment in the deserted hall, and then ran quickly up-stairs to what had been her bed-room.

Everything there was unchanged as on the night she left it. On the dressing-table stood her band-box, as she remembered to have left it when she took out her bonnet. On the mantel lay the other glove she had forgotten in her flight. The two lower drawers of the bureau were half open—she had forgotten to shut them—and on its marble top

lay her shawl pin and a soiled cuff. What other
recollections came upon her I know not, but she
suddenly grew quite white, shivered, and listened
with a beating heart and her hand upon the door.
Then she stepped to the mirror and half fearfully,
half curiously, parted with her fingers the braids of
her blonde hair above her little pink ear, until she
came upon an ugly, half-healed scar. She gazed at
this, moving her pretty head up and down to get a
better light upon it, until the slight cast in her
velvety eyes became very strongly marked indeed.
Then she turned away with a light, reckless, foolish
laugh, and ran to the closet where hung her precious dresses. These she inspected nervously, and
missing suddenly a favourite black silk from its accustomed peg for a moment, thought she should
have fainted. But discovering it the next instant,
lying upon a trunk where she had thrown it, a feeling of thankfulness to a Superior Being who protects the friendless, for the first time sincerely
thrilled her. Then, albeit she was hurried for time,
she could not resist trying the effect of a certain
lavender neck-ribbon upon the dress she was then
wearing before the mirror. And then suddenly she
became aware of a child's voice close beside her
and she stopped. And then the child's voice repeated, "Is it mamma?"

Mrs. Tretherick faced quickly about. Standing
in the doorway was a little girl of six or seven.
Her dress had been originally fine, but was torn
and dirty, and her hair, which was a very violent
red, was tumbled serio-comically about her fore-

head. For all this she was a picturesque little thing, even through whose childish timidity there was a certain self-sustained air which is apt to come upon children who are left much to themselves. She was holding under her arm a rag doll, apparently of her own workmanship and nearly as large as herself—a doll with a cylindrical head and features roughly indicated with charcoal. A long shawl, evidently belonging to a grown person, dropped from her shoulders and swept the floor.

The spectacle did not excite Mrs. Tretherick's delight. Perhaps she had but a small sense of humor. Certainly, when the child, still standing in the doorway, again asked "Is it mamma?" she answered sharply, "No, it isn't," and turned a severe look upon the intruder.

The child retreated a step, and then, gaining courage with the distance, said, in deliciously imperfect speech—

"Dow 'way then—why don't you dow away?"

But Mrs. Tretherick was eyeing the shawl. Suddenly she whipped it off the child's shoulders and said angrily:

"How dared you take my things—you bad child?"

"Is it yours? Then you are my mamma! ain't you? You are mamma!" she continued gleefully, and before Mrs. Tretherick could avoid her, she had dropped her doll, and, catching the woman's skirts with both hands, was dancing up and down before her.

"What's your name, child?" said Mrs. Tretherick, coldly, removing the small and not very white hands from her garments.

"Tarry."

"Tarry?"

"Yeth. Tarry. Tarowline."

"Caroline?"

"Yeth. Tarowline Tretherick."

"Whose child *are* you?" demanded Mrs. Tretherick still more coldly, to keep down a rising fear.

"Why, yours," said the little creature with a laugh. "I'm your little durl. You're my mamma —my new mamma—don't you know my ole mamma's dorn away, never to tum back any more. I don't live wid my ol' mamma now. I live wid you and papa."

"How long have you been here?" asked Mrs. Tretherick, snappishly.

"I fink it's free days," said Carry, reflectively.

"You think!—don't you know?"—sneered Mrs. Tretherick. "Then where did you come from?"

Carry's lip began to work under this sharp cross-examination. With a great effort and a small gulp she got the better of it and answered:

"Papa—papa fetched me—from Miss Simmons —from Sacramento, last week."

"Last week! you said three days just now," returned Mrs. Tretherick with severe deliberation.

"I mean a monf," said Carry, now utterly adrift in sheer helplessness and confusion.

"Do you know what you are talking about?" demanded Mrs. T. shrilly, restraining an impulse to shake the little figure before her and precipitate the truth by specific gravity.

But the flaming red head here suddenly disappeared in the folds of Mrs. Tretherick's dress, as if it were trying to extinguish itself for ever.

"There now—stop that sniffling," said Mrs. Tretherick, extricating her dress from the moist embraces of the child, and feeling exceedingly uncomfortable. "Wipe your face now and run away and don't bother. Stop," she continued, as Carry moved away, "where's your papa!"

"He's dorn away too. He's sick. He's been dorn"—she hesitated,—"two—free—days."

"Who takes care of you, child?" said Mrs. T., eyeing her curiously.

"John—the Chinaman. I tresses myselth; John tooks and makes the beds."

"Well, now, run away and behave yourself, and don't bother me any more," said Mrs. Tretherick, remembering the object of her visit. "Stop—where are you going?" she added, as the child began to ascend the stairs, dragging the long doll after her by one helpless leg.

"Doin up stairs to play and be dood, and not bother mamma."

"I ain't your mamma," shouted Mrs. Tretherick, and then she swiftly re-entered her bedroom and slammed the door.

Once inside, she drew forth a large trunk from the closet, and set to work with querulous and fretful haste to pack her wardrobe. She tore her best dress in taking it from the hook on which it hung; she scratched her soft hands twice with an ambushed pin. All the while she kept up an indignant commentary on the events of the past few moments. She said to herself she saw it all. Tretherick had sent for this child of his first wife —this child of whose existence he had never seemed to care — just to insult her — to fill her place. Doubtless the first wife herself would follow soon, or perhaps there would be a third. Red hair—not auburn, but *red*—of course the child— this Caroline—looked like its mother, and if so she was anything but pretty. Or the whole thing had been prepared—this red-haired child—the image of its mother—had been kept at a convenient distance at Sacramento, ready to be sent for when needed. She remembered his occasional visits there — on business, as he said. Perhaps the mother already was there—but no—she had gone East. Nevertheless Mrs. Tretherick, in her then state of mind, preferred to dwell upon the fact that she might be there. She was dimly conscious also of a certain satisfaction in exaggerating her feelings. Surely no woman had ever been so shamefully abused. In fancy she sketched a picture of herself sitting alone and deserted, at sunset, among the fallen columns of a ruined temple,—in a melancholy yet graceful attitude, while her husband drove rapidly away in a luxurious coach and four, with a red-haired woman at his side. Sitting upon the trunk she had just packed, she partly composed a lugubrious poem, describing her sufferings as, wandering alone and poorly clad, she came upon her husband and "another," flaunting in silks and diamonds. She pictured herself dying of consumption, brought on by sorrow—a beautiful wreck, yet still fascinating, gazed upon adoringly by the editor of the *Avalanche* and Col. Starbottle. And where was Colonel Starbottle all this while,—why didn't he come? He at least understood her. He—she laughed the reckless, light laugh of a few moments before, and then her face suddenly grew grave, as it had not a few moments before.

What was that little red-haired imp doing all this time? Why was she so quiet? She opened the door noiselessly and listened. She fancied that she heard, above the multitudinous small noises, and creakings, and warpings of the vacant house, a smaller voice singing on the floor above. This, as she remembered, was only an open attic that had been used as a store-room. With a half-guilty consciousness, she crept softly upstairs, and, pushing the door partly open, looked within.

Athwart the long, low-studded attic, a slant sunbeam from a single small window lay, filled with dancing motes and only half illuminating the barren, dreary apartment. In the ray of this sunbeam she saw the child's glowing hair, as if crowned by a red aureole, as she sat upon the floor with her exaggerated doll between her knees. She appeared to be talking to it, and it was not long before Mrs. Tretherick observed that she was rehearsing the interview of a half-hour before. She catechized the doll severely—cross-examining it in regard to the duration of its stay there, and generally on the measure of time. The imitation of Mrs. T.'s manner was exceedingly successful, and the conversation almost a literal reproduction, with a single exception. After she had informed the doll that she was not her mother, at the close of the interview she added pathetically "that if she was dood—very dood—she might be her mamma and love her very much."

I have already hinted that Mrs. Tretherick was deficient in a sense of humor. Perhaps it was for this reason that this whole scene affected her most unpleasantly, and the conclusion sent the blood tingling to her cheek. There was something, too, inconceivably lonely in the situation; the unfurnished vacant room, the half light, the monstrous doll, whose very size seemed to give a pathetic significance to its speechlessness, the smallness of the one animate self-centered figure,—all these touched more or less deeply the half-poetic sensibilities of the woman. She could not help utilizing the impression as she stood there, and thought what a fine poem might be constructed from this material, if the room were a little darker, the child lonelier—say, sitting beside a dead mother's bier and the wind wailing in the turrets. And then she suddenly heard footsteps at the door below, and recognized the tread of the Colonel's cane.

She flew swiftly down the stairs and encountered the Colonel in the hall. Here she poured into his astonished ear a voluble and exaggerated statement of her discovery and indignant recital of her wrongs. "Don't tell me the whole thing wasn't arranged beforehand — for I know it was!" she almost screamed. "And think," she added, "of the heartlessness of the wretch—leaving his own child alone here in that way."

"It's a blank shame!" stammered the Colonel, without the least idea of what he was talking about. In fact, utterly unable as he was to comprehend a reason for the woman's excitement with his estimate of her character, I fear he showed it more plainly than he intended. He stammered, expanded his chest, looked stern, gallant, tender, but all unintelligently. Mrs. Tretherick for an instant experienced a sickening doubt of the existence of natures in perfect affinity.

"It's of no use," said Mrs. Tretherick with sudden vehemence, in answer to some inaudible remark of the Colonel's, and withdrawing her hand from the fervent grasp of that ardent and sympathetic man. "It's of no use; my mind is made up. You can send for my trunk as soon as you like, but *I* shall stay here and confront that man with the proof of his vileness. I will put him face to face with his infamy."

I do not know whether Col. Starbottle thoroughly appreciated the convincing proof of Tretherick's unfaithfulness and malignity afforded by the damning evidence of the existence of Tretherick's own child in his own house. He was dimly aware, however, of some unforeseen obstacle to the perfect expression of the infinite longing of his own sentimental nature. But before he could say anything, Carrie appeared on the landing above them, looking timidly and yet half-critically at the pair.

"That's her," said Mrs. Tretherick excitedly. In her deepest emotions, either in verse or prose, she rose above a consideration of grammatical construction.

"Ah!" said the Colonel, with a sudden assumption of parental affection and jocularity that was glaringly unreal and affected. "Ah! pretty little girl, pretty little girl! how do you do? how are you? you find yourself pretty well, do you, pretty little girl?" The Colonel's impulse also was to expand his chest and swing his cane, until it occurred to him that this action might be ineffective with a child of six or seven. Carrie, however, took no immediate notice of this advance, but further discomposed the chivalrous Colonel by running quickly to Mrs. Tretherick, and hiding herself, as if for protection, in the folds of her gown. Nevertheless, the Colonel was not vanquished. Falling back into an attitude of respectful admiration, he pointed out a marvelous resemblance to the "Madonna and Child." Mrs. Tretherick simpered, but did not dislodge Carrie as before. There was an awkward pause for a moment, and then Mrs. Tretherick, motioning significantly to the child, said in a whisper: "Go, now. Don't come here again, but meet me to-night at the hotel." She extended her hand; the Colonel bent over it gallantly, and raising his hat, the next moment was gone.

"Do you think," said Mrs. Tretherick, with an embarrassed voice and a prodigious blush, looking down and addressing the fiery curls just visible in the folds of her dress, "do you think you will be 'dood' if I let you stay in here and sit with me?"

"And let me call you mamma?" queried Carry, looking up.

"And let you call me mamma!" assented Mrs. Tretherick with an embarrassed laugh.

"Yeth," said Carry promptly.

They entered the bed-room together. Carry's eye instantly caught sight of the trunk.

"Are you dowin away adain, mamma," she said with a quick nervous look, and a clutch at the woman's dress.

"No-o," said Mrs. Tretherick, looking out of the window.

"Only playing your dowin away," suggested Carry with a laugh. "Let me play, too."

Mrs. T. assented. Carry flew into the next room, and presently reappeared, dragging a small trunk, into which she gravely proceeded to pack her clothes. Mrs. T. noticed that they were not many. A question or two regarding them brought out some further replies from the child, and before many minutes had elapsed Mrs. Tretherick was in possession of all her earlier history. But to do this Mrs. Tretherick had been obliged to take Carry upon her lap, pending the most confidential disclosures. They sat thus a long time after Mrs. Tretherick had apparently ceased to be interested in Carry's disclosures, and, when lost in thought, she allowed the child to rattle on unheeded, and ran her fingers through the scarlet curls.

"You don't hold me right, mamma," said Carry at last, after one or two uneasy shiftings of position.

"How should I hold you?" asked Mrs. Tretherick, with a half-amused, half-embarrassed laugh.

"This way," said Carry, curling up into position with one arm around Mrs. Tretherick's neck and her cheek resting on her bosom; "this way—there." After a little preparatory nestling, not unlike some small animal, she closed her eyes and went to sleep.

For a few moments the woman sat silent, scarcely daring to breathe, in that artificial attitude. And then, whether from some occult sympathy in the touch, or God best knows what, a sudden fancy began to thrill her. She began by remembering an old pain that she had forgotten, an old horror that she had resolutely put away all these years. She recalled days of sickness and distrust, days of an overshadowing fear, days of preparation for something that was to be prevented,—that *was* prevented, with mortal agony and fear. She thought of a life that might have been—she dared not say *had* been—and wondered! It was six years ago; if it had lived it would have been as old as Carry. The arms which were folded loosely around the sleeping child began to tremble and tighten their clasp. And then the deep potential impulse came, and with a half-sob, half-sigh, she threw her arms out and drew the body of the sleeping child down, down, into her breast, down again and again as if she would hide it in the grave dug there years before. And the gust that shook her passed, and then, ah me! the rain.

A drop or two fell upon the curls of Carry, and she moved uneasily in her sleep. But the woman soothed her again — it was *so* easy to do it now — and they sat there quiet and undisturbed — so quiet that they might have seemed incorporate of the lonely silent house, the slowly declining sunbeams, and the general air of desertion and abandonment, yet a desertion that had in it nothing of age, decay, or despair.

Col. Starbottle waited at the Fiddletown Hotel all that night in vain. And the next morning, when Mr. Tretherick returned to his husks, he found the house vacant and untenanted except by motes and sunbeams.

When it was fairly known that Mrs. Tretherick had run away, taking Mr. Tretherick's own child with her, there was some excitement and much diversity of opinion in Fiddletown. *The Dutch Flat Intelligencer* openly alluded to the "forcible abduction" of the child with the same freedom, and it is to be feared the same prejudice, with which it had criticised the abductor's poetry. All of Mrs. Tretherick's own sex, and perhaps a few of the opposite sex whose distinctive quality was not, however, very strongly indicated, fully coincided in the views of the *Intelligencer*. The majority, however, evaded the moral issue; that Mrs. Tretherick had shaken the red dust of Fiddletown from her dainty slippers was enough for them to know. They mourned the loss of the fair abductor more than her offence. They promptly rejected Tretherick as an injured husband and disconsolate father, and even went so far as to openly cast discredit in the sincerity of his grief. They reserved an ironical condolence for Colonel Starbottle, overbearing that excellent man with untimely and demonstrative sympathy in bar-rooms, saloons and other localities not generally deemed favorable to the display of sentiment. "She was alliz a skittish thing, Kernel," said one sympathizer with a fine affectation of gloomy concern and great readiness of illustration, "and it's kinder nat'ril thet she'd get away some day and stampede that theer colt, but she should shake *you*, Kernel, thet she should just shake you —is what gits me. And they do say thet you jist hung around thet hotel all night, and payrolled them corriders and histed yourself up and down them stairs, and meandered in and out o' thet piazzy, and all for nothing?" It was another generous and tenderly commiserating spirit that poured additional oil and wine on the Colonel's wounds. "The boys yer let on thet Mrs. Tretherick prevailed on ye to pack her trunk and a baby over from the house to the stage offis, and that the chap ez did go off with her thanked you and offered you two short bits and sed ez how he liked your looks and ud employ you agin—and now you say it aint so? Well—I'll tell the boys it aint so, and I'm glad I met you, for stories *do* get round."

Happily for Mrs. Tretherick's reputation, however, the Chinaman in Tretherick's employment, who was the only eye-witness of her flight, stated that she was unaccompanied except by the child. He further deposed that obeying her orders he had stopped the Sacramento coach and secured a passage for herself and child to San Francisco. It was true that Ah Fe's testimony was of no legal value. But nobody doubted it. Even those who were skeptical of the Pagan's ability to recognize the sacredness of the truth admitted his passionless, unprejudiced unconcern. But it would appear from an hitherto unrecorded passage of this veracious chronicle that herein they were mistaken.

It was about six months after the disappearance of Mrs. Tretherick that Ah Fe, while working in Tretherick's lot, was hailed by two passing Chinamen. They were the ordinary mining coolies, equipped with long poles and baskets for their usual pilgrimages. An animated conversation at once ensued between Ah Fe and his brother Mongolians —a conversation characterized by that usual shrill volubility and apparent animosity which was at once the delight and scorn of the intelligent Caucasian who did not understand a word of it. Such at least was the feeling with which Mr. Tretherick on his veranda, and Col. Starbottle who was passing, regarded their heathenish jargon. The gallant Colonel simply kicked them out of his way; the irate Tretherick with an oath threw a stone at the group and dispersed them. But not before one or two slips of yellow rice paper marked with hieroglyphics were exchanged, and a small parcel put into Ah Fe's hands. When Ah Fe opened this, in the dim solitude of his kitchen, he found a little girl's apron, freshly washed, ironed and folded. On the corner of the hem were the initials "C. T." Ah Fe tucked it away in a corner of his blouse, and proceeded to wash his dishes in the sink with a smile of guileless satisfaction.

Two days after this Ah Fe confronted his master. "Me no likee Fiddletown. Me belly sick. Me go now." Mr. Tretherick violently suggested a profane locality. Ah Fe gazed at him placidly and withdrew.

Before leaving Fiddletown, however, he accidentally met Col. Starbottle and dropped a few incoherent phrases which apparently interested that gentleman. When he concluded, the Col. handed him a letter and a twenty-dollar gold piece. "If you bring me an answer I'll double that—Sabe, John?" Ah Fe nodded. An interview equally accidental, with precisely the same result, took place between Ah Fe and another gentleman, whom I suspect to have been the youthful editor of the *Avalanche*. Yet I regret to state that after proceeding some distance on his journey, Ah Fe calmly broke the seals of both letters, and after trying to read them upside down and sideways, finally divided them into accurate squares, and in this condition disposed of them to a brother Celestial whom he met on the road for a trifling gratuity. The agony of Col. Starbottle on finding his wash-bill made out on the unwritten side of one of these squares, and delivered to him with his weekly clean clothes, and the subsequent discovery that the remaining portions of his letter were circulated by the same method from the Chinese laundry of one Fung Ti of Fiddletown, has been described to me as peculiarly affecting. Yet I am satisfied that a higher nature, rising above the levity induced by the mere contemplation of the insignificant details of this breach of trust, would find ample retributive justice in the difficulties that subsequently attended Ah Fe's pilgrimage.

On the road to Sacramento he was twice playfully thrown from the top of the stage-coach by an intelligent but deeply intoxicated Caucasian, whose moral nature was shocked at riding with one addicted to opium smoking. At Hangtown he was beaten by a passing stranger — purely an act of Christian supererogation. At Dutch Flat he was robbed by well-known hands from unknown motives. At Sacramento he was arrested on suspicion of being something or other, and discharged with a severe reprimand — possibly for not being it, and so delaying the course of justice. At San Francisco he was freely stoned by children of the public schools, but by carefully avoiding these monuments of enlightened progress he at last reached in comparative safety the Chinese quarters, where his abuse was confined to the police and limited by the strong arm of the law.

The next day he entered the wash-house of Chy Fook as an assistant, and on the following Friday was sent with a basket of clean clothes to Chy Fook's several clients.

It was the usual foggy afternoon as he climbed the long wind-swept hill of California street — one of those bleak gray intervals that made the summer a misnomer to any but the liveliest San Franciscan fancy. There was no warmth or color in earth or sky; no light nor shade within or without, only one monotonous, universal neutral tint over everything. There was a fierce unrest in the wind-whipped streets, there was a dreary vacant quiet in the gray houses. When Ah Fe reached the top of the hill the Mission ridge was already hidden, and the chill sea-breeze made him shiver. As he put down his basket to rest himself, it is possible that to his defective intelligence and heathen experience this "God's own climate," as it was called, seemed to possess but scant tenderness, softness or mercy. But it is possible that Ah Fe illogically confounded this season with his old persecutors, the school children, who, being released from studious confinement, at this hour were generally most aggressive. So he hastened on, and, turning a corner, at last stopped before a small house.

It was the usual San Franciscan urban cottage. There was the little strip of cold green shrubbery before it; the chilly bare veranda, and above this again the grim balcony on which no one sat. Ah Fe rang the bell; a servant appeared, glanced at his basket, and reluctantly admitted him as if he were some necessary domestic animal. Ah Fe silently mounted the stairs, and, entering the open door of the front chamber, put down the basket and stood passively on the threshold.

A woman who was sitting in the cold gray light of the window, with a child in her lap, rose listlessly and came toward him. Ah Fe instantly recognized Mrs. Tretherick, but not a muscle of his immobile face changed nor did his slant eyes lighten as he met her own placidly. She evidently did not recognize him as she began to count the clothes. But the child, curiously examining him, suddenly uttered a short glad cry,

"Why it's John! Mamma—it's our old John what we had in Fiddletown."

For an instant Ah Fe's eyes and teeth electrically lightened. The child clapped her hands and caught at his blouse. Then he said, shortly, "Me John—Ah Fe—allee same. Me know you. How do?"

Mrs. Tretherick dropped the clothes nervously and looked hard at Ah Fe. Wanting the quick-witted instinct of affection that sharpened Carrie's perception, she even then could not distinguish him above his fellows. With a recollection of past pain and an obscure suspicion of impending danger, she asked him when he had left Fiddletown.

"Longee time. No likee Fiddletown, no likee Tlevelick. Likee San Flisco. Like washee. Likee Tally."

Ah Fe's laconics pleased Mrs. Tretherick. She did not stop to consider how much an imperfect knowledge of English added to his curt directness and sincerity. But she said, "Don't tell anybody you have seen me," and took out her pocket-book.

Ah Fe, without looking at it, saw that it was nearly empty. Ah Fe, without examining the apartment, saw that it was scantily furnished. Ah Fe, without removing his eyes from blank vacancy, saw that both Mrs. Tretherick and Carrie were poorly dressed. Yet it is my duty to state that Ah Fe's long fingers closed promptly and firmly over the half-dollar which Mrs. Tretherick extended to him.

Then he began to fumble in his blouse with a series of extraordinary contortions. After a few moments he extracted from apparently no particular place a child's apron, which he laid upon the basket with the remark,

"One piecee washman flagittee."

Then he began anew his fumblings and contortions. At last his efforts were rewarded by his producing, apparently from his right ear, a many-folded piece of tissue paper. Unwrapping this carefully, he at last disclosed two twenty-dollar gold pieces, which he handed to Mrs. Tretherick.

"You leavee money top side of blulow, Fiddletown, me findee money. Me fetchee money to you. All lightee."

"But I left no money on the top of the bureau, John," said Mrs. Tretherick earnestly. "There must be some mistake. It belongs to some other person. Take it back, John."

Ah Fe's brows darkened. He drew away from Mrs. Tretherick's extended hand and began hastily to gather up his basket.

"Me no takee back. No, no. Bimeby pleesman he catchee me! He say, 'God damn thief—catchee flowty dollar—come to jailee.' Me no takee back. You leavee money top side blulow,

Fiddletown. Me fetchee money you. Me no takee back."

Mrs. Tretherick hesitated. In the confusion of her flight she *might* have left the money in the manner he had said. In any event she had no right to jeopardize this honest Chinaman's safety by refusing it. So she said, "Very well, John, I will keep it. But you must come again and see me" —here Mrs. T. hesitated with a new and sudden revelation of the fact that any man could wish to see any other than herself,—"and, and—Carry!"

Ah Fe's face lightened. He even uttered a short ventriloquistic laugh without moving his mouth. Then shouldering his basket he shut the door carefully and slid quietly down stairs. In the lower hall he however found an unexpected difficulty in opening the front door, and after fumbling vainly at the lock for a moment, looked around for some help or instruction. But the Irish handmaid who had let him in was contemptuously oblivious of his needs and did not appear.

There occurred a mysterious and painful incident which I shall simply record without attempting to explain. On the hall table a scarf, evidently the property of the servant before alluded to, was lying. As Ah Fe tried the lock with one hand, the other rested lightly on the table. Suddenly, and apparently of its own volition, the scarf began to creep slowly towards Ah Fe's hand. From Ah Fe's hand it began to creep up his sleeve, slowly and with an insinuating, snake-like motion, and then disappeared somewhere in the recesses of his blouse. Without betraying the least interest or concern in this phenomenon, Ah Fe still repeated his experiments upon the lock. A moment later the tablecloth of red damask, moved by apparently the same mysterious impulse, slowly gathered itself under Ah Fe's fingers and sinuously disappeared by the same hidden channel. What further mystery might have followed, I cannot say, for at this moment Ah Fe discovered the secret of the lock, and was enabled to open the door coincident with the sound of footsteps upon the kitchen stairs. Ah Fe did not hasten his movements, but patiently shouldering his basket, closed the door carefully behind him again, and stepped forth into the thick encompassing fog that now shrouded earth and sky.

From her high casement window Mrs. Tretherick watched Ah Fe's figure until it disappeared in the gray cloud. In her present loneliness she felt a keen sense of gratitude toward him, and may have ascribed to the higher emotions and the consciousness of a good deed that certain expansiveness of the chest and swelling of the bosom that was really due to the hidden presence of the scarf and tablecloth under his blouse. For Mrs. Tretherick was still poetically sensitive. As the gray fog deepened into night she drew Carrie closer towards her, and above the prattle of the child pursued a vein of sentimental and egotistic recollection at once bitter and dangerous. The sudden apparition of Ah Fe linked her again with her past life at Fiddletown. Over the dreary interval between she was now wandering—a journey so piteous, wilful, thorny and useless, that it was no wonder that at last Carrie stopped suddenly in the midst of her voluble confidences to throw her small arms around the woman's neck and bid her not to cry.

Heaven forefend that I should use a pen that should be ever dedicated to an exposition of unalterable moral principle to transcribe Mrs. Tretherick's own theory of this interval and episode, with its feeble palliations, its illogical deductions, its fond excuses and weak apologies. It would seem, however, that her experience had been hard. Her slender stock of money was soon exhausted. At Sacramento she found that the composition of verse, although appealing to the highest emotion of the human heart, and compelling the editorial breast to the noblest commendation in the editorial pages, was singularly inadequate to defray the expenses of herself and Carrie. Then she tried the stage, but failed signally. Possibly her conception of the passions was different from that which obtained with a Sacramento audience, but it was certain that her charming presence, so effective at short range, was not sufficiently pronounced for the footlights. She had admirers enough in the green-room, but awakened no abiding affection among the audience. In this strait it occurred to her that she had a voice —a contralto of no very great compass or cultivation, but singularly sweet and touching, and she finally obtained position in a church choir. She held it for three months, greatly to her pecuniary advantage, and, it is said, much to the satisfaction of the gentlemen in the back pews who faced toward her during the singing of the last hymn.

I remember her quite distinctly at this time. The light that slanted through the oriel of St. Dives choir was wont to fall tenderly on her beautiful head with its stacked masses of deerskin-colored hair, on the low black arches of her brows, and to deepen the pretty fringes that shaded her eyes of Genoa velvet. Very pleasant it was to watch the opening and shutting of that small straight mouth, with its quick revelation of little white teeth, and to see the foolish blood faintly deepen her satin cheek as you watched. For Mrs. Tretherick was very sweetly conscious of admiration, and, like most pretty women, gathered herself under your eye like a racer under the spur.

And then of course there came trouble. I have it from the soprano—a little lady who possessed even more than the usual unprejudiced judgment of her sex—that Mrs. Tretherick's conduct was simply shameful; that her conceit was unbearable; that if she considered the rest of the choir as slaves, she, the soprano, would like to know it; that her conduct on Easter Sunday with the basso had attracted the attention of the whole congregation, and that she herself had noticed Doctor Cope twice look up during the service; that her, the soprano's friends had objected to her singing in the choir with a person who had been on the stage, but she had waived this. Yet she had it from the best authority that Mrs. Tretherick had run away from her husband, and that this red-haired child who sometimes came in the choir was not her own. The tenor confided to me, behind the organ, that Mrs. Tretherick had a way of sustaining a note at the end of a line, in order that her voice might linger longer with the congregation—an act that could be attributed only to a defective moral nature; that as a man—he was a very popular dry-goods clerk on week-days, and sang a good deal from apparently behind his eyebrows on the Sabbath—that as a man, sir, he would put up with it no longer. The basso alone—a short German with a heavy voice, for which he seemed reluctantly responsible, and rather grieved at its possession—stood up for Mrs. Tretherick and averred that they were jealous of her because she was "bretty." The climax was at last reached in an open quarrel, wherein Mrs. Tretherick used her tongue with such precision of statement and epithet that the soprano burst into hysterical tears, and had to be supported from the choir by her husband and the tenor. This act was marked intentionally to the congregation by the omission of the usual soprano solo. Mrs. Tretherick went home flushed with triumph, but on reaching her room frantically told Carrie that they were beggars henceforward; that she—her mother—had just taken the very bread out of her darling's mouth, and ended by bursting into a flood of penitent tears. They did not come so quickly as in her old poetical days, but when they came they stung deeply She was roused by a formal visit from a vestryman—one of the Music Committee. Mrs. Tretherick dried her long lashes, put on a new neck ribbon, and went down to the parlor. She stayed there two hours—a fact that might have occasioned some remark but that the vestryman was married and had a family of grown-up daughters. When Mrs. Tretherick returned to her room, she sang to herself in the glass and scolded Carrie. But she retained her place in the choir.

It was not long, however. In due course of time her enemies received a powerful addition to their forces in the committeeman's wife. That lady called upon several of the church members and on Dr. Cope's family. The result was that at a later meeting of the Music Committee Mrs. Tretherick's voice was declared inadequate to the size of the building and she was invited to resign. She did so. She had been out of a situation for two months and her scant means were almost exhausted when Ah Fe's unexpected treasure was tossed into her lap.

The gray fog deepened into night, and the street lamps started into shivering life as, absorbed in these unprofitable memories, Mrs. Tretherick still sat drearily at her window. Even Carrie had slipped away unnoticed, and her abrupt entrance with the damp evening paper in her hand roused Mrs. Tretherick and brought her back to an active realization of the present. For Mrs. Tretherick was wont to scan the advertisements in the faint hope of finding some avenue of employment—she knew not what—open to her needs, and Carrie had noted this habit.

Mrs. Tretherick mechanically closed the shutters,

lit the lights and opened the paper. Her eye fell instinctively on the following paragraph in the telegraphic column:—

"Fiddletown, 7th. Mr. James Tretherick, an old resident of this place, died last night of delirium tremens. Mr. Tretherick was addicted to intemperate habits, said to have been induced by domestic trouble."

Mrs. Tretherick did not start. She quietly turned over another page of the paper and glanced at Carrie. The child was absorbed in a book. Mrs. Tretherick uttered no word, but during the remainder of the evening was unusually silent and cold. When Carrie was undressed and in bed, Mrs. Tretherick suddenly dropped on her knees beside the bed, and taking Carrie's flaming head between her hands, said,

"Should you like to have another papa, Carrie, darling?"

"No," said Carrie, after a moment's thought.

"But a papa to help mamma take care of you— to love you, to give you nice clothes, to make a lady of you when you grow up?"

Carrie turned her sleepy eyes toward the questioner. "Should *you*, mamma?"

Mrs. Tretherick suddenly flushed to the roots of her hair. "Go to sleep," she said sharply, and turned away.

But at midnight the child felt two white arms close tightly around her, and was drawn down into a bosom that heaved, fluttered and at last was broken up by sobs.

"Don't ky, mamma," whispered Carrie, with a vague retrospect of their recent conversation. "Don't ky. I fink I *should* like a new papa if he loved you very much—very, very much!"

A month afterward, to everybody's astonishment, Mrs. Tretherick was married. The happy bridegroom was one Col. Starbottle, recently elected to represent Calaveras County in the legislative councils of the State. As I cannot record the event in finer language than that used by the correspondent of the *Sacramento Globe*, I venture to quote some of his graceful periods. "The relentless shafts of the sly god have been lately busy among our gallant Solons. We quote 'one more unfortunate.' The latest victim is the Hon. A. Starbottle of Calaveras. The fair enchantress in the case is a beautiful widow—a former votary of Thespis and lately a fascinating St. Cecilia of one of the most fashionable churches of San Francisco, where she commanded a high salary."

The *Dutch Flat Intelligencer* saw fit, however, to comment upon the fact with that humorous freedom characteristic of an unfettered press. "The new Democratic war-horse from Calaveras has lately advented in the Legislature with a little bill to change the name of Tretherick to Starbottle. They call it a marriage certificate down there. Mr. Tretherick has been dead just one month, but we presume the gallant Col. is not afraid of ghosts." It is but just to Mrs. Tretherick to state that the Colonel's victory was by no means an easy one

To a natural degree of coyness on the part of the lady was added the impediment of a rival — a prosperous undertaker from Sacramento, who had first seen and loved Mrs. Tretherick at the theatre and church; his professional habits debarring him from ordinary social intercourse and indeed any other than the most formal public contact with the sex. As this gentleman had made a snug fortune during the felicitous prevalence of a severe epidemic, the Colonel regarded him as a dangerous rival. Fortunately, however, the undertaker was called in professionally to lay out a brother Senator who had unhappily fallen by the Colonel's pistol in an affair of honor, and either deterred by physical consideration from rivalry, or wisely concluding that the Colonel was professionally valuable, he withdrew from the field.

The honeymoon was brief, and brought to a close by an untoward incident. During their bridal trip Carrie had been placed in the charge of Col. Starbottle's sister. On their return to the city, immediately on reaching their lodgings, Mrs. Starbottle announced her intention of at once proceeding to Mrs. Culpepper's to bring the child home. Col. Starbottle, who had been exhibiting for some time a certain uneasiness which he had endeavored to overcome by repeated stimulation, finally buttoned his coat tightly across his breast, and after walking unsteadily once or twice up and down the room, suddenly faced his wife with his most imposing manner.

"I have deferred," said the Colonel, with an

exaggeration of port that increased with his inward fear, and a growing thickness of speech, "I have deferr—I may say poshponed statement o' fack thash my duty ter dishclose ter ye. I did no wish to mar sushine mushal happ'ness—to bligh bud o' promise, to darken conjuglar sky by unpleasht revelashun. Musht be done—by G—d, m'm, musht do it now. The chile is gone!"

"Gone!" echoed Mrs. Starbottle.

There was something in the tone of her voice— in the sudden drawing together of the pupils of her eyes, that for a moment nearly sobered the Colonel and partly collapsed his chest.

"I'll splain all in a minit," he said with a deprecating wave of the hand, "everything shall be splained. The-the-the-melencholly event wish preshipitate our happ'ness—the myster'us prov'nice wish releash you—releash chile! hunerstan?—releash chile. The mom't Tretherick die—all claim you have in chile through him—die too. Thash law. Whose chile b'long to? Tretherick? Tretherick dead. Chile can't b'long dead man. Damn nonshense b'long dead man. I'sh your chile? no! who's chile then? Chile b'long to 'ts mother. Unnerstan?"

"Where is she?" said Mrs. Starbottle, with a very white face and a very low voice.

"I'll 'splain all. Chile b'long to 'ts mother. Thash law. I'm lawyer, leshlator, and American sis'n. Ish my duty as lawyer, as leshlator, and 'merikan sis'n to reshtore chile to suff'rin mother at any coss—any coss."

"Where is she?" repeated Mrs. Starbottle with her eyes still fixed on the Colonel's face.

"Gone to 'ts m'o'r. Gone East on shteamer yesserday. Waffed by fav'rin gales to suff'rin p'rent. Thash so!"

Mrs. Starbottle did not move. The Colonel felt his chest slowly collapsing but steadied himself against a chair, and endeavored to beam with chivalrous gallantry not unmixed with magisterial firmness upon her as she sat.

"Your feelin's, m'm, do honor to yer sex, but conshider situashun. Conshider m'ors feelings—conshider *my* feelin's." The Colonel paused, and flourishing a white handkerchief placed it negligently in his breast, and then smiled tenderly above it, as over laces and ruffles, on the woman before him. "Why should dark shedder cass bligh on two sholes with single beat? Chile's fine chile, good chile, but summonelse chile! chile's gone, Clar'; but all ish'n't gone, Clar'. Conshider dearesht, you all's have me!"

Mrs. Starbottle started to her feet. "*You!*" she cried, bringing out a chest note that made the chandeliers ring, "You that I married to give my darling food and clothes. *You!* a dog that I whistled to my side to keep the men off me! *You!*"

She choked up, and then dashed past him into the inner room which had been Carrie's; then she swept by him again into her own bed-room, and then suddenly reappeared before him erect, menacing, with a burning fire over her cheek-bones, a quick straightening of her arched brows and mouth, a squaring of jaw and ophidian flattening of the head.

"Listen!" she said, in a hoarse half-grown boy's voice. "Hear me! If you ever expect to set eyes on me again you must find the child. If you ever expect to speak to me again—to touch me—you must bring her back. For where she goes, I go—you hear me!—where she has gone, look for me!"

She struck out past him again, with a quick feminine throwing out of her arms from the elbows down, as if freeing herself from some imaginary bonds, and dashing into her chamber slammed and locked the door. Colonel Starbottle, although no coward, stood in superstitious fear of an angry woman, and recoiling as she swept by, lost his unsteady foothold and rolled helplessly on the sofa. Here, after one or two unsuccessful attempts to regain his foothold, he remained, uttering from time to time profane but not entirely coherent or intelligible protests, until at last he succumbed to the exhausting quality of his emotions, and the narcotic quantity of his potations.

Meantime, within, Mrs. Starbottle was excitedly gathering her valuables and packing her trunk, even as she had done once before in the course of this remarkable history. Perhaps some recollection of this was in her mind, for she stopped to lean her burning cheeks upon her hand, as if she saw again the figure of the child standing in the doorway, and heard once more a childish voice asking, "Is it mamma?" But the epithet now stung her to the quick, and with a quick, passionate gesture she dashed it away with a tear that had gathered in her eye. And then it chanced that in turning over some clothes she came upon the child's slipper with a broken sandal string. She uttered a great cry here — the first she had uttered — and caught it to her breast, kissing it passionately again and again, and rocking from side to side with a motion peculiar to her sex. And then she took it to the window, the better to see it through her now streaming eyes. Here she was taken with a sudden fit of coughing that she could not stifle with the handkerchief she put to her feverish lips. And then she suddenly grew very faint, the window seemed to recede before her, the floor to sink beneath her feet, and staggering to the bed, she fell prone upon it with the sandal and handkerchief pressed to her breast. Her face was quite pale, the orbit of her eyes dark, and there was a spot upon her lip, another on her handkerchief and still another on the white counterpane of the bed.

The wind had risen, rattling the window sashes, and swaying the white curtains in a ghostly way. Later, a gray fog stole softly over the roofs, soothing the wind-roughened surfaces, and enwrapping all things in an uncertain light and a measureless peace. She lay there very quiet, — for all her troubles, still a very pretty bride. And on the other side of the bolted door the gallant bridegroom, from his temporary couch, snored peacefully.

A week before Christmas day, 1870, the little town of Genoa, in the State of New York, exhibited, perhaps more strongly than at any other time, the bitter irony of its founders and sponsors. A driving snow-storm that had whitened every windward hedge, bush, wall and telegraph pole, played around this soft Italian capital, whirled in and out of the great staring wooden Doric columns of its post-office and hotel, beat upon the cold green shutters of its best houses, and powdered the angular, stiff, dark figures in its streets. From the level of the street the four principal churches of the town stood out starkly, even while their misshapen spires were kindly hidden in the low driving storm. Near the railroad station the new Methodist chapel, whose resemblance to an enormous locomotive was further heightened by the addition of a pyramidal row of front steps, like a cowcatcher, stood as if waiting for a few more houses to be hitched on to proceed to a pleasanter location. But the pride of Genoa—the great Crammer Institute for Young Ladies—stretched its bare brick length and reared its cupola plainly from the bleak Parnassian hill above the principal avenue. There was no evasion in the Crammer Institute of the fact that it was a public institution. A visitor upon its doorstep, a pretty face at its window, were clearly visible all over the township.

The shriek of the engine of the 4 o'clock Northern express brought but few of the usual loungers to the depot. Only a single passenger alighted and was driven away in the solitary waiting sleigh toward the Genoa Hotel. And then the train sped away again—with that passionate indifference to human sympathies or curiosity peculiar to express trains—the one baggage truck was wheeled into the station again, the station door was locked and the station master went home.

The locomotive whistle however awakened the guilty consciousness of three young ladies of the Crammer Institute who were even then surreptitiously regaling themselves in the bake-shop and confectionery saloon of Mistress Phillips in a by-lane. For even the admirable regulations of the Institute failed to entirely develop the physical and moral natures of its pupils; they conformed to the excellent dietary rules in public, and in private drew upon the luxurious rations of their village caterer; they attended church with exemplary formality and flirted informally during service with the village beaux; they received the best and most judicious instruction during school hours, and devoured the trashiest novels during recess. The result of which was an aggregation of quite healthy, quite human and very charming young creatures, that reflected infinite credit on the Institute. Even Mistress Phillips, to whom they owed vast sums, exhilarated by the exuberant spirits and youthful freshness of her guests, declared that the sight of "them young things" did her good, and had even been known to shield them by shameless equivocation.

"Four o'clock! girls, and if we're not back to prayers by five we'll be missed," said the tallest of these foolish virgins, with an aquiline nose and certain quiet *élan* that bespoke the leader, as she rose from her seat. "Have you got the books, Addy?" Addy displayed three dissipated-looking novels under her waterproof. "And the provisions, Carrie?" Carrie showed a suspicious parcel filling the pocket of her sack. "All right, then. Come girls, trudge. Charge it," she added, nodding to her host, as they passed toward the door. "I'll pay you when my quarter's allowance comes."

"No, Kate," interposed Carrie, producing her purse, "let me pay—it's my turn."

"Never," said Kate, arching her black brows loftily—"even if you do have rich relatives and regular remittances from California. Never. Come, girls—forward, march!"

As they opened the door a gust of wind nearly took them off their feet. Kind-hearted Mrs. Phillips was alarmed. "Sakes alive! galls, ye mussn't go out in sich weather; better let me send word to the Institoot and make ye up a nice bed to-night in my parlor." But the last sentence was lost in a chorus of half-suppressed shrieks as the girls, hand in hand, ran down the steps into the storm and were at once whirled away.

The short December day, unlit by any sunset glow, was failing fast. It was quite dark already, and the air was thick with driving snow. For some distance their high spirits, youth, and even inexperience kept them bravely up, but in ambitiously attempting a short cut from the high road across an open field their strength gave out, the laugh grew less frequent, and tears began to stand in Carrie's brown eyes. When they reached the road again they were utterly exhausted. "Let us go back," said Carrie.

"We'd never get across that field again," said Addy.

"Let's stop at the first house, then," said Carrie.

"The first house," said Addy, peering through the gathering darkness, "is Squire Robinson's." She darted a mischievous glance at Carrie that even in her discomfort and fear brought the quick blood to her cheek.

"O yes," said Kate, with gloomy irony, "certainly, stop at the Squire's by all means, and be invited to tea, and be driven home after tea by your dear friend Mr. Harry, with a formal apology from Mrs. Robinson, and hopes that the young ladies may be excused this time. No," continued Kate, with sudden energy, "that may suit *you*—but I'm going back as I came—by the window—or not at all." Then she pounced suddenly, like a hawk, on Carrie, who was betraying a tendency to sit down on a snow-bank and whimper, and shook her briskly. "You'll be going to sleep next. Stay,—hold your tongues, all of you—what's that?"

It was the sound of sleigh-bells. Coming down toward them out of the darkness was a sleigh with a single occupant. "Hold down your heads, girls, if it's anybody that knows us—we're lost." But it was not, for a voice strange to their ears, but withal very kindly and pleasant, asked if its owner could be of any help to them. As they turned toward him they saw it was a man wrapped in a handsome sealskin cloak, wearing a sealskin cap—his face, half concealed by a muffler of the same material, disclosing only a pair of long moustaches and two keen dark eyes. "It's a son of old Santa Claus," whispered Addy. The girls tittered audibly as they tumbled into the sleigh—they had regained their former spirits. "Where shall I take you?" said the stranger, quietly. There was a hurried whispering, and then Kate said boldly, "To the Institute." They drove silently up the hill until the long ascetic building loomed up before them. The stranger reined up suddenly. "You know the way better than I," he said; "where do you go in?"—"Through the back window," said Kate, with sudden and appalling frankness. "I see!" responded their strange driver quietly, and alighting quickly, removed the bells from the horses. "We can drive as near as you please now," he added by way of explanation. "He certainly is a son of Santa Claus," whispered Addy; "hadn't we better ask after his father?" "Hush," said Kate, decidedly. "He is an angel, I dare say." She added, with a delicious irrelevance, which was however perfectly understood by her feminine auditors, "We are looking like three frights."

Cautiously skirting the fences, they at last pulled up a few feet from a dark wall. The stranger proceeded to assist them to alight. There was still some light from the reflected snow, and as he handed his fair companions to the ground each was conscious of undergoing an intense though respectful scrutiny. He assisted them gravely to open the window, and then discreetly retired to the sleigh until the difficult and somewhat discomposing ingress was made. He then walked to the window. "Thank you and good night" whispered three voices. A single figure still lingered. The stranger leaned over the window-sill. "Will you permit me to light my cigar here? it might attract attention if I struck a match outside." By the upspringing light he saw the figure of Kate very charmingly framed in by the window. The match burnt slowly out in his fingers. Kate smiled mischievously. The astute young woman had detected the pitiable subterfuge. For what else did she stand at the head of her class, and had doting parents paid three years' tuition?

The storm had passed, and the sun was shining quite cheerily in the eastern recitation-room the next morning, when Miss Kate, whose seat was nearest the window, placing her hand pathetically upon her heart, affected to fall in bashful and extreme agitation upon the shoulder of Carrie her neighbor. "*He has come,*" she gasped in a thrilling whisper. "Who?" asked Carrie sympathetically, who never clearly understood when Kate was in earnest. "Who?—why the man who rescued us last night! I saw him drive to the door this moment. Don't speak—I shall be better in a moment, there!" she said, and the shameless hypocrite passed her hand pathetically across her forehead with a tragic air.

"What can he want?" asked Carrie, whose curiosity was excited.

"I don't know," said Kate, suddenly relapsing

into gloomy cynicism. "Possibly to put his five daughters to school. Perhaps to finish his young wife and warn her against us."

"He didn't look old, and he didn't seem like a married man," rejoined Addy thoughtfully.

"That was his art, you poor creature!" returned Kate scornfully; "you can never tell anything of these men—they are so deceitful. Besides, it's just my fate!"

"Why Kate," began Carrie, in serious concern.

"Hush, Miss Walker is saying something," said Kate laughing.

"The young ladies will please give attention," said a slow perfunctory voice. "Miss Carrie Tretherick is wanted in the parlor."

Meantime Mr. Jack Prince, the name given on the card and various letters and credentials submitted to the Rev. Mr. Crammer, paced the somewhat severe apartment known publicly as the "Reception Parlor," and privately to the pupils as "Purgatory." His keen eyes had taken in the various rigid details, from the flat steam "Radiator" like an enormous japanned soda-cracker that heated one end of the room, to the monumental bust of Dr. Crammer that hopelessly chilled the other; from the Lord's Prayer, executed by a former writing-master in such gratuitous variety of elegant calligraphic trifling as to considerably abate the serious value of the composition, to three views of Genoa from the Institute, which nobody ever recognized, taken on the spot by the drawing teacher; from two illuminated texts of Scripture in an English letter, so gratuitously and hideously remote as to chill all human interest, to a large photograph of the senior class, in which the prettiest girls were Ethiopian in complexion, and sat (apparently) on each other's heads and shoulders;—his fingers had turned listlessly the leaves of school catalogues, the *sermons* of Dr. Crammer, the *poems* of Henry Kirke White, the *Lays of the Sanctuary* and *Lives of Celebrated Women;*—his fancy, and it was a nervously active one, had gone over the partings and greetings that must have taken place here, and wondered why the apartment had yet caught so little of the flavor of humanity;—indeed, I am afraid he had almost forgotten the object of his visit when the door opened and Carrie Tretherick stood before him.

It was one of those faces he had seen the night before,—prettier even than it had seemed then,—and yet I think he was conscious of some disappointment, without knowing exactly why. Her abundant waving hair was of a guinea-golden tint, her complexion of a peculiar flower-like delicacy, her brown eyes of the color of sea-weed in deep water. It certainly was not her beauty that disappointed him.

Without possessing his sensitiveness to impression, Carrie was, on her part, quite as vaguely ill at ease. She saw before her one of those men whom the sex would vaguely generalize as "nice"—that is to say, correct in all the superficial appointments of style, dress, manners and feature. Yet there was a decidedly unconventional quality about him — he was totally unlike anything or anybody that she could remember, and, as the attributes of originality are often as apt to alarm as to attract people, she was not entirely prepossessed in his favor.

"I can hardly hope," he began pleasantly, "that you remember me. It is eleven years ago, and you were a very little girl. I am afraid I cannot even claim to have enjoyed that familiarity that might exist between a child of six and a young man of twenty-one. I don't think I was fond of children. But I knew your mother very well. I was editor of the *Avalanche* in Fiddletown when she took you to San Francisco."

"You mean my stepmother — she wasn't my mother, you know," interposed Carrie hastily.

Mr. Prince looked at her curiously. "I mean your stepmother," he said gravely. "I never had the pleasure of meeting your mother."

"No, *mother* hasn't been in California these twelve years."

There was an intentional emphasizing of the title and of its distinction, that began to coldly interest Prince after his first astonishment was past.

"As I come from your stepmother now," he went on, with a slight laugh, "I must ask you to go back for a few moments to that point. After your father's death, your mother—I mean your stepmother—recognized the fact that your mother, the first Mrs. Tretherick, was legally and morally your guardian, and although much against her inclination and affections, placed you again in her charge."

"My stepmother married again within a month after father died, and sent me home," said Carrie with great directness, and the faintest toss of her head.

Mr. Prince smiled so sweetly, and apparently so sympathetically, that Carrie began to like him. With no other notice of the interruption he went on: "After your stepmother had performed this act of simple justice, she entered into an agreement with your mother to defray the expenses of your education until your eighteenth year, when you were to elect and choose which of the two should thereafter be your guardian, and with whom you would make your home. This agreement, I think, you are already aware of, and I believe knew at the time."

"I was a mere child, then," said Carrie.

"Certainly," said Mr. Prince with the same smile; "still the conditions, I think, have never been oppressive to you nor your mother, and the only time they are likely to give you the least uneasiness will be when you come to make up your mind in the choice of your guardian. That will be on your eighteenth birthday—the 20th, I think, of the present month."

Carrie was silent.

"Pray do not think that I am here to receive your decision—even if it be already made. I only came to inform you that your stepmother, Mrs. Starbottle, will be in town to-morrow, and will pass a few days at the hotel. If it is your wish to see her before you make up your mind, she will be glad to meet you. She does not, however, wish to do anything to influence your judgment."

"Does mother know she is coming?" said Carrie hastily.

"I do not know," said Prince gravely; "I only know that if you conclude to see Mrs. Starbottle, it will be with your mother's permission. Mrs. Starbottle will keep sacredly this part of the agreement, made ten years ago. But her health is very poor, and the change and country quiet of a few days may benefit her." Mr. Prince bent his keen bright eyes upon the young girl, and almost held his breath until she spoke again.

"Mother's coming up to-day or to-morrow," she said, looking up.

"Ah!" said Mr. Prince, with a sweet and languid smile.

"Is Col. Starbottle here too?" asked Carrie, after a pause.

"Col. Starbottle is dead — your stepmother is again a widow."

"Dead," repeated Carrie.

"Yes," replied Mr. Prince, "your stepmother has been singularly unfortunate in surviving her affections."

Carrie did not know what he meant, and looked so. Mr. Prince smiled reassuringly.

Presently Carrie began to whimper.

Mr. Prince softly stepped beside her chair.

"I am afraid," he said, with a very peculiar light in his eye, and a singular dropping of the corners of his moustache, "I am afraid you are taking this too deeply. It will be some days before you are called upon to make a decision. Let us talk of something else. I hope you caught no cold last evening."

Carrie's face shone out again in dimples.

"You must have thought us so queer! It was too bad to give you so much trouble."

"None whatever, I assure you. My sense of propriety," he added demurely, "which might have been outraged had I been called upon to help three young ladies out of a schoolroom window at night, was deeply gratified at being able to assist them in again." The door-bell rang loudly, and Mr. Prince rose. "Take your own time, and think well before you make your decision." But Carrie's ear and attention were given to the sound of voices in the hall. At the same moment the door was thrown open and a servant announced, "Mrs. Tretherick and Mr. Robinson."

The afternoon train had just shrieked out its usual indignant protest at stopping at Genoa at all, as Mr. Jack Prince entered the outskirts of the town and drove towards his hotel. He was wearied and cynical; a drive of a dozen miles through unpicturesque outlying villages, past small economic farmhouses and hideous villas that violated his fastidious taste, had, I fear, left that gentleman in a captious state of mind. He would have even avoided his taciturn landlord as he drove up to the door, but that functionary waylaid him on the steps. "There's a lady in the sittin' room waitin' for ye." Mr. Prince hurried up-stairs and entered the room as Mrs. Starbottle flew towards him.

She had changed sadly in the last ten years. Her figure was wasted to half its size; the beautiful curves of her bust and shoulders were broken or inverted; the once full, rounded arm was shrunken in its sleeve, and the golden hoops that encircled her wan wrists almost slipped from her hands as her long, scant fingers closed convulsively around Jack's. Her cheek-bones were painted that afternoon with the hectic of fever; somewhere in the hollows of those cheeks were buried the dimples of long ago, but their graves were forgotten; her lustrous eyes were still beautiful, though the orbits were deeper than before; her mouth was still sweet, although the lips parted more easily over the little teeth, and even in breathing—and showed more of them than she was wont to do before. The glory of her blonde hair was still left; it was finer, more silken and ethereal, yet it failed even in its plenitude to cover the hollows of the blue-veined temples.

"Clara," said Jack reproachfully.

"Oh, forgive me, Jack," she said, falling into a chair but still clinging to his hand, "forgive me, dear, but I could not wait longer. I should have died, Jack, died before another night. Bear with me a little longer,—it will not be long,—but let me stay. I may not see her, I know—I shall not speak to her—but it's so sweet to feel that I am at last near her—that I breathe the same air with my darling—I am better already, Jack, I am indeed. And you have seen her to-day? How did she look? what did she say?—tell me all—everything, Jack.

Was she beautiful?—they say she is! Has she grown? Would you have known her again? Will she come, Jack? Perhaps she has been here already—perhaps—" she had risen with tremulous excitement, and was glancing at the door. "Perhaps she is here now. Why don't you speak, Jack —tell me all."

The keen eyes that looked down into hers were glistening with an infinite tenderness that none perhaps but she would have deemed them capable of. "Clara," he said, gently and cheerily, "try and compose yourself. You are trembling now with the fatigue and excitement of your journey. I have seen Carrie—she is well and beautiful! Let that suffice you now."

His gentle firmness composed and calmed her now as it had often done before. Stroking her thin hand, he said after a pause, "Did Carrie ever write to you?"

"Twice—thanking me for some presents; they were only school-girl letters," she added, nervously answering the interrogation of his eyes.

"Did she ever know of your own troubles—of your poverty! of the sacrifices you made to pay her bills; of your pawning your clothes and jewels; of your——"

"No, no," interrupted the woman quickly—"no! How could she? I have no enemy cruel enough to tell her that."

"But if she—or if Mrs. Tretherick—had heard of it? If Carrie thought you were poor and unable to support her properly—it might influence her decision. Young girls are fond of the position that wealth can give. She may have rich friends—maybe a lover."

Mrs. Starbottle winced at the last sentence, "But," she said eagerly, grasping Jack's hand, "when you found me sick and helpless at Sacramento—when you—God bless you for it, Jack!—offered to help me to the East, you said you knew of something— you had some plan—that would make me and Carrie independent."

"Yes," said Jack, hastily, "but I want you to get strong and well first. And now that you are calmer, you shall listen to my visit to the school."

It was then that Mr. Jack Prince proceeded to describe the interview already recorded with a singular felicity and discretion that shames my own account of that proceeding. Without suppressing a single fact, without omitting a word or detail, he yet managed to throw a poetic veil over that prosaic episode—to invest the heroine with a romantic roseate atmosphere, which, though not perhaps entirely imaginary, still I fear exhibited that genius which ten years ago had made the columns of the *Fiddletown Avalanche* at once fascinating and instructive. It was not until he saw the heightening color and heard the quick breathing of his eager listener that he felt a pang of self-reproach. "God help her and forgive me," he muttered between his clenched teeth, "but how can I tell her *all* now!"

That night when Mrs. Starbottle laid her weary head upon her pillow she tried to picture to herself Carrie at the same moment sleeping peacefully in the great school-house on the hill, and it was a rare comfort to this yearning foolish woman to know that she was so near. But at this moment Carrie was sitting on the edge of her bed, half undressed, pouting her pretty lips, and twisting her long, leonine locks between her fingers, as Miss Kate Van Corlear, dramatically wrapped in a long white counterpane, her black eyes sparkling, and her thorough-bred nose thrown high in air, stood over her like a wrathful and indignant ghost. For Carrie had that evening imparted her woes and her history to Miss Kate, and that young lady had "proved herself no friend," by falling into a state of fiery indignation over Carrie's "ingratitude," and openly and shamelessly espousing the claims of Mrs. Starbottle. "Why if the half you tell me is true, your mother and those Robinsons are making of you not only a little coward but a little snob, Miss. Respectability forsooth! look you! my family are centuries before the Trethericks, but if my family had ever treated me in this way, and then asked me to turn my back on my best friend, I'd whistle them down the wind," and here Kate snapped her fingers, bent her black brows, and glared around the room, as if in search of a recreant Van Corlear.

"You just talk this way because you have taken a fancy to that Mr. Prince," said Carrie.

In the debasing slang of the period that had even found its way into the virgin cloisters of the Crammer Institute, Miss Kate, as she afterwards expressed it, instantly "went for her."

First with a shake of her head she threw her

long black hair over one shoulder, then dropping one end of the counterpane from the other like a vestal tunic, she stepped before Carrie with a purposely exaggerated classic stride. "And what if I have, Miss? What if I happen to know a gentleman when I see him? What if I happen to know that among a thousand such traditional, conventional, feeble editions of their grandfathers as Mr. Harry Robinson, you cannot find one original, independent, individualized gentleman like your Prince! Go to bed, Miss! and pray to Heaven that he may be *your* Prince indeed! Ask to have a contrite and grateful heart, and thank the Lord in particular for having sent you such a friend as Kate Van Corlear." Yet after an imposing dramatic exit, she reappeared the next moment as a straight white flash, kissed Carrie between the brows, and was gone.

The next day was a weary one to Jack Prince. He was convinced in his mind that Carrie would not come, yet to keep this consciousness from Mrs. Starbottle, to meet her simple hopefulness with an equal degree of apparent faith, was a hard and difficult task. He would have tried to divert her mind by taking her on a long drive, but she was fearful that Carrie might come during her absence, and her strength, he was obliged to admit, had failed greatly. As he looked into her large and awe-inspiring clear eyes, a something he tried to keep from his mind,—to put off day by day from contemplation,—kept asserting itself directly to his inner consciousness. He began to doubt the expediency and wisdom of his management; he recalled every incident of his interview with Carrie, and half believed that its failure was due to himself. Yet Mrs. Starbottle was very patient and confident; her very confidence shook his faith in his own judgment. When her strength was equal to the exertion, she was propped up in her chair by the window, where she could see the school and the entrance to the hotel. In the intervals she would elaborate pleasant plans for the future, and would sketch a country home. She had taken a strange fancy, as it seemed to Prince, to the present location, but it was notable that the future always thus outlined was one of quiet and repose. She believed she would get well soon; in fact she thought she was now much better than she had been, but it might be long before she should be quite strong again. She would whisper on in this way until Jack would dash madly down into the bar-room, order liquors that he did not drink, light cigars that he did not smoke, talk with men that he did not listen to, and behave generally as our stronger sex is apt to do in periods of delicate trials and perplexity.

The day closed with a clouded sky and a bitter searching wind. With the night fell a few wandering flakes of snow. She was still content and hopeful, and as Jack wheeled her from the window to the fire, she explained to him how that, as the school-term was drawing near its close, Carrie was probably kept closely at her lessons during the day, and could only leave the school at night. So she sat up the greater part of the evening and combed her silken hair, and, as far as her strength would allow, made an undress toilette to receive her guest. "We must not frighten the child, Jack," she said apologetically and with something of her old coquetry.

It was with a feeling of relief that, at ten o'clock, Jack received a message from the landlord, saying that the doctor would like to see him for a moment down stairs. As Jack entered the grim, dimly-lighted parlor, he observed the hooded figure of a woman near the fire. He was about to withdraw again, when a voice that he remembered very pleasantly said:—

"Oh, it's all right. I'm the doctor."

The hood was thrown back, and Prince saw the shining black hair and black audacious eyes of Kate Van Corlear.

"Don't ask any questions. I'm the doctor, and there's my prescription," and she pointed to the half-frightened, half-sobbing Carrie in the corner; "to be taken at once!"

"Then Mrs. Tretherick has given her permission?"

"Not much, if I know the sentiments of that lady," replied Kate, saucily.

"Then how did you get away?" asked Prince gravely.

"BY THE WINDOW."

When Mr. Prince had left Carrie in the arms of her stepmother, he returned to the parlor.

"Well?" demanded Kate.

"She will stay—*you* will, I hope, also, to-night."

"As I shall not be eighteen and my own mistress on the 20th, and as I haven't a sick stepmother, I won't."

"Then you will give me the pleasure of seeing you safely through the window again?"

When Mr. Prince returned an hour later, he found Carrie sitting on a low stool at Mrs. Starbottle's feet. Her head was in her stepmother's lap, and she had sobbed herself to sleep. Mrs. Starbottle put her finger to her lip. "I told you she would come. God bless you, Jack, and good night."

The next morning Mrs. Tretherick indignant, the Rev. Asa Crammer, Principal, injured, and Mr. Joel Robinson, Senior, complacently respectable, called upon Mr. Prince. There was a stormy meeting, ending in a demand for Carrie. "We certainly cannot admit of this interference," said Mrs. Tretherick, a fashionably-dressed, indistinctive-looking woman; "it is several days before the expiration of our agreement, and we do not feel, under the circumstances, justified in releasing Mrs. Starbottle from its conditions." "Until the expiration of the school term, we must consider Miss Tretherick as complying entirely with its rules and discipline," imposed Dr. Crammer. "The whole proceeding is calculated to injure the prospects and compromise the position of Miss Tretherick in society," suggested Mr. Robinson.

In vain Mr. Prince urged the failing condition

of Mrs. Starbottle, her absolute freedom from complicity with Carrie's flight, the pardonable and natural instincts of the girl, and his own assurance that they were willing to abide by her decision. And then, with a rising color in his cheek, a dangerous look in his eye, but a singular calmness in his speech, he added:

"One word more. It becomes my duty to inform you of a circumstance which would certainly justify me, as an executor of the late Mr. Tretherick, in fully resisting your demands. A few months after Mr. Tretherick's death, through the agency of a Chinaman in his employment, it was discovered that he had made a will, which was subsequently found among his papers. The insignificant value of his bequest—mostly land, then quite valueless—prevented his executors from carrying out his wishes, or from even proving the will, or making it otherwise publicly known, until within the last two or three years, when the property had enormously increased in value. The provisions of that bequest are simple, but unmistakable. The property is divided between Carrie and her stepmother, with the explicit condition that Mrs. Starbottle shall become her legal guardian, provide for her education, and in all details stand to her *in loco parentis.*"

"What is the value of this bequest?" asked Mr. Robinson. "I cannot tell exactly, but not far from half a million, I should say," returned Prince. "Certainly, with this knowledge, as a friend of Miss Tretherick, I must say that her conduct is as judicious as it is honorable to her," responded Mr. Robinson. "I shall not presume to question the wishes or throw any obstacles in the way of carrying out the intentions of my dead husband," added Mrs. Tretherick, and the interview was closed.

When its result was made known to Mrs. Starbottle, she raised Jack's hand to her feverish lips. "It cannot add to *my* happiness now, Jack, but tell me, why did you keep it from her?" Jack smiled but did not reply.

Within the next week the necessary legal formalities were concluded, and Carrie was restored to her stepmother. At Mrs. Starbottle's request a small house in the outskirts of the town was procured, and thither they removed to wait the spring and Mrs. Starbottle's convalescence. Both came tardily that year.

Yet she was happy and patient. She was fond of watching the budding of the trees beyond her window—a novel sight to her Californian experience—and of asking Carrie their names and seasons. Even at this time she projected for that summer, which seemed to her so mysteriously withheld, long walks with Carrie through the leafy woods whose gray, misty ranks she could see along the hill-top. She even thought she could write poetry about them—and recalled the fact as evidence of her gaining strength; and there is, I believe, still treasured by one of the members of this little household, a little carol so joyous, so simple and so innocent, that it might have been an echo of the robin that called to her from the window, as perhaps it was.

And then without warning there dropped from Heaven a day so tender, so mystically soft, so dreamily beautiful, so throbbing and alive with the fluttering of invisible wings, so replete and bounteously overflowing with an awakening and joyous resurrection not taught by man or limited by creed—that they thought it fit to bring her out and lay her in that glorious sunshine that sprinkled like the droppings of a bridal torch the happy lintels and doors. And there she lay, beatified and calm.

Wearied by watching, Carrie had fallen asleep by her side, and Mrs. Starbottle's thin fingers lay like a benediction on her head. Presently she called Jack to her side.

"Who was that," she whispered, "who just came in?".

"Miss Van Corlear," said Jack, answering the look in her great hollow eyes.

"Jack," she said, after a moment's silence, "sit by me a moment, dear Jack; I've something I must say. If I ever seemed hard or cold or coquettish to you in the old days, it was because I loved you, Jack, too well to mar your future by linking it with my own. I always loved you, dear Jack, even when I seemed least worthy of you. That is gone now; but I had a dream lately, Jack, a foolish woman's dream, that you might find what I lacked in *her*," and she glanced lovingly at the sleeping girl at her side,—"that you might love her as you have loved me. But even that is not to be, Jack—is it?" and she glanced wistfully in his face. Jack pressed her hand but did not speak. After a few moments' silence she again said, "Perhaps you are right in your choice. She is a good-hearted girl — Jack — but a little bold."

And with this last flicker of foolish weak humanity in her struggling spirit she spoke no more. When they came to her a moment later, a tiny bird that had lit upon her breast flew away, and the hand that they lifted from Carrie's head fell lifeless at her side.

A MONTE FLAT PASTORAL.

HOW OLD MAN PLUNKETT WENT HOME.

I THINK we all loved him. Even after he mismanaged the affairs of the Amity Ditch Company, we commiserated him, although most of us were stockholders and lost heavily. I remember that the blacksmith went so far as to say that "them chaps as put that responsibility on the old man oughter be lynched." But the blacksmith was not a stockholder, and the expression was looked upon as the excusable extravagance of a large sympathizing nature, that, when combined with a powerful frame, was unworthy of notice. At least that was the way they put it. Yet I think there was a general feeling of regret that this misfortune would interfere with the old man's long cherished plan of "going home."

Indeed for the last ten years he had been "going home." He was going home after a six months' sojourn at Monte Flat. He was going home after the first rains. He was going home when the rains were over. He was going home when he had cut the timber on Buckeye Hill, when there was pasture on Dow's Flat, when he struck pay-dirt on Eureka Hill, when the Amity Company paid its first dividend, when the election was over, when he had received an answer from his wife. And so the years rolled by, the spring rains came and went, the woods of Buckeye Hill were level with the ground, the pasture on Dow's Flat grew sere and dry, Eureka Hill yielded its pay-dirt and swamped its owner, the first dividends of the Amity Company were made from the assessments of stockholders, there were new county officers at Monte Flat, his wife's answer had changed into a persistent question, and still old man Plunkett remained.

It is only fair to say that he had made several distinct essays towards going. Five years before he had bidden good-bye to Monte Hill with much effusion and hand-shaking. But he never got any further than the next town. Here he was induced to trade the sorrel colt he was riding for a bay mare—a transaction that at once opened to his lively fancy a vista of vast and successful future speculation. A few days after, Abner Dean of Angel's received a letter from him stating that he was going to Visalia to buy horses. "I am satisfied," wrote Plunkett, with that elevated rhetoric for which his correspondence was remarkable, "I am satisfied that we are at last developing the real resources of California. The world will yet look to Dow's Flat as the great stock-raising centre. In view of the interests involved, I have deferred my departure for a month." It was two before he again returned to us, penniless. Six months later he was again enabled to start for the Eastern States, and this time he got as far as San Francisco. I have before me a letter which I received a few days after his arrival, from which I venture to give an extract: "You know, my dear boy, that I have always believed that gambling, as it is absurdly called, is still in its infancy in California. I have always maintained that a perfect system might be invented by which the game of poker may be made to yield a certain percentage to the intelligent player. I am not at liberty at present to disclose the system, but before leaving this city I intend to perfect it." He seems to have done so, and returned to Monte Flat with two dollars and thirty-seven cents, the absolute remainder of his capital after such perfection.

It was not until 1868 that he appeared to have finally succeeded in going home. He left us by the overland route—a route which he declared would give great opportunity for the discovery of undeveloped resources. His last letter was dated Virginia City. He was absent three years. At the close of a very hot day in midsummer he alighted from the Wingdam stage with hair and beard powdered with dust and age. There was a certain shyness about his greeting, quite different from his usual frank volubility, that did not, however, impress us as any accession of character. For some days he was reserved regarding his recent visit, contenting himself with asserting, with more or less aggressiveness, that he had "always said he was going home and now he had been there." Later he grew more communicative, and spoke freely and critically of the manners and customs of New York and Boston, commented on the social changes in the years of his absence, and, I remember, was very hard upon what he deemed the follies incidental to a high state of civilization. Still later he darkly alluded to the moral laxity of the higher planes of Eastern society, but it was not long before he completely tore away the veil and revealed the naked wickedness of New York social life in a way I even now shudder to recall. Vinous intoxication, it appeared, was a common habit of the first ladies of the city; immoralities which he scarcely dared name were daily practiced by the refined of both sexes; niggardliness and greed were the common vices of the rich. "I have always asserted," he continued, "that corruption must exist where luxury and riches are rampant, and capital is not used to develop the natural resources of the country. Thank you—I will take mine without sugar." It is possible that some of these painful details crept into the local journals. I remember an editorial in the *Monte Flat Monitor*, entitled "The Effete East," in which the fatal decadence of New York and New England was elaborately stated, and California offered as a means of natural salvation. "Perhaps," said the *Monitor*, "we might add that Calaveras county offers superior inducements to the Eastern visitor with capital."

Later he spoke of his family. The daughter he had left a child had grown into beautiful womanhood; the son was already taller and larger than his father, and in a playful trial of strength, "the young rascal," added Plunkett, with a voice broken with paternal pride and humorous objurgation, had twice thrown his doting parent to the ground. But it was of his daughter he chiefly spoke. Perhaps emboldened by the evident interest which masculine Monte Flat held in feminine beauty, he expatiated at some length on her various charms and accomplishments, and finally produced her photograph,—that of a very pretty girl,—to their infinite peril. But his account of his first meeting with her was so peculiar that I must fain give it after his own methods, which were, perhaps, some shades less precise and elegant than his written style.

"You see, boys, it's always been my opinion that a man oughter be able to tell his own flesh and blood by instinct. It's ten years since I'd seen my Melindy, and she was then only seven and about so high. So when I went to New York, what did I do? Did I go straight to my house and ask for my wife and daughter, like other folks? No, sir! I rigged myself up as a peddler, as a peddler, sir, and I rung the bell. When the servant came to the door, I wanted—don't you see—to show the ladies some trinkets. Then there was a voice over the banister, says, "Don't want anything — send him away." "Some nice laces, ma'am, smuggled," I says looking up. "Get out you wretch," says she. I knew the voice, boys, it was my wife; sure as a gun,—thar wasn't any instinct thar. "May be the young ladies want somethin'," I said. "Did you hear me!" says she, and with that she jumps forward and I left. It's ten years, boys, since I've seen the old woman, but somehow, when she fetched that leap, I natcrally left."

He had been standing beside the bar,—his usual attitude,—when he made this speech, but at this point he half-faced his auditors with a look that was very effective. Indeed a few who had exhibited some signs of skepticism and lack of interest at once assumed an appearance of intense gratification and curiosity as he went on.

"Well, by hangin' round there for a day or two, I found out at last it was to be Melindy's birthday next week, and that she was goin' to have a big party. I tell ye what, boys, it weren't no slouch of a reception. The whole house was bloomin' with flowers, and blazin' with lights, and there was no end of servants and plate and refreshments and fixin's—"

"Uncle Joe."

"Well?"

"Where did they get the money?"

Plunkett faced his interlocutor with a severe glance. "I always said," he replied slowly, "that when I went home, I'd send on ahead of me a draft for ten thousand dollars. I always said that, didn't I? Eh? And I said I was goin' home—and I've been home—haven't I? Well?"

Either there was something irresistibly conclusive in this logic or else the desire to hear the remainder of Plunkett's story was stronger; but there was no more interruption. His ready good-humor quickly returned, and, with a slight chuckle, he went on.

"I went to the biggest jewelry shop in town, and I bought a pair of diamond earrings and put them in my pocket, and went to the house. 'What name?' says the chap who opened the door, and he looked like a cross 'twixt a restaurant waiter and a parson. 'Skeesicks,' said I. He takes me in and pretty soon my wife comes sailin' into the parlor and says: 'Excuse me, but I don't think I recognize the name.' She was mighty polite for I had on a red wig and side-whiskers. 'A friend of your husband's from California, ma'am, with a present for your daughter, Miss——,' and I made as I had forgot the name. But all of a sudden a voice said, 'That's too thin,' and in walked Melindy. 'It's playin' it rather low down, father, to pretend you don't know your daughter's name—ain't it now? How are you, old man?' And with that she tears off my wig and whiskers, and throws her arms around my neck,—instinct, sir, pure instinct!"

Emboldened by the laughter which followed his description of the filial utterances of Melinda, he again repeated her speech, with more or less elaboration, joining in with, and indeed often leading, the hilarity that accompanied it, and returning to it with more or less incoherency, several times during the evening.

And so at various times, and at various places, —but chiefly in bar-rooms,—did this Ulysses of Monte Flat recount the story of his wanderings. There were several discrepancies in his statement, there was sometimes considerable prolixity of detail, there was occasional change of character and scenery, there was once or twice an absolute change in the denouement, but always the fact of his having visited his wife and children remained. Of course in a skeptical community like that of Monte Flat—a community accustomed to great expectation and small realization, a community wherein, to use the local dialect, "they got the color and struck hardpan," more frequently than any other mining camp—in such a community the fullest credence was not given to old man Plunkett's facts. There was only one exception to the general unbelief—Henry York, of Sandy Bar. It was he who was always an attentive listener; it was his scant purse that had often furnished Plunkett with means to pursue his unprofitable speculations; it was to him that the charms of Melinda were more frequently rehearsed; it was he that had borrowed her photograph—and it was he that, sitting alone in his little cabin one night, kissed that photograph until his honest, handsome face glowed again in the firelight.

It was dusty in Monte Flat. The ruins of the long, dry season were crumbling everywhere; everywhere the dying summer had strewn its red ashes a foot deep or exhaled its last breath in a red cloud above the troubled highways. The alders and cottonwoods that marked the line of the water-courses were grimy with dust and looked as if they might have taken root in the open air; the gleaming stones of the parched water-courses themselves were as dry bones in the valley of death. The dusty sunset at times painted the flanks of the distant hills a dull coppery hue; on other days there was an odd, indefinable earthquake halo on the volcanic cones of the further coast spurs; again an acrid, resinous smoke from the burning wood on Heavytree Hill, smarted the eyes and choked the free breath of Monte Flat, or a fierce wind, driving everything— including the shriveled summer like a curled leaf— before it, swept down the flanks of the Sierras and chased the inhabitants to the doors of their cabins, and shook its red fist in at their windows. And on such a night as this,—the dust having, in some way, choked the wheels of material progress in Monte Flat,—most of the inhabitants were gathered listlessly in the gilded bar-room of the Moquelumne Hotel, spitting silently at the red-hot stove that tempered the mountain winds to the shorn lambs of Monte Flat, and waiting for the rain.

Every method known to the Flat of beguiling the time until the advent of this long-looked-for phenomenon had been tried. It is true the methods were not many—being limited chiefly to that form of popular facetiæ known as practical joking; and even this had assumed the seriousness of a business pursuit. Tommy Roy, who had spent two hours in digging a ditch in front of his own door,—into which a few friends casually dropped during the evening,—looked *ennuyé* and dissatisfied; the four prominent citizens, who, disguised as footpads, had stopped the County Treasurer on the Wingdam road, were jaded from their playful efforts, next morning; the principal physician and lawyer of Monte Flat, who had entered into an unhallowed conspiracy to compel the Sheriff of Calaveras and his *posse* to serve a writ of ejectment on a grizzly bear, feebly disguised under the name of "one Major Ursus," who haunted the groves of Heavytree Hill, wore an expression of resigned weariness. Even the editor of the *Monte Flat Monitor* who had that morning written a glowing account of a battle with the Wipneck Indians for the benefit of Eastern readers — even *he* looked grave and worn. When, at last, Abner Dean of Angel's, who had been on a visit to San Francisco, walked into the room, he was, of course, victimized in the usual way by one or two apparently honest questions which ended in his answering them, and then falling into the trap of asking another to his utter and complete shame and mortification — but that was all. Nobody laughed, and Abner, although a victim, did not lose his good-humor. He turned quietly on his tormentors and said,

"I've got something better than that — you know old man Plunkett?"

Everybody simultaneously spat at the stove and nodded his head.

"You know he went home three years ago?" Two or three changed the position of their legs from the backs of different chairs, and one man said "Yes."

"Had a good time home?"

Everybody looked cautiously at the man who had said "yes," and he, accepting the responsibility with a faint-hearted smile, said "yes," again, and breathed hard. "Saw his wife and child, — purty gal?" said Abner, cautiously. "Yes," answered the man, doggedly. "Saw her photograph, perhaps?" continued Abner Dean, quietly.

The man looked hopelessly around for support. Two or three who had been sitting near him and evidently encouraging him with a look of interest, now shamelessly abandoned him and looked another way. Henry York flushed a little and veiled his brown eyes. The man hesitated, and then with a sickly smile that was intended to convey the fact that he was perfectly aware of the object of this questioning, and was only humoring it from abstract good feeling, returned "yes," again.

"Sent home—let's see,—ten thousand dollars, wasn't it?" Abner Dean went on. "Yes," reiterated the man, with the same smile.

"Well, I thought so," said Abner, quietly, "but the fact is, you see, that he never went home at all —nary time."

Everybody stared at Abner in genuine surprise and interest, as with provoking calmness and a half-lazy manner he went on.

"You see thar was a man down in 'Frisco as knowed him and saw him in Sonora during the whole of that three years. He was herding sheep or tending cattle, or spekilating all that time, and hadn't a red cent. Well it 'mounts to this—that 'ar Plunkett ain't been east of the Rocky mountains since '49."

The laugh which Abner Dean had the right to confidently expect came, but it was bitter and sardonic. I think indignation was apparent in the minds of his hearers. It was felt, for the first time, that there was a limit to practical joking. A deception carried on for a year, compromising the sagacity of Monte Flat was deserving the severest reprobation. Of course nobody had believed Plunkett—but then the supposition that it might be believed in adjacent camps that they *had* believed him was gall and bitterness. The lawyer thought that an indictment for obtaining money under false pretences might be found, the physician had long suspected him of insanity, and was not certain but that he ought to be confined. The four prominent merchants thought that the business interests of Monte Flat demanded that something should be done. In the midst of an excited and angry discussion the door slowly opened and old man Plunkett staggered into the room.

He had changed pitifully in the last six months. His hair was a dusty yellowish gray, like the chimisal on the flanks of Heavytree Hill; his face was waxen white and blue and puffy under the eyes; his clothes were soiled and shabby—streaked in front with the stains of hurried luncheons eaten standing, and fluffy behind with the wool and hair of hurriedly extemporized couches. In obedience to that odd law that the more seedy and soiled a man's garments become the less does he seem inclined to part with them, even during that portion of the twenty-four hours when they are deemed least essential, Plunkett's clothes had gradually taken on the appearance of a kind of bark or an out-growth from within for which their possessor was not entirely responsible. Howbeit as he entered the room he attempted to button his coat over a dirty shirt and passed his fingers, after the manner of some animal, over his cracker-strewn beard—in recognition of a cleanly public sentiment. But even as he did so the weak smile faded from his lips, and his hand, after fumbling aimlessly around a button, dropped helplessly at his side. For as he leaned his back against the bar and faced the group, he for the first time became aware that every eye but one was fixed upon him. His quick nervous apprehension at once leaped to the truth. His miserable secret was out and abroad in the very air about him. As a last resort he glanced despairingly at Henry York, but his flushed face was turned toward the windows.

No word was spoken. As the bar-keeper silently swung a decanter and glass before him, he took a cracker from a dish and mumbled it with affected unconcern. He lingered over his liquor until its potency stiffened his relaxed sinews, and dulled the nervous edge of his apprehension, and then he suddenly faced around. "It don't look as if we were goin' to hev any rain much afore Christmas," he said with defiant ease.

No one made any reply.

"Just like this in '52 and again in '60. It's always been my opinion that these dry seasons come reg'lar. I've said it afore. I say it again. It's jist as I said about going home, you know," he added with desperate recklessness.

"Thar's a man," said Abner Dean, lazily, "ez sez you never went home. Thar's a man ez sez you've been three years in Sonora. Thar's a man ez sez you haint seen your wife and daughter since '49. Thar's a man ez sez you've been playin' this camp for six months."

There was a dead silence. Then a voice said, quite as quietly,

"That man lies."

It was not the old man's voice. Everybody turned as Henry York slowly rose, stretching out his six feet of length, and, brushing away the ashes that had fallen from his pipe upon his breast, deliberately placed himself beside Plunkett, and faced the others.

"That man ain't here," continued Abner Dean, with listless indifference of voice and a gentle preoccupation of manner as he carelessly allowed his right hand to rest on his hip near his revolver. "That man ain't here, but if I'm called upon to make good what he says, why I'm on hand."

All rose as the two men,—perhaps the least externally agitated of them all,—approached each other. The lawyer stepped in between them.

"Perhaps there's some mistake here. York, do you *know* that the old man has been home?"

"Yes."

"How do you know it?"

York turned his clear, honest, frank eyes on his questioner and without a tremor told the only direct and unmitigated lie of his life. "Because I've seen him there."

The answer was conclusive. It was known that York had been visiting the East during the old man's absence. The colloquy had diverted attention from Plunkett, who, pale and breathless, was staring at his unexpected deliverer. As he turned again toward his tormentors there was something in the expression of his eye that caused those that were nearest to him to fall back and sent a strange, indefinable thrill through the boldest and most reckless. As he made a step forward the physician almost unconsciously raised his hand with a warning gesture, and old man Plunkett, with his eyes fixed upon the red-hot stove, and an odd smile playing about his mouth, began.

"Yes — of course you did. Who says you didn't? It ain't no lie; I said I was goin' home, and I've been home. Haven't I? My God! I have. Who says I've been lyin'! Who says I'm dreamin'! Is it true — why don't you speak? It is true after all. You say you saw me there, why don't you speak again. Say! Say! — is it true? It's going now, O my God — it's going again. It's going now. Save me!" and with a fierce cry, he fell forward in a fit upon the floor.

When the old man regained his senses he found himself in York's cabin. A flickering fire of pine boughs lit up the rude rafters and fell upon a photograph tastefully framed with fir cones and hung above the brush whereon he lay. It was the portrait of a young girl. It was the first object to meet the old man's gaze, and it brought with it a flush of such painful consciousness, that he started and glanced quickly around. But his eyes only encountered those of York — clear, gray, critical and patient, and they fell again.

"Tell me, old man," said York, not unkindly, but with the same cold, clear tone in his voice that his eye betrayed a moment ago, "tell me, is *that* a lie too," and he pointed to the picture.

The old man closed his eyes and did not reply. Two hours before the question would have stung him into some evasion or bravado. But the revelation contained in the question, as well as the tone of York's voice, was to him now, in his pitiable condition, a relief. It was plain even to his confused brain that York had lied when he had endorsed his story in the bar-room—it was clear to him now that he had not been home—that he was not, as he had begun to fear, going mad. It was such a relief that with characteristic weakness his former recklessness and extravagance returned. He began to chuckle—finally to laugh uproariously.

York, with his eyes still fixed on the old man, withdrew the hand with which he had taken his.

"Didn't we fool 'em nicely, eh, Yorky! He! he! The biggest thing yet ever played in this camp! I always said I'd play 'em all some day, and I have—played 'em for six months. Ain't it rich—ain't it the richest thing you ever seed? Did you see Abner's face when he spoke 'bout that man as seed me in Sonora?—warn't it good as the minstrels? O it's too much!" and striking his leg with the palm of his hand he almost threw himself from the bed in a paroxysm of laughter—a paroxysm that nevertheless appeared to be half real and half affected.

"Is that photograph hers," said York in a low voice, after a slight pause.

"Hers? No! It's one of the San Francisco actresses, he! he! Don't you see—I bought it for two bits in one of the bookstores. I never thought they'd swaller *that* too! but they did! Oh, but the old man played 'em this time, didn't he—eh?" and he peered curiously in York's face.

"Yes, and he played *me* too," said York, looking steadily in the old man's eye.

"Yes, of course," interposed Plunkett, hastily, "but you know, Yorky, you got out of it well! You've sold 'em too. We've both got 'em on a string now,—you and me,—got to stick together now. You did it well, Yorky, you did it well. Why when you said you'd seen me in York city, I'm d—d if I didn't——"

"Didn't what?" said York, gently, for the old man had stopped with a pale face and wandering eye.

"Eh?"

"You say when I said I had seen you in New York you thought——"

"You lie!" said the old man fiercely, "I didn't say I thought anything. What are you trying to go back on me for? Eh?" His hands were trembling as he rose muttering from the bed and made his way toward the hearth.

"Gimme some whisky," he said presently, "and dry up. You oughter treat anyway. Them fellows oughter treated last night. By hookey I'd made 'em—only I fell sick."

York placed the liquor and a tin cup on the table beside him, and going to the door turned his back upon his guest and looked out on the night. Although it was clear moonlight the familiar prospect never to him seemed so dreary. The dead waste of the broad, Wingdam highway never seemed so monotonous—so like the days that he had passed and were to come to him—so like the old man in its suggestion of going sometime and never getting there. He turned, and going up to Plunkett put his hand upon his shoulder and said,

"I want you to answer one question fairly and squarely?"

The liquor seemed to have warmed the torpid blood in the old man's veins and softened his acerbity, for the face he turned up to York was mellowed in its rugged outline and more thoughtful in expression, as he said:

"Go on, my boy."

"Have you a wife and—daughter?"

"Before God I have!"

The two men were silent for a moment; both gazing at the fire. Then Plunkett began rubbing his knees slowly.

"The wife, if it comes to that, ain't much," he began cautiously, "being a little on the shoulder, you know, and wantin', so to speak, a liberal California education—which makes, you know, a bad combination. It's always been my opinion that there ain't any worse. Why, she's as ready with her tongue as Abner Dean is with his revolver, only with the difference that she shoots from principle, as she calls it, and the consequence is, she's always layin' for you. It's the effete East, my boy, that's ruinin' her—it's them ideas she gets in New York and Boston that's made her and me what we are. I don't mind her havin' 'em if she didn't shoot. But havin' that propensity, them principles oughtn't to be lying round loose no more'n firearms."

"But your daughter?" said York.

The old man's hands went up to his eyes here, and then both hands and head dropped forward on the table. "Don't say anything 'bout her, my boy, don't ask me now—" With one hand concealing his eyes he fumbled about with the other in his pockets for his handkerchief—but vainly. Perhaps it was owing to this fact that he repressed his tears, for when he removed his hand from his eyes they were quite dry. Then he found his voice.

"She's a beautiful girl, beautiful—though I say it, and you shall see her, my boy, you shall see her, sure. I've got things about fixed now. I shall have my plan for reducin' ores perfected in a day or two, and I've got proposals from all the smeltin' works here;" here he hastily produced a bundle of papers that fell upon the floor, "and I'm goin' to send for 'em. I've got the papers here as will give me ten thousand dollars clear in the next month," he added, as he strove to collect the valuable documents again. "I'll have 'em here by Christmas, if I live, and you shall eat your Christmas dinner with me, York, my boy,—you shall, sure."

With his tongue now fairly loosened by liquor and the suggestive vastness of his prospects, he rambled on more or less incoherently, elaborating and amplifying his plans—occasionally even speaking of them as already accomplished, until the moon rode high in the heavens, and York led him again to his couch. Here he lay for some time muttering to himself, until at last he sank into a heavy sleep. When York had satisfied himself of the fact, he gently took down the picture and frame and, going to the hearth, tossed them on the dying embers, and sat down to see them burn.

The fir cones leaped instantly into flame; then the features that had entranced San Francisco audiences nightly flashed up and passed away,—as such things are apt to pass,—and even the cynical smile on York's lips faded too. And then there came a supplemental and unexpected flash as the embers fell together, and by its light York saw a paper upon the floor. It was one that had fallen from the old man's pocket. As he picked it up listlessly, a photograph slipped from its folds. It was the portrait of a young girl, and on its reverse was written, in a scrawling hand, "Melinda to Father."

It was at best a cheap picture, but ah me! I fear even the deft graciousness of the highest art could not have softened the rigid angularities of that youthful figure, its self-complacent vulgarity, its cheap finery, its expressionless ill-favor. York did not look at it the second time. He turned to the letter for relief.

It was misspelled, it was unpunctuated, it was almost illegible, it was fretful in tone and selfish in sentiment. It was not, I fear, even original in the story of its woes. It was the harsh recital of poverty, of suspicion, of mean makeshifts and compromises, of low pains and lower longings, of sorrows that were degrading, of a grief that was pitiable. Yet it was sincere in a certain kind of vague yearning for the presence of the degraded man to whom it was written—an affection that was more like a confused instinct than a sentiment.

York folded it again carefully and placed it beneath the old man's pillow. Then he returned to his seat by the fire. A smile that had been playing upon his face, deepening the curves behind his moustache and gradually overrunning his clear brown eyes, presently faded away. It was last to go from his eyes, and it left there,—oddly enough to those who did not know him,—a tear.

He sat there for a long time, leaning forward, his head upon his hands. The wind that had been striving with the canvas roof, all at once lifted its edges and a moonbeam slipped suddenly in, and lay for a moment like a shining blade upon his shoulder. And knighted by its touch, straightway plain Henry York arose,—sustained, high-purposed and self-reliant!

The rains had come at last. There was already a visible greenness on the slopes of Heavytree Hill, and the long, white track of the Wingdam road was lost in outlying pools and ponds a hundred rods from Monte Flat. The spent water-courses, whose white bones had been sinuously trailed over the flat, like the vertebræ of some forgotten Saurian, were full again; the dry bones moved once more in the valley, and there was joy in the ditches, and a pardonable extravagance in the columns of the *Monte Flat Monitor*. "Never before in the history of the county has the yield been so satisfactory. Our contemporary of the *Hillside Beacon*, who yesterday facetiously alluded to the fact (?) that our best citizens were leaving town, in 'dug-outs,' on account of the flood, will be glad to hear that our distinguished fellow-townsman, Mr. Henry York, now on a visit to his relatives in the East, lately took with him, in his 'dug-out,' the modest sum of fifty thousand dollars, the result of one week's clean-up. We can imagine," continued that sprightly journal, "that no such misfortune is likely to overtake Hillside this season. And yet we believe the *Beacon* man wants a railroad." A few journals broke out into poetry. The operator at Simpson's Crossing telegraphed to the Sacramento *Universe:* "All day the low clouds have shook their garnered fullness down." A San Francisco journal lapsed into noble verse, thinly disguised as editorial prose: "Rejoice, the gentle rain has come, the bright and pearly rain, which scatters blessings on the hills, and sifts them o'er the plain. Rejoice, etc." Indeed, there was only one to whom the rain had not brought blessing, and that was Plunkett. In some mysterious and darksome way, it had interfered with the perfection of his new method of reducing ores, and thrown the advent of that invention back another season. It had brought him down to an habitual seat in the bar-room, where, to heedless and inattentive ears, he sat and discoursed of the East and his family.

No one disturbed him. Indeed, it was rumored that some funds had been lodged with the landlord, by a person or persons unknown, whereby his few wants were provided for. His mania,—for that was the charitable construction which Monte Flat put upon his conduct,—was indulged, even to the extent of Monte Flat's accepting his invitation to dine with his family on Christmas Day—an invitation extended frankly to every one with whom the old man drank or talked. But one day, to everybody's astonishment, he burst into the bar-room, holding an open letter in his hand. It read as follows:

"Be ready to meet your family at the new cottage on Heavytree Hill on Christmas Day. Invite what friends you choose   HENRY YORK."

The letter was handed round in silence. The old man, with a look alternating between hope and fear, gazed in the faces of the group. The Doctor looked up significantly, after a pause. "It's a forgery, evidently," he said, in a low voice; "he's cunning enough to conceive it—they always are—but you'll find he'll fail in executing it. Watch his face! Old man," he said suddenly, in a loud, peremptory tone, "this is a trick—a forgery—and you know it. Answer me squarely, and look me in the eye. Isn't it so?"

The eyes of Plunkett stared a moment, and then dropped weakly. Then, with a feebler smile, he said: "You're too many for me, boys. The Doc's right. The little game's up. You can take the old man's hat"; and so, tottering, trembling, and chuckling, he dropped into silence and his accustomed seat. But the next day he seemed to have forgotten this episode, and talked as glibly as ever of the approaching festivity.

And so the days and weeks passed until Christmas,—a bright, clear day, warmed with south winds, and joyous with the resurrection of springing grasses,—broke upon Monte Flat. And then there was a sudden commotion in the hotel bar-room, and Abner Dean stood beside the old man's chair, and shook him out of a slumber to his feet. "Rouse up, old man; York is here, with your wife and daughter at the cottage on Heavytree. Come, old man. Here, boys, give him a lift"; and in another moment a dozen strong and willing hands had raised the old man, and bore him in triumph to the street, up the steep grade of Heavytree Hill, and deposited him, struggling and confused, in the porch of a little cottage. At the same instant, two women rushed forward, but were restrained by a gesture from Henry York. The old man was struggling to his feet. With an effort, at last, he stood erect, trembling, his eye fixed, a gray pallor on his cheek, and a deep resonance in his voice.

"It's all a trick, and a lie! They ain't no flesh and blood or kin o' mine. It ain't my wife, nor child. My daughter's a beautiful girl—a beautiful girl—d'ye hear? She's in New York, with her mother, and I'm going to fetch her here. I said I'd go home, and I've been home—d'ye hear me?—I've been home! It's a mean trick you're playin' on the old man. Let me go, d'ye hear? Keep them women off me! Let me go! I'm going—I'm going home!"

His hands were thrown up convulsively in the air, and, half turning round, he fell sideways on the porch, and so to the ground. They picked him up hurriedly; but too late. He had gone home.

BABY SYLVESTER

It was at a little mining camp in the California Sierras that he first dawned upon me in all his grotesque sweetness.

I had arrived early in the morning, but not in time to intercept the friend who was the object of my visit. He had gone "prospecting," — so they told me on the river—and would not probably return until late in the afternoon. They could not say what direction he had taken; they could not suggest that I would be likely to find him if I followed. But it was the general opinion that I had better wait.

I looked around me. I was standing upon the bank of the river; and, apparently, the only other human beings in the world were my interlocutors, who were even then just disappearing from my horizon down the steep bank toward the river's dry bed. I approached the edge of the bank.

Where could I wait?

O, anywhere; down with them on the river-bar, where they were working, if I liked! Or I could make myself at home in any of those cabins that I found lying round loose. Or, perhaps it would be cooler and pleasanter for me in my friend's cabin on the hill. Did I see those three large sugar-pines? And, a little to the right, a canvas roof and chimney over the bushes? Well, that was my friend's, — that was Dick Sylvester's cabin. I could stake my horse in that little hollow, and just hang round there till he came. I would find some books in the shanty; I could amuse myself with them. Or I could play with the baby.

Do what?

But they had already gone. I leaned over the bank and called after their vanishing figures:

"What did you say I could do?"

The answer floated slowly up on the hot, sluggish air:

"Pla-a-y with the ba-by."

The lazy echoes took it up and tossed it languidly from hill to hill, until Bald Mountain opposite made some incoherent remark about the baby, and then all was still.

I must have been mistaken. My friend was not a man of family; there was not a woman within forty miles of the river camp; he never was so passionately devoted to children as to import a luxury so expensive. I must have been mistaken.

I turned my horse's head toward the hill. As we slowly climbed the narrow trail, the little settlement might have been some exhumed Pompeian suburb, so deserted and silent were its habitations. The open doors plainly disclosed each rudely-furnished interior,—the rough pine table, with the scant equipage of the morning meal still standing; the wooden bunk, with its tumbled and disheveled blankets. A golden lizard—the very genius of desolate stillness—had stopped breathless upon the threshold of one cabin; a squirrel peeped impudently into the window of another; a woodpecker, with the general flavor of undertaking which distinguishes that bird, withheld his sepulchral hammer from the coffin-lid of the roof on which he was professionally engaged, as we passed. For a moment, I half-regretted that I had not accepted the invitation to the river-bed; but, the next moment, a breeze swept up the long, dark cañon, and the waiting files of the pines beyond bent toward me in salutation. I think my horse understood as well as myself that it was the cabins that made the solitude human, and therefore unbearable, for he quickened his pace, and with a gentle trot brought me to the edge of the wood and the three pines that stood like videttes before the Sylvester outpost.

Unsaddling my horse in the little hollow, I unslung the long *riata* from the saddle-bow, and tethering him to a young sapling, turned toward the cabin. But I had gone only a few steps when I heard a quick trot behind me, and poor Pomposo, with every fibre tingling with fear, was at my heels. I looked hurriedly around. The breeze had died away, and only an occasional breath from the deep-chested woods, more like a long sigh than any articulate sound, or the dry singing of a cicala in the heated cañon, were to be heard. I examined the ground carefully for rattlesnakes, but in vain. Yet here was Pomposo shivering from his arched neck to his sensitive haunches, his very flanks pulsating with terror. I soothed him as well as I could, and then walked to the edge of the wood and peered into its dark recesses. The bright flash of a bird's wing, or the quick dart of a squirrel, was all I saw. I confess it was with something of superstitious expectation that I again turned toward the cabin. A fairy child, attended by Titania and her train, lying in an expensive cradle, would not have surprised me; a Sleeping Beauty, whose awakening would have repeopled these solitudes with life and energy, I am afraid I began to confidently look for, and would have kissed without hesitation.

But I found none of these. Here was the evidence of my friend's taste and refinement in the hearth swept scrupulously clean, in the picturesque arrangement of the fur skins that covered the floor and furniture, and the striped *serápe** lying on the wooden couch. Here were the walls fancifully papered with illustrations from the *London News;* here was the wood-cut portrait of Mr. Emerson over the chimney, quaintly framed with blue jays' wings; here were his few favorite books on the swinging shelf; and here, lying upon the couch, the latest copy of *Punch*. Dear Dick! The flour-sack was sometimes empty, but the gentle satirist seldom missed his weekly visit.

I threw myself on the couch and tried to read. But I soon exhausted my interest in my friend's

* A fine Mexican blanket, used as an outer garment for riding.

library, and lay there staring through the open door on the green hillside beyond. The breeze again sprang up, and a delicious coolness, mixed with the rare incense of the woods, stole through the cabin. The slumbrous droning of bumble-bees outside the canvas roof, the faint cawing of rooks on the opposite mountain, and the fatigue of my morning ride, began to droop my eyelids. I pulled the *serápe* over me, as a precaution against the freshening mountain breeze, and in a few moments was asleep.

I do not remember how long I slept. I must have been conscious, however, during my slumber, of my inability to keep myself covered by the *serápe*, for I awoke once or twice, clutching it with a despairing hand as it was disappearing over the foot of the couch. Then I became suddenly aroused to the fact that my efforts to retain it were resisted by some equally persistent force, and, letting it go, I was horrified at seeing it swiftly drawn under the couch. At this point I sat up completely awake; for immediately after, what seemed to be an exaggerated muff began to emerge from under the couch. Presently it appeared fully, dragging the *serápe* after it. There was no mistaking it now—it was a baby bear. A mere suckling, it was true,—a helpless roll of fat and fur,—but, unmistakably, a grizzly cub.

I cannot recall anything more irresistibly ludicrous than its aspect as it slowly raised its small wondering eyes to mine. It was so much taller on its haunches than its shoulders,—its fore-legs were so disproportionately small,—that in walking, its hind-feet invariably took precedence. It was perpetually pitching forward over its pointed, inoffensive nose, and recovering itself always, after these involuntary somersaults, with the gravest astonishment. To add to its preposterous appearance, one of its hind-feet was adorned by a shoe of Sylvester's, into which it had accidentally and inextricably stepped. As this somewhat impeded its first impulse to fly, it turned to me; and then, possibly recognizing in the stranger the same species as its master, it paused. Presently, it slowly raised itself on its hind-legs, and vaguely and deprecatingly waved a baby paw, fringed with little hooks of steel. I took the paw and shook it gravely. From that moment we were friends. The little affair of the *serápe* was forgotten.

Nevertheless, I was wise enough to cement our friendship by an act of delicate courtesy. Following the direction of his eyes, I had no difficulty in finding, on a shelf near the ridge-pole, the sugar-box and the square lumps of white sugar that even the poorest miner is never without. While he was eating them I had time to examine him more closely. His body was a silky, dark, but exquisitely modulated grey, deepening to black in his paws and muzzle. His fur was excessively long, thick, and soft as eider down; the cushions of flesh beneath, perfectly infantine in their texture and contour. He was so very young that the palms of his half-human feet were still tender as a baby's. Except for the bright blue, steely hooks, half-sheathed in his little toes, there was not a single harsh outline or detail

in his plump figure. He was as free from angles
as one of Leda's offspring. Your caressing hand
sank away in his fur with dreamy languor. To look
at him long was an intoxication of the senses; to
pat him was a wild delirium; to embrace him, an
utter demoralization of the intellectual faculties.

When he had finished the sugar, he rolled out
of the door with a half-diffident, half-inviting look
in his eye, as if he expected me to follow. I did
so, but the sniffing and snorting of the keen-scented
Pomposo in the hollow, not only revealed the cause
of his former terror, but decided me to take another
direction. After a moment's hesitation, he concluded
to go with me, although I am satisfied, from a certain impish look in his eye, that he fully understood
and rather enjoyed the fright of Pomposo. As he
rolled along at my side, with a gait not unlike a
drunken sailor, I discovered that his long hair concealed a leather collar around his neck, which bore
for its legend the single word, "Baby!" I recalled
the mysterious suggestion of the two miners. This,
then, was the "baby" with whom I was to "play."

How we "played;" how Baby allowed me to
roll him down hill, crawling and puffing up again
each time, with perfect good humor; how he climbed
a young sapling after my Panama hat, which I had
"shied" into one of the topmost branches; how
after getting it he refused to descend until it suited
his pleasure; how when he did come down he persisted in walking about on three legs, carrying my
hat, a crushed and shapeless mass, clasped to his
breast with the remaining one; how I missed him

at last, and finally discovered him seated on a table in one of the tenantless cabins, with a bottle of syrup between his paws, vainly endeavoring to extract its contents—these and other details of that eventful day I shall not weary the reader with now. Enough that when Dick Sylvester returned, I was pretty well fagged out, and the baby was rolled up, an immense bolster at the foot of the couch, asleep. Sylvester's first words after our greeting were:

"Isn't he delicious?"

"Perfectly. Where did you get him?"

"Lying under his dead mother, five miles from here," said Dick, lighting his pipe. "Knocked her over at fifty yards; perfectly clean shot—never moved afterwards! Baby crawled out, scared but unhurt. She must have been carrying him in her mouth, and dropped him when she faced me, for he wasn't more than three days old, and not steady on his pins. He takes the only milk that comes to the settlement—brought up by Adams Express at seven o'clock every morning. They say he looks like me. Do you think so?" asked Dick, with perfect gravity, stroking his hay-colored moustachios, and evidently assuming his best expression.

I took leave of the baby early the next morning in Sylvester's cabin, and out of respect to Pomposo's feelings, rode by without any postscript of expression. But the night before I had made Sylvester solemnly swear, that in the event of any separation between himself and Baby, it should revert to me. "At the same time," he had added, "it's only fair to say that I don't think of dying just yet, old fellow, and I don't know of anything else that would part the cub and me."

Two months after this conversation, as I was turning over the morning's mail at my office in San Francisco, I noticed a letter bearing Sylvester's familiar hand. But it was post-marked "Stockton," and I opened it with some anxiety at once. Its contents were as follows:

O FRANK!—Don't you remember what we agreed upon anent the baby? Well, consider me as dead for the next six months, or gone where cubs can't follow me—East. I know you love the baby; but do you think, dear boy,—now, really, do you think you *could* be a father to it? Consider this well. You are young, thoughtless, well-meaning enough; but dare you take upon yourself the functions of guide, genius or guardian to one so young and guileless? Could you be the mentor to this Telemachus? Think of the temptations of a metropolis. Look at the question well, and let me know speedily, for I've got him as far as this place, and he's kicking up an awful row in the hotel-yard, and rattling his chain like a maniac. Let me know by telegraph at once. SYLVESTER.

P.S.—Of course he's grown a little, and doesn't take things always as quietly as he did. He dropped rather heavily on two of Watson's "purps" last week, and snatched old Watson himself, bald-headed, for interfering. You remember Watson: for an intelligent man, he knows very little of California fauna. How are you fixed for bears on Montgomery street,—I mean in regard to corrals and things? S.

P.P.S.—He's got some new tricks. The boys have been teaching him to put up his hands with them. He slings an ugly left. S.

I am afraid that my desire to possess myself of Baby overcame all other considerations, and I telegraphed an affirmative at once to Sylvester. When I reached my lodgings late that afternoon, my landlady was awaiting me with a telegram. It was two lines from Sylvester:

   All right. Baby goes down on night-boat. Be a father to him.   S.

It was due, then, at one o'clock that night. For a moment I was staggered at my own precipitation. I had as yet made no preparations,—had said nothing to my landlady about her new guest. I expected to arrange everything in time; and now, through Sylvester's indecent haste, that time had been shortened twelve hours.

Something, however, must be done at once. I turned to Mrs. Brown. I had great reliance in her maternal instincts; I had that still greater reliance, common to our sex, in the general tender-heartedness of pretty women. But I confess I was alarmed. Yet, with a feeble smile, I tried to introduce the subject with classical ease and lightness. I even said, "If Shakespeare's Athenian clown, Mrs. Brown, believed that a lion among ladies was a dreadful thing, what must——" But here I broke down, for Mrs. Brown, with the awful intuition of her sex, I saw at once was more occupied with my manner than my speech. So I tried a business *brusquerie*, and, placing the telegram in her hand, said hurriedly, "We must do something about this at once. It's perfectly absurd, but he will be here at one tonight. Beg thousand pardons, but business prevented my speaking before——" and paused, out of breath and courage.

Mrs. Brown read the telegram gravely, lifted her pretty eyebrows, turned the paper over and looked on the other side, and then, in a remote and chilling voice, asked me if she understood me to say that the mother was coming also.

"O dear no," I exclaimed, with considerable relief; "the mother is dead, you know. Sylvester—that is my friend, who sent this—shot her when the Baby was only three days old——" But the expression of Mrs. Brown's face at this moment was so alarming, that I saw that nothing but the fullest explanation would save me. Hastily, and I fear not very coherently, I told her all.

She relaxed sweetly. She said I had frightened her with my talk about lions. Indeed, I think my picture of poor Baby—albeit a trifle highly-colored —touched her motherly heart. She was even a little vexed at what she called Sylvester's "hard-heartedness." Still, I was not without some apprehension. It was two months since I had seen him, and Sylvester's vague allusion to his "slinging an ugly left" pained me. I looked at sympathetic little Mrs. Brown, and the thought of Watson's pups covered me with guilty confusion.

Mrs. Brown had agreed to sit up with me until he arrived. One o'clock came, but no Baby. Two o'clock—three o'clock passed. It was almost four when there was a wild clatter of horses' hoofs outside, and with a jerk a wagon stopped at the door. In an instant I had opened it and confronted a stranger. Almost at the same moment, the horses attempted to run away with the wagon.

The stranger's appearance was, to say the least, disconcerting. His clothes were badly torn and frayed; his linen sack hung from his shoulders like a herald's apron; one of his hands was bandaged; his face scratched, and there was no hat on his disheveled head. To add to the general effect, he had evidently sought relief from his woes in drink, and he swayed from side to side as he clung to the door-handle; and, in a very thick voice, stated that he had "suthin" for me outside. When he had finished, the horses made another plunge.

Mrs. Brown thought they must be frightened at something.

"Frightened!" laughed the stranger, with bitter irony. "Oh no! Hossish aint frightened! On'y ran away four timesh comin' here. Oh no! Nobody's frightened. Everythin's all ri'. Aint it, Bill?" he said, addressing the driver. "On'y been overboard twish; knocked down a hatchway once. Thash nothin'! On'y two men unner doctor's han's at Stockton. Thash nothin'! Six hunner dollarsh cover all dammish."

I was too much disheartened to reply, but moved toward the wagon. The stranger eyed me with an astonishment that almost sobered him.

"Do you reckon to tackle that animile yourself?" he asked, as he surveyed me from head to foot.

I did not speak, but, with an appearance of boldness I was far from feeling, walked to the wagon and called "Baby!"

"All ri'. Cash loose them straps, Bill, and stan' clear."

The straps were cut loose, and Baby—the remorseless, the terrible—quietly tumbled to the ground, and rolling to my side, rubbed his foolish head against me.

I think the astonishment of the two men was beyond any vocal expression. Without a word the drunken stranger got into the wagon and drove away.

And Baby? He had grown, it is true, a trifle larger; but he was thin, and bore the marks of evident ill-usage. His beautiful coat was matted and unkempt, and his claws—those bright steel hooks—had been ruthlessly pared to the quick. His eyes were furtive and restless, and the old expression of stupid good humor had changed to one of intelligent distrust. His intercourse with mankind had evidently quickened his intellect without broadening his moral nature.

I had great difficulty in keeping Mrs. Brown from smothering him in blankets and ruining his digestion with the delicacies of her larder; but I at last got him completely rolled up in the corner of my room and asleep. I lay awake some time later with plans for his future. I finally determined to take him to Oakland, where I had built a little cottage and always spent my Sundays, the very next day. And in the midst of a rosy picture of domestic felicity, I fell asleep.

When I awoke it was broad day. My eyes at once sought the corner where Baby had been lying. But he was gone. I sprang from the bed, looked under it, searched the closet, but in vain. The door was still locked; but there were the marks of his blunted claws upon the sill of the window, that I had forgotten to close. He had evidently escaped that way,—but where? The window opened upon a balcony, to which the only other entrance was through the hall. He must be still in the house.

My hand was already upon the bell-rope, but I stayed it in time. If he had not made himself known, why should I disturb the house? I dressed myself hurriedly, and slipped into the hall. The first object that met my eyes was a boot lying upon the stairs. It bore the marks of Baby's teeth; and as I looked along the hall, I saw too plainly that the usual array of freshly-blackened boots and shoes before the lodgers' doors was not there. As I ascended the stairs I found another, but with the blacking carefully licked off. On the third floor were two or three more boots, slightly mouthed; but at this point Baby's taste for blacking had evidently palled. A little further on was a ladder, leading to an open scuttle. I mounted the ladder, and reached the flat roof, that formed a continuous level over the row of houses to the corner of the street. Behind the chimney on the very last roof something was lurking. It was the fugitive Baby. He was covered with dust and dirt and fragments of glass. But he was sitting on his hind-legs, and was eating an enormous slab of pea-nut candy, with a look of mingled guilt and infinite satisfaction. He even, I fancied, slightly stroked his stomach with his disengaged fore-paw, as I approached. He knew that I was looking for him, and the expression of his eye said plainly, "The past, at least, is secure."

I hurried him, with the evidences of his guilt, back to the scuttle, and descended on tip-toe to the floor beneath. Providence favored us; I met no one on the stairs, and his own cushioned tread was inaudible. I think he was conscious of the dangers of detection, for he even forebore to breathe, or much less chew the last mouthful he had taken; and he skulked at my side, with the syrup dropping from his motionless jaws. I think he would have silently choked to death just then, for my sake: and it was not until I had reached my room again, and threw myself panting on the sofa, that I saw how near strangulation he had been. He gulped once or twice, apologetically, and then walked to the corner of his own accord, and rolled himself up like an immense sugar-plum, sweating remorse and treacle at every pore.

I locked him in when I went to breakfast, when I found Mrs. Brown's lodgers in a state of intense excitement over certain mysterious events of the night before, and the dreadful revelations of the morning. It appeared that burglars had entered the block from the scuttles; that being suddenly alarmed, they had quitted our house without committing any depredation, dropping even the boots they had collected in the halls; but that a desperate attempt had been made to force the till in the confectioner's shop on the corner, and that the glass show-cases had been ruthlessly smashed. A courageous servant in No. 4 had seen a masked burglar, on his hands and knees, attempting to enter their scuttle; but on her shouting, "Away wid yees," he instantly fled.

I sat through this recital with cheeks that burned uncomfortably; nor was I the less embarrassed on raising my eyes to meet Mrs. Brown's fixed curiously and mischievously on mine. As soon as I could make my escape from the table, I did so; and running rapidly up stairs, sought refuge from any possible inquiry in my own room. Baby was still asleep in the corner. It would not be safe to remove him until the lodgers had gone down town; and I was revolving in my mind the expediency of keeping him until night veiled his obstrusive eccentricity from the public eye, when there came a cautious tap at my door. I opened it. Mrs. Brown slipped in quietly, closed the door softly, stood with her back against it and her hand on the knob, and beckoned me mysteriously towards her. Then she asked, in a low voice:

"Is hair-dye poisonous?"

I was too confounded to speak.

"O do! you know what I mean," she said, impatiently. "This stuff." She produced suddenly from behind her a bottle with a Greek label—so long as to run two or three times spirally around it from top to bottom. "He says it isn't a dye; it's a vegetable preparation, for invigorating——"

"Who says?" I asked, despairingly.

"Why, Mr. Parker, of course," said Mrs. Brown, severely, with the air of having repeated the name a great many times,—"the old gentleman in the room above. The simple question I want to ask," she continued, with the calm manner of one who has just convicted another of gross ambiguity of language, "is only this: If some of this stuff were put in a saucer and left carelessly on the table, and a child or a baby or a cat, or any young animal, should come in at the window and drink it up—a whole saucer full—because it had a sweet taste, would it be likely to hurt them?"

I cast an anxious glance at Baby, sleeping peacefully in the corner, and a very grateful one at Mrs. Brown, and said I didn't think it would.

"Because," said Mrs. Brown, loftily, as she opened the door, "I thought if it was poisonous, remedies might be used in time. Because," she added suddenly, abandoning her lofty manner and wildly rushing to the corner, with a frantic embrace of the unconscious Baby, "because if any nasty stuff should turn its boofull hair a horrid green or a naughty pink, it would break its own muzzer's heart, it would!"

But before I could assure Mrs. Brown of the inefficiency of hair-dye as an internal application, she had darted from the room.

That night, with the secrecy of defaulters, Baby and I decamped from Mrs. Brown's. Distrusting the too emotional nature of that noble animal, the horse, I had recourse to a hand-cart, drawn by a stout Irishman, to convey my charge to the ferry. Even then, Baby refused to go unless I walked by the cart, and at times rode in it.

"I wish," said Mrs. Brown, as she stood by the door wrapped in an immense shawl, and saw us depart, "I wish it looked less solemn—less like a pauper's funeral."

I must admit, that as I walked by the cart that night, I felt very much as if I were accompanying the remains of some humble friend to his last resting-place; and that, when I was obliged to ride in it, I never could entirely convince myself that I was not helplessly overcome by liquor, or the victim of an accident, *en route* to the hospital. But, at last, we reached the ferry. On the boat I think no one discovered Baby except a drunken man, who approached me to ask for a light for his cigar, but who suddenly dropped it and fled in dismay to the gentlemen's cabin, where his incoherent ravings were luckily taken for the earlier indications of *delirium tremens.*

It was nearly midnight when I reached my little cottage on the outskirts of Oakland; and it was with a feeling of relief and security that I entered, locked the door, and turned him loose in the hall, satisfied that henceforward his depredations would be limited to my own property. He was very quiet that night, and after he had tried to mount the hat-rack, under the mistaken impression that it was intended for his own gymnastic exercise, and knocked all the hats off, he went peaceably to sleep on the rug.

In a week, with the exercise afforded him by the run of a large, carefully-boarded enclosure, he recovered his health, strength, spirits, and much of his former beauty. His presence was unknown to my neighbors, although it was noticeable that horses invariably "shied" in passing to the windward of my house, and that the baker and milkman had great difficulty in the delivery of their wares in the morning, and indulged in unseemly and unnecessary profanity in so doing.

At the end of the week, I determined to invite a few friends to see the Baby, and to that purpose wrote a number of formal invitations. After descanting, at some length, on the great expense and danger attending his capture and training, I offered a programme of the performances of the "Infant Phenomenon of Sierran Solitudes," drawn up into the highest professional profusion of alliteration and capital letters. A few extracts will give the reader some idea of his educational progress:

1. He will, rolled up in a Round Ball, roll down the Wood Shed, Rapidly, illustrating His manner of Escaping from His Enemy in his Native Wilds.
2. He will Ascend the Well Pole, and remove from the Very Top a Hat, and as much of the Crown and Brim thereof as May be Permitted.
3. He will perform in a pantomime, descriptive of the Conduct of the Big Bear, The Middle-Sized Bear, and The Little Bear of the Popular Nursery Legend.
4. He will shake his chain Rapidly, showing his Manner of striking Dismay and Terror in the Breasts of Wanderers in Ursine Wildernesses.

The morning of the exhibition came, but an hour before the performance the wretched Baby was missing. The Chinese cook could not indicate his whereabouts. I searched the premises thoroughly, and then, in despair, took my hat and hurried out into the narrow lane that led toward the open fields and the woods beyond. But I found no trace nor track of Baby Sylvester. I returned, after an hour's fruitless search, to find my guests already assembled on the rear verandah. I briefly recounted my disappointment, my probable loss, and begged their assistance.

"Why," said a Spanish friend, who prided himself on his accurate knowledge of English, to Barker, who seemed to be trying vainly to rise from his reclining position on the verandah, "Why do you not disengage yourself from the verandah of our friend? and why, in the name of Heaven, do you attach to yourself so much of this thing, and make to yourself such unnecessary contortion? Ah," he continued, suddenly withdrawing one of his own feet from the verandah with an evident effort, "I am myself attached! Surely it is something here!"

It evidently was. My guests were all rising with difficulty,—the floor of the verandah was covered with some glutinous substance. It was—syrup!

I saw it all in a flash. I ran to the barn; the keg of "golden syrup," purchased only the day before, lay empty upon the floor. There were sticky tracks all over the enclosure, but still no Baby.

"There's something moving the ground over there by that pile of dirt," said Barker.

He was right; the earth was shaking in one corner of the enclosure like an earthquake. I approached cautiously. I saw, what I had not before noticed, that the ground was thrown up; and there, in the middle of an immense grave-like cavity, crouched Baby Sylvester, still digging, and slowly, but surely, sinking from sight in a mass of dust and clay.

What were his intentions? Whether he was stung by remorse, and wished to hide himself from my reproachful eyes, or whether he was simply trying to dry his syrup-besmeared coat, I never shall know, for that day, alas! was his last with me.

He was pumped upon for two hours, at the end of which time he still yielded a thin treacle. He was then taken and carefully enwrapped in blankets and locked up in the store-room. The next morning he was gone! The lower portion of the window sash and pane were gone too. His successful experiments on the fragile texture of glass at the confectioner's, on the first day of his entrance to civilization, had not been lost upon him. His first essay at combining cause and effect ended in his escape.

Where he went, where he hid, who captured him if he did not succeed in reaching the foot-hills beyond Oakland, even the offer of a large reward, backed by the efforts of an intelligent police, could not discover. I never saw him again from that day until——

Did I see him? I was in a horse-car on Sixth avenue, a few days ago, when the horses suddenly became unmanageable and left the track for the sidewalk, amid the oaths and execrations of the driver. Immediately in front of the car a crowd had gathered around two performing bears and a showman. One of the animals—thin, emaciated, and the mere wreck of his native strength—attracted my attention. I endeavored to attract his. He turned a pair of bleared, sightless eyes in my direction, but there was no sign of recognition. I leaned from the car-window and called, softly, "Baby!" But he did not heed. I closed the window. The car was just moving on, when he suddenly turned, and, either by accident or design, thrust a callous paw through the glass.

"It's worth a dollar-and-half to put in a new pane," said the conductor, "if folks will play with bears!——"

WAN LEE, THE PAGAN.

As I opened Hop Sing's letter, there fluttered to the ground a square strip of yellow paper covered with hieroglyphics which at first glance I innocently took to be the label from a pack of Chinese firecrackers. But the same envelope also contained a smaller strip of rice paper, with two Chinese characters traced in India ink, that I at once knew to be Hop Sing's visiting card. The whole, as afterwards literally translated, ran as follows:

> "To the stranger the gates of my house are not closed; the rice jar is on the left, and the sweetmeats on the right as you enter.
> Two sayings of the Master:
> Hospitality is the virtue of the son and the wisdom of the ancestor.
> The Superior man is light hearted after the crop-gathering; he makes a festival.
> When the stranger is in your melon patch observe him not too closely; inattention is often the highest form of civility.
> Happiness, Peace and Prosperity.
> HOP SING.

Admirable, certainly, as was this morality and proverbial wisdom, and although this last axiom was very characteristic of my friend Hop Sing who was that most somber of all humorists, a Chinese philosopher, I must confess that, even after a very free translation, I was at a loss to make any immediate application of the message. Luckily I discovered a third enclosure in the shape of a little note in English and Hop Sing's own commercial hand. It ran thus:

THE pleasure of your company is requested at No.—Sacramento St. on Friday Evening at 8 o'clock. A cup of tea at 9—sharp.

HOP SING."

This explained all. It meant a visit to Hop Sing's warehouse, the opening and exhibition of some rare Chinese novelties and *curios*, a chat in the back office, a cup of tea of a perfection unknown beyond these sacred precincts, cigars, and a visit to the Chinese Theater or Temple. This was in fact the favorite programme of Hop Sing when he exercised his functions of hospitality as the chief factor or Superintendent of the Ning Foo Company.

At eight o'clock on Friday evening I entered the warehouse of Hop Sing. There was that deliciously commingled mysterious foreign odor that I had so often noticed; there was the old array of uncouth looking objects, the long procession of jars and crockery, the same singular blending of the grotesque and the mathematically neat and exact, the same endless suggestions of frivolity and fragility, the same want of harmony in colors that were each, in themselves, beautiful and rare. Kites in the shape of enormous dragons and gigantic butterflies; kites so ingeniously arranged as to utter at intervals, when facing the wind, the cry of a hawk; kites so large as to be beyond any boy's power of restraint—so large that you understood why kite-flying in China was an amusement for adults; gods of china and bronze so gratuitously ugly as to be beyond any human interest or sympathy from their very impossibility; jars of sweetmeats covered all over with moral sentiments from Confucius; hats that looked like baskets, and baskets that looked like hats; silks so light that I hesitate to record the incredible number of square yards that you might pass through the ring on your little finger—these and a great many other indescribable objects were all familiar to me. I pushed my way through the dimly-lighted warehouse until I reached the back office or parlor, where I found Hop Sing waiting to receive me.

Before I describe him I want the average reader to discharge from his mind any idea of a Chinaman that he may have gathered from the pantomime. He did not wear beautifully scalloped drawers fringed with little bells—I never met a Chinaman who did; he did not habitually carry his forefinger extended before him at right angles with his body, nor did I ever hear him utter the mysterious sentence "Ching a ring a ring chaw," nor dance under any provocation. He was on the whole, a rather grave, decorous, handsome gentleman. His complexion, which extended all over his head except where his long pig-tail grew, was like a very nice piece of glazed brown paper-muslin. His eyes were black and bright, and his eye-lids set at an angle of 15°; his nose straight and delicately formed, his mouth small, and his teeth white and clean. He wore a dark blue silk blouse; and in the streets on cold days, a short jacket of astrakhan fur. He wore also a pair of drawers of blue brocade gathered tightly over his calves and ankles, offering a general sort of suggestion that he had forgotten his trousers that morning, but, that so gentlemanly were his manners, his friends had forborne to mention the fact to him. His manner was urbane, although quite serious. He spoke French and English fluently. In brief, I doubt if you could have found the equal of this Pagan shop-keeper among the Christian traders of San Francisco.

There were a few others present: a Judge of the Federal Court, an editor, a high government official, and a prominent merchant. After we had drunk our tea, and tasted a few sweetmeats from a mysterious jar, that looked as if it might contain a preserved mouse among its other nondescript treasures, Hop Sing arose and, gravely beckoning us to follow him, began to descend to the basement. When we got there, we were amazed at finding it brilliantly lighted, and that a number of chairs were arranged in a half-circle on the asphalt pavement. When he had courteously seated us he said:

"I have invited you to witness a performance which I can at least promise you no other foreigners but yourselves have ever seen. Wang, the court juggler, arrived here yesterday morning. He has never given a performance outside of the palace before. I have asked him to entertain my friends this evening. He requires no theater, stage accessories, or any confederate—nothing more than you see here. Will you be pleased to examine the ground yourselves, gentlemen."

Of course we examined the premises. It was the ordinary basement or cellar of the San Francisco store-house, cemented to keep out the damp. We poked our sticks into the pavement and rapped on the walls to satisfy our polite host, but for no other purpose. We were quite content to be the victims of any clever deception. For myself, I knew I was ready to be deluded to any extent, and if I had been offered an explanation of what followed, I should have probably declined it.

Although I am satisfied that Wang's general performance was the first of that kind ever given on American soil, it has probably since become so familiar to many of my readers that I shall not bore them with it here. He began by setting to flight, with the aid of his fan, the usual number of butterflies made before our eyes of little bits of tissue paper, and kept them in the air during the remainder of the performance. I have a vivid recollection of the Judge trying to catch one that had lit on his knee, and of its evading him with the pertinacity of a living insect. And even at this time Wang, still plying his fan, was taking chickens out of hats, making oranges disappear, pulling endless yards of silk from his sleeve, apparently filling the whole area of the basement with goods that appeared mysteriously from the ground, from his own sleeves, from nowhere! He swallowed knives to the ruin of his digestion for years to come, he dislocated every limb of his body, he reclined in the air, apparently upon nothing. But his crowning performance, which I have never yet seen repeated, was the most weird, mysterious and astounding. It is my apology for this long introduction, my sole excuse for writing this article, the genesis of this veracious history.

He cleared the ground of its encumbering articles for a space of about fifteen feet square, and then invited us all to walk forward and again examine it. We did so gravely; there was nothing but the cemented pavement below to be seen or felt. He then asked for the loan of a handkerchief, and, as I chanced to be nearest him, I offered mine. He took it, and spread it open upon the floor. Over this he spread a large square of silk, and over this again a large shawl nearly covering the space he had cleared. He then took a position at one of the points of this rectangle, and began a monotonous chant, rocking his body to and fro in time with the somewhat lugubrious air.

We sat still and waited. Above the chant we could hear the striking of the city clocks, and the occasional rattle of a cart in the street overhead. The absolute watchfulness and expectation, the dim mysterious half-light of the cellar falling in a grewsome way upon the misshapen bulk of a Chinese deity in the background, a faint smell of opium smoke mingling with spice, and the dreadful uncertainty of what we were really waiting for, sent an uncomfortable thrill down our backs, and made us look at each other with a forced and unnatural smile. This feeling was heightened when Hop Sing slowly rose, and, without a word, pointed with his finger to the centre of the shawl.

There was something beneath the shawl. Surely —and something that was not there before. At first a mere suggestion in relief, a faint outline; but growing more and more distinct and visible every moment. The chant still continued, the perspiration began to roll from the singer's face, gradually the hidden object took upon itself a shape and bulk that raised the shawl in its centre some five or six inches. It was now unmistakably the outline of a small but perfect human figure, with extended arms and legs. One or two of us turned pale, there was a feeling of general uneasiness, until the editor broke the silence by a gibe that, poor as it was, was received with spontaneous enthusiasm. Then the chant suddenly ceased, Wang arose, and, with a quick, dexterous movement, stripped both shawl and silk away, and discovered, sleeping peacefully upon my handkerchief, a tiny Chinese baby!

The applause and uproar which followed this revelation ought to have satisfied Wang, even if his audience was a small one; it was loud enough to awaken the baby—a pretty little boy about a year old, looking like a Cupid cut out of sandal wood. He was whisked away almost as mysteriously as he appeared. When Hop Sing returned my handkerchief to me with a bow, I asked if the juggler was the father of the baby. "No sabe!" said the imperturbable Hop Sing, taking refuge in that Spanish form of non-committalism so common in California.

"But does he have a new baby for every performance?" I asked. "Perhaps; who knows?" "But what will become of this one?" "Whatever you choose, gentlemen," replied Hop Sing, with a courteous inclination, "it was born here,—you are its godfathers."

There were two characteristic peculiarities of any Californian assemblage in 1856; it was quick to take a hint, and generous to the point of prodigality in its response to any charitable appeal. No matter how sordid or avaricious the individual, he could not resist the infection of sympathy. I doubled the points of my handkerchief into a bag, dropped a coin into it, and, without a word, passed it to the Judge. He quietly added a twenty dollar gold piece, and passed it to the next; when it was returned to me it contained over a hundred dollars. I knotted the money in the kandkerchief, and gave it to Hop Sing.

"For the baby, from its godfathers."

"But what name," said the Judge. There was a running fire of "Erebus," "Nox," "Plutus," "Terra

Cotta," "Antæus," etc., etc. Finally the question was referred to our host.

"Why not keep his own name?" he said quietly—"Wan Lee." And he did.

And thus was Wan Lee, on the night of Friday, the 5th of March, 1856, born into this veracious chronicle.

The last forme of "The Northern Star" for the 19th of July, 1865,—the only daily paper published in Klamath County,—had just gone to press, and at three A. M. I was putting aside my proofs and manuscripts, preparatory to going home, when I discovered a letter lying under some sheets of paper which I must have overlooked. The envelope was considerably soiled, it had no post-mark, but I had no difficulty in recognizing the hand of my friend Hop Sing. I opened it hurriedly, and read as follows:

"MY DEAR SIR: I do not know whether the bearer will suit you, but unless the office of 'devil' in your newspaper is a purely technical one, I think he has all the qualities required. He is very quick, active and intelligent; understands English better than he speaks it, and makes up for any defect by his habits of observation and imitation. You have only to show him how to do a thing once, and he will repeat it, whether it is an offence or a virtue. But you certainly know him already; you are one of his god-fathers, for is he not Wan Lee, the reputed son of Wang the Conjurer, to whose performances I had the honor to introduce you? But, perhaps, you have forgotten it.

"I shall send him with a gang of coolies to Stockton, thence by express to your town. If you can use him there, you will do me a favor, and probably save his life, which is at present in great peril from the hands of the younger members of your Christian and highly civilized race who attend the enlightened schools in San Francisco.

"He has acquired some singular habits and customs from his experience of Wang's profession, which he followed for some years, until he became too large to go in a hat, or be produced from his father's sleeve. The money you left with me has been expended on his education; he has gone through the Tri-literal Classics, but, I think, without much benefit. He knows but little of Confucius, and absolutely nothing of Mencius. Owing to the negligence of his father, he associated, perhaps, too much with American children.

"I should have answered your letter before, by post, but I thought that Wan Lee himself would be a better messenger for this.

"Yours respectfully,

"HOP SING."

And this was the long-delayed answer to my letter to Hop Sing. But where was "the bearer?" How was the letter delivered? I summoned hastily the foreman, printers and office-boy, but without eliciting anything; no one had seen the letter delivered, nor knew anything of the bearer. A few days later I had a visit from my laundry-man, Ah Ri.

"You wantee debbil? All lightee; me catchee him."

He returned in a few moments with a bright-looking Chinese boy, about ten years old, with whose appearance and general intelligence I was so greatly impressed that I engaged him on the spot. When the business was concluded, I asked his name.

"Wan Lee," said the boy.

"What! Are you the boy sent out by Hop Sing? What the devil do you mean by not coming here before, and how did you deliver that letter?"

Wan Lee looked at me and laughed. "Me pitchee in top side window."

I did not understand. He looked for a moment perplexed, and then snatching the letter out of my hand, ran down the stairs. After a moment's pause, to my great astonishment, the letter came flying in the window, circled twice around the room, and then dropped gently like a bird upon my table. Before I had got over my surprise Wan Lee reappeared, smiled, looked at the letter and then at me, said, "So, John," and then remained gravely silent. I said nothing further, but it was understood that this was his first official act.

His next performance, I grieve to say, was not

attended with equal success. One of our regular paper-carriers fell sick, and, at a pinch, Wan Lee was ordered to fill his place. To prevent mistakes he was shown over the route the previous evening, and supplied at about daylight with the usual number of subscribers' copies. He returned after an hour, in good spirits and without the papers. He had delivered them all, he said.

Unfortunately for Wan Lee, at about eight o'clock indignant subscribers began to arrive at the office. They had received their copies; but how? In the form of hard-pressed cannon balls, delivered by a single shot and a mere *tour de force* through the glass of bed-room windows. They had received them full in the face, like a base ball, if they happened to be up and stirring; they had received them in quarter sheets, tucked in at separate windows; they had found them in the chimney, pinned against the door, shot through attic windows, delivered in long slips through convenient keyholes, stuffed into ventilators, and occupying the same can with the morning's milk. One subscriber, who waited for some time at the office door, to have a personal interview with Wan Lee (then comfortably locked in my bed-room), told me, with tears of rage in his eyes, that he had been awakened at five o'clock by a most hideous yelling below his windows; that on rising, in great agitation, he was startled by the sudden appearance of "The Northern Star," rolled hard and bent into the form of a boomerang or East Indian club, that sailed into the window, described a number of fiendish circles in the room, knocked over the light, slapped the baby's face, "took" him (the subscriber) "in the jaw," and then returned out of the window, and dropped helplessly in the area. During the rest of the day wads and strips of soiled paper, purporting to be copies of "The Northern Star" of that morning's issue, were brought indignantly to the office. An admirable editorial on "The Resources of Humboldt County" which I had constructed the evening before, and which, I have reason to believe, might have changed the whole balance of trade during the ensuing year, and left San Francisco bankrupt at her wharves, was in this way lost to the public.

It was deemed advisable for the next three weeks to keep Wan Lee closely confined to the printing-office and the purely mechanical part of the business. Here he developed a surprising quickness and adaptability, winning even the favor and good will of the printers and foreman, who at first looked upon his introduction into the secrets of their trade as fraught with the gravest political significance. He learned to set type readily and neatly, his wonderful skill in manipulation aiding him in the mere mechanical act, and his ignorance of the language confining him simply to the mechanical effort—confirming the printer's axiom that the printer who considers or follows the ideas of his copy makes a poor compositor. He would set up deliberately long diatribes against himself, composed by his fellow-printers, and hung on his hook as copy, and even such short sentences as "Wan Lee is the devil's own imp," "Wan Lee is a Mongolian rascal," and bring the proof to me with happiness beaming from every tooth and satisfaction shining in his huckleberry eyes.

It was not long, however, before he learned to retaliate on his mischievous persecutors. I remember one instance in which his reprisal came very near involving me in a serious misunderstanding. Our foreman's name was Webster, and Wan Lee presently learned to know and recognize the individual and combined letters of his name. It was during a political campaign, and the eloquent and fiery Col. Starbottle, of Siskyou, had delivered an effective speech, which was reported especially for "The Northern Star." In a very sublime peroration Col. Starbottle had said: "In the language of the god-like Webster, I repeat,"—and here followed the quotation, which I have forgotten. Now, it chanced that Wan Lee, looking over the galley after it had been revised, saw the name of his chief persecutor, and, of course, imagined the quotation his. After the forme was locked up, Wan Lee took advantage of Webster's absence to remove the quotation, and substitute a thin piece of lead, of the same size as the type, engraved with Chinese characters, making a sentence which, I had reason to believe, was an utter and abject confession of the incapacity and offensiveness of the Webster family generally, and exceedingly eulogistic of Wan Lee himself personally.

The next morning's paper contained Col. Starbottle's speech in full, in which it appeared that the "god-like" Webster had on one occasion uttered his thoughts in excellent but perfectly enigmatical Chinese. The rage of Col. Starbottle knew no bounds. I have a vivid recollection of that admirable man walking into my office and demanding a retraction of the statement.

"But, my dear sir," I asked, "are you willing to deny, over your own signature, that Webster ever uttered such a sentence? Dare you deny that, with Mr. Webster's well-known attainments, a knowledge of Chinese might not have been among the number? Are you willing to submit a translation suitable to the capacity of our readers, and deny, upon your honor as a gentleman, that the late Mr. Webster ever uttered such a sentiment? If you are, sir, I am willing to publish your denial."

The Col. was not, and left, highly indignant.

Webster, the foreman, took it more coolly. Happily he was unaware that for two days after, Chinamen from the laundries, from the gulches, from the kitchens, looked in the front office door with faces beaming with sardonic delight; that three hundred extra copies of the "Star" were ordered for the washhouses on the river. He only knew that during the day Wan Lee occasionally went off into convulsive spasms, and that he was obliged to kick him into consciousness again. A week after the occurrence I called Wan Lee into my office.

"Wan," I said, gravely, "I should like you to give me, for my own personal satisfaction, a translation of that Chinese sentence which my gifted countryman, the late god-like Webster, uttered upon a public occasion." Wan Lee looked at me intently, and then the slightest possible twinkle crept into his black eyes. Then he replied, with equal gravity:

"Mishtel Webstel,—he say: 'China boy makee me belly much foolee. China boy makee me heap sick.'" Which I have reason to think was true.

But I fear I am giving but one side, and not the best, of Wan Lee's character. As he imparted it to me, his had been a hard life. He had known scarcely any childhood—he had no recollection of a father or mother. The conjurer Wang had brought him up. He had spent the first seven years of his life in appearing from baskets, in dropping out of hats, in climbing ladders, in putting his little limbs out of joint in posturing. He had lived in an atmosphere of trickery and deception; he had learned to look upon mankind as dupes of their senses; in fine, if he had thought at all, he would have been a skeptic; if he had been a little older, he would have been a cynic; if he had been older still, he would have been a philosopher. As it was, he was a little imp! A good-natured imp it was, too—an imp whose moral nature had never been awakened, an imp up for a holiday, and willing to try virtue as a diversion. I don't know that he had any spiritual nature; he was very superstitious: he carried about with him a hideous little porcelain god, which he was in the habit of alternately reviling and propitiating. He was too intelligent for the commoner Chinese vices of stealing or gratuitous lying. Whatever discipline he practised was taught by his intellect.

I am inclined to think that his feelings were not altogether unimpressible,—although it was almost impossible to extract an expression from him,—and I conscientiously believe he became attached to those that were good to him. What he might have become under more favorable conditions than the bondsman of an over-worked, under-paid, literary man, I don't know; I only know that the scant, irregular, impulsive kindnesses that I showed him were gratefully received. He was very loyal and patient—two qualities rare in the average American servant. He was like Malvolio, "sad and civil" with me; only once, and then under great provocation, do I remember of his exhibiting any impatience. It was my habit, after leaving the office at night, to take him with me to my rooms, as the bearer of any supplemental or happy after-thought in the editorial way, that might occur to me before the paper went to press. One night I had been scribbling away past the usual hour of dismissing Wan Lee, and had become quite oblivious of his presence in a chair near my door, when suddenly I became aware of a voice saying, in plaintive accents, something that sounded like "Chy Lee."

I faced around sternly.

"What did you say?"

"Me say 'Chy Lee.'"

"Well?" I said impatiently.

"You sabe 'How do, John?'"

"Yes."

"You sabe 'So long, John?'"

"Yes."

"Well, 'Chy Lee' allee same!"

I understood him quite plainly. It appeared that "Chy Lee" was a form of "good night," and that Wan Lee was anxious to go home. But an instinct of mischief which I fear I possessed in common with him, impelled me to act as if oblivious of the hint. I muttered something about not understanding him, and again bent over my work. In a few minutes I heard his wooden shoes pattering pathetically over the floor. I looked up. He was standing near the door.

"You no sabe, 'Chy Lee?'"

"No," I said, sternly.

"You sabe muchee big foolee!—allee same!"

And with this audacity upon his lips, he fled. The next morning, however, he was as meek and patient as before, and I did not recall his offence. As a probable peace-offering, he blacked all my boots,—a duty never required of him,—including a pair of buff deer-skin slippers and an immense pair of horseman's jack-boots, on which he indulged his remorse for two hours.

I have spoken of his honesty as being a quality of his intellect rather than his principle, but I recall about this time two exceptions to the rule. I was anxious to get some fresh eggs, as a change to the heavy diet of a mining town, and knowing that Wan Lee's countrymen were great poultry raisers, I applied to him. He furnished me with them regularly every morning, but refused to take any pay, saying that the man did not sell them—a remarkable instance of self-abnegation, as eggs were then worth half a dollar apiece. One morning, my neighbor, Forster, dropped in upon me at breakfast, and took occasion to bewail his own ill fortune, as his hens had lately stopped laying, or wandered off in the bush. Wan Lee, who was present during our colloquy, preserved his characteristic sad taciturnity. When my neighbor had gone, he turned to me with a slight chuckle: "Flostel's hens—Wan Lee's hens —allee same!" His other offence was more serious and ambitious. It was a season of great irregularities in the mails, and Wan Lee had heard me deplore the delay in the delivery of my letters and newspapers. On arriving at my office one day, I was amazed to find my table covered with letters, evidently just from the post-office, but unfortunately not one addressed to me. I turned to Wan Lee, who was surveying them with a calm satisfaction, and demanded an explanation. To my horror he pointed to an empty mail bag in the corner, and said: "Postman he say 'no lettee, John—no lettee, John.' Postman plentee lie! Postman no good. Me catchee lettee last night—allee same!" Luckily it was still early; the mails had not been distributed; I had a hurried interview with the Postmaster, and Wan Lee's bold attempt at robbing the U. S. Mail was finally condoned, by the purchase of a new mail bag, and the whole affair thus kept a secret.

If my liking for my little Pagan page had not been sufficient, my duty to Hop Sing was enough to cause me to take Wan Lee with me when I returned to San Francisco, after my two years' experience with "The Northern Star." I do not think he contemplated the change with pleasure. I attributed his feelings to a nervous dread of crowded public streets,—when he had to go across town for me on an errand, he always made a long circuit of the outskirts,—to his dislike for the discipline of the Chinese and English school to which I proposed to send him, to his fondness for the free, vagrant life of the mines, to sheer wilfulness! That it might have been a superstitious premonition did not occur to me until long after.

Nevertheless it really seemed as if the opportunity I had long looked for and confidently expected had come—the opportunity of placing Wan Lee under gently restraining influences, of subjecting him to a life and experience that would draw out of him what good my superficial care and ill-regulated kindness could not reach. Wan Lee was placed at the school of a Chinese Missionary—an intelligent and kind-hearted clergyman, who had shown great interest in the boy, and who, better than all, had a wonderful faith in him. A home was found for him in the family of a widow, who had a bright and interesting daughter about two years younger than Wan Lee. It was this bright, cheery, innocent and artless child that touched and reached a depth in the boy's nature that hitherto had been unsuspected — that awakened a moral susceptibility which had lain for years insensible alike to the teachings of society or the ethics of the theologian.

These few brief months, bright with a promise that we never saw fulfilled, must have been happy ones to Wan Lee. He worshiped his little friend with something of the same superstition, but without any of the caprice that he bestowed upon his porcelain pagan god. It was his delight to walk behind her to school, carrying her books—a service always fraught with danger to him from the little hands of his Caucasian Christian brothers. He made her the most marvelous toys, he would cut out of carrots and turnips the most astonishing roses and tulips, he made lifelike chickens out of melon-seeds, he constructed fans and kites, and was singularly proficient in the making of dolls' paper dresses. On the other hand, she played and sang to him, taught him a thousand little prettinesses and refinements only known to girls, gave him a yellow ribbon for his pig-tail, as best suiting his complexion, read to him, showed him wherein he was original and valuable, took him to Sunday School with her, against the precedents of the school, and, small-womanlike, triumphed. I wish I could add here, that she effected his conversion, and made him give up his porcelain idol, but I am telling a true story, and this little girl was quite content to fill him with her own Christian goodness, without letting him know that he was changed. So they got along very well together—this little Christian girl with her shining cross hanging around her plump, white, little neck, and this dark little pagan, with his hideous porcelain god hidden away in his blouse.

There were two days of that eventful year which will long be remembered in San Francisco—two days when a mob of her citizens set upon and killed unarmed, defenceless foreigners, because they were foreigners and of another race, religion and color, and worked for what wages they could get. There were some public men so timid, that, seeing this, they thought that the end of the world had come; there were some eminent statesmen whose names I am ashamed to write here, who began to think that the passage in the Constitution which guarantees civil and religious liberty to every citizen or foreigner was a mistake. But there were also some men who were not so easily frightened, and in twenty-four hours we had things so arranged that the timid men could wring their hands in safety, and the eminent statesmen utter their doubts without hurting anybody or anything. And in the midst of this I got a note from Hop Sing, asking me to come to him immediately.

I found his warehouse closed and strongly guarded by the police against any possible attack of the rioters. Hop Sing admitted me through a barred grating with his usual imperturbable calm, but, as it seemed to me, with more than his usual seriousness. Without a word he took my hand and led me to the rear of the room, and thence down stairs into the basement. It was dimly lighted, but there was something lying on the floor covered by a shawl. As I approached he drew the shawl away with a sudden gesture, and revealed Wan Lee, the Pagan, lying there dead!

Dead, my reverend friends, dead! Stoned to death in the streets of San Francisco, in the year of grace, eighteen hundred and sixty-nine, by a mob of half-grown boys and Christian school children!

As I put my hand reverently upon his breast, I felt something crumbling beneath his blouse. I looked enquiringly at Hop Sing. He put his hand between the folds of silk and drew out something with the first bitter smile I had ever seen on the face of that pagan gentleman.

It was Wan Lee's porcelain god, crushed by a stone from the hands of those Christian iconoclasts!

IN VERSE.

LUKE.

(IN THE COLORADO PARK, 1873.)

Wot's that you're readin'?—a novel? A novel—
   well darn my skin!
You a man grown and bearded and histin' such
   stuff ez that in—
Stuff about gals and their sweethearts! No wonder
   you're thin ez a knife.
Look at me!—clar two hundred—and never read
   one in my life!

That's my opinion o' novels. And ez to their lyin'
   round here,
They belonged to the Jedge's daughter—the Jedge
   who came up last year
On account of his lungs and the mountains and
   the balsam o' pine and fir;
And his daughter—well, she read novels, and that's
   what's the matter with her.

Yet she was sweet on the Jedge, and stuck by him
    day and night,
Alone in the cabin up yer—till she grew like a
    ghost, all white.
She wus only a slip of a thing, ez light and ez up
    and away
Ez rifle smoke blown through the woods, but she
    wasn't my kind—no way!

Speakin' o' gals, d'ye mind that house ez you rise
    the hill,
A mile and a half from White's, and jist above
    Mattingly's mill?
You do? Well now *thar's* a gal! What, you saw
    her? O, come now, thar, quit!
She was only bedevlin' you boys, for to me she
    don't cotton one bit.

Now she's what I call a gal—ez pretty and plump
    ez a quail;
Teeth ez white ez a hound's and they'd go through
    a tenpenny nail;
Eyes that kin snap like a cap. So she asked to
    know "whar I was hid."
She did! O, it's jist like her sass, for she's peart
    ez a Katy-did.

But what was I talking of?—O! the Jedge and his
    daughter—she read
Novels the whole day long, and I reckon she read
    them abed,

And sometimes she read them out loud to the
    Jedge on the porch where he sat,
And 'twas how "Lord Augustus" said this, and how
    "Lady Blanche" she said that.

But the sickest of all that I heerd, was a yarn thet
    they read 'bout a chap,
"Leather-stocking" by name and a hunter chock
    full o' the greenest o' sap;
And they asked me to hear, but I says, "Miss
    Mabel, not any for me;
When I likes I kin sling my own lies, and thet chap
    and I shouldn't agree."

Yet somehow-or-other she was always sayin' I
    brought her to mind
Of folks about whom she had read, or suthin belike
    of thet kind,
And thar warn't no end o' the names that she give
    me thet summer up here,
"Robin Hood," "Leather-stocking," "Rob Roy,"—
    O, I tell you, the critter was queer.

And yet ef she hadn't been spiled, she was harmless
    enough in her way,
She could jabber in French to her dad, and they
    said that she knew how to play,
And she worked me that shot-pouch up thar—which
    the man doesn't live ez kin use,
And slippers—you see 'em down yer—ez would
    cradle an Injin's pappoose.

Yet along o' them novels, you see, she was wastin'
    and mopin' away,
And then she got shy with her tongue, and at last
    had nothin' to say;
And whenever I happened around, her face it was
    hid by a book,
And it warn't until she left that she give me ez
    much ez a look.

And this was the way it was. It was night when I
    kem up here
To say to 'em all "good-bye," for I reckoned to go
    for deer
At "sun up" the day they left. So I shook 'em all
    round by the hand,
'Cept Mabel, and she was sick, ez they give me to
    understand.

But jist ez I passed the house next morning at
    dawn, some one,
Like a little waver o' mist, got up on the hill with
    the sun;
Miss Mabel it was, alone—all wrapped in a mantle
    o' lace—
And she stood there straight in the road, with a
    touch o' the sun in her face.

And she looked me right in the eye—I'd seen
    suthin like it before
When I hunted a wounded doe to the edge o' the
    Clear Lake shore,

And I had my knee on its neck, and jist was raisin'
   my knife
When it give me a look like that, and—well, it got
   off with its life.

"We are going to-day," she said, "and I thought I
   would say good-bye
To you in your own house, Luke—these woods,
   and the bright blue sky!
You've always been kind to us, Luke, and papa has
   found you still
As good as the air he breathes, and wholesome as
   Laurel Tree Hill.

"And we'll always think of you, Luke, as the thing
   we could not take away;
The balsam that dwells in the woods, the rainbow
   that lives in the spray.
And you'll sometimes think of *me*, Luke, as you
   know you once used to say,
A rifle smoke blown through the woods, a moment,
   but never to stay."

And then we shook hands. She turned, but a-sud-
   dent she tottered and fell,
And I caught her sharp by the waist, and held her
   a minit—well,
It was only a minit, you know, that ez cold and ez
   white she lay
Ez a snow-flake here on my breast, and then—well,
   she melted away—

And was gone * * * And thar are her books; but I
    says not any for me,
Good enough may be for some, but them and I
    mightn't agree.
They spiled a decent gal ez might hev made some
    chap a wife,
And look at me!—clar two hundred—and never
    read one in my life!

"THE BABES IN THE WOODS."

(BIG PINE FLAT, 1871.)

"SOMETHING characteristic," eh?
   Humph! I reckon you mean by that,
Something that happened in our way,
   Here at the crossin' of Big Pine Flat.
Times aren't now as they used to be,
   When gold was flush and the boys were frisky,
And a man would pull out his battery
   For anything—maybe the price of whisky.

Nothing of that sort, eh? That's strange.
   Why, I thought you might be diverted,
Hearing how Jones, of Red Rock Range,
   Drawed his "Hint to the Unconverted,"
And saying, "Whar will you have it?" shot
   Cherokee Bob at the last Debating!
What was the question? I forgot—
   But Jones didn't like Bob's way of stating

Nothing of that kind, eh? You mean
    Something milder? Let's see—Oh, Joe!
Tell to the stranger that little scene
    Out of the "Babes in the Woods." You know,
"Babes" was the name that we gave 'em, sir,
    Two lean lads in their teens, and greener
Than even the belt of spruce and fir
    Where they built their nest, and each day grew
        leaner.

No one knew where they came from. None
    Cared to ask if they had a mother.
Runaway schoolboys, maybe. One
    Tall and dark as a spruce; the other
Blue and gold in the eyes and hair,
    Soft and low in his speech, but rarely
Talking with us; and we didn't care
    To get at their secret at all unfairly.

For they were so quiet, so sad and shy,
    Content to trust each other solely,
That somehow we'd always shut one eye,
    And never seem to observe them wholly,
As they passed to their work. 'Twas a wornout
        claim,
    And it paid them grub. They could live with-
        out it,
For the boys had a way of leaving game
    In their tent, and forgetting all about it.

Yet no one asked for their secret. Dumb
  It lay in their big eyes' heavy hollows.
It was understood that no one should come
  To their tent unawares, save the bees and swallows.
So they lived alone. Until one warm night
  I was sitting here at the tent-door, so, sir,
When out of the sunset's rosy light
  Up rose the sheriff of Mariposa.

I knew at once there was something wrong,
  For his hand and his voice shook just a little,
And there isn't much you can fetch along
  To make the sinews of Jack Hill brittle.
"Go warn the Babes!" he whispered, hoarse;
  "Tell I'm coming—to get and scurry,
For I've got a story that's bad, and worse,
  I've got a warrant: G—d d—n it, hurry."

Too late! they had seen him cross the hill;
  I ran to their tent and found them lying
Dead in each other's arms, and still
  Clasping the drug they had taken flying.
And there lay their secret cold and bare,
  Their life, their trial—the old, old story!
For the sweet blue eyes, and the golden hair,
  Was a *woman's* shame and a *woman's* glory.

"Who were they?" Ask no more, or ask
  The sun that visits their grave so lightly;

Ask of the whispering reeds, or task
  The mourning crickets that chirrup nightly.
All of their life but its Love forgot,
  Everything tender and soft and mystic,
These are our Babes in the Woods, you've got,
  Well—Human Nature—that's characteristic.

GUILD'S SIGNAL.

WILLIAM GUILD was engineer of the train which on the 19th of April plunged into Meadow Brook, on the line of the Stonington and Providence Railroad. It was his custom, as often as he passed his home, to whistle an "all's well" to his wife. He was found, after the disaster, dead, with his hand on the throttle-valve of his engine.

Two low whistles, quaint and clear,
That was the signal the engineer—
  That was the signal that Guild, 'tis said—
Gave to his wife at Providence,
As through the sleeping town, and thence,
    Out in the night,
    On to the light,
  Down past the farms, lying white, he sped!

As a husband's greeting, scant, no doubt,
Yet to the woman looking out,

Watching and waiting, no serenade,
Love song or midnight roundelay
Said what that whistle seemed to say:
   "To my trust true,
      So love to you!
Working or waiting, good night!" it said.

Brisk young bagmen, tourists fine,
Old commuters along the line,
   Brakemen and porters glanced ahead,
Smiled as the signal, sharp, intense,
Pierced through the shadows of Providence—
         "Nothing amiss—
            Nothing!—it is
Only Guild calling his wife," they said.

Summer and Winter, the old refrain
Rang o'er the billows of ripening grain,
   Pierced through the budding boughs o'erhead,
Flew down the track when the red leaves burned
Like living coals from the engine spurned;
         Sang as it flew:
         "To our trust true,
   First of all, duty. Good night!" it said.

And then, one night, it was heard no more
From Stonington over Rhode Island shore,
   And the folk in Providence smiled and said,

As they turned in their beds, "The engineer
Has once forgotten his midnight cheer,"
    One only knew,
    To his trust true,
Guild lay under his engine, dead.

TRUTHFUL JAMES TO THE EDITOR

(YREKA, 1873.)

WHICH it is not my style
    To produce needless pain
By statements that rile,
    Or that go 'gin the grain,
But here's Captain Jack still a livin', and Nye has no skelp on his brain!

    On that Caucasian head
        There is no crown of hair.
    It has gone, it has fled!
        And Echo sez "where?"
And I asks, "Is this Nation a White Man's, and is generally things on the square?"

    She was known in the camp
        As "Nye's other squaw,"
    And folks of that stamp
        Hez no rights in the Law,
But is treacherous, sinful and slimly, as Nye might hev' well known before.

But she said that she knew
    Where the Injins was hid,
And the statement was true,
    For it seemed that she did;
Since she led William where he was covered by
    seventeen Modocs, and—slid!

Then they reached for his hair;
    But Nye sez, "By the Law
Of Nations, forbear!
    I surrenders—no more:
And I looks to be treated, you hear me?—as a
    pris'ner, a pris'ner of war!"

But Captain Jack rose
    And he sez "It's too thin.
Such statements as those
    It's too late to begin.
There's a *Modoc indictment* agin you, O Paleface,
    and you're goin' in!

"You stole Schonchin's squaw
    In the year 'sixty-two;
It was in 'sixty-four
    That Long Jack you went through,
And you burned Nasty Jim's rancheria and his wives
    and his pappooses too.

"This gun in my hand
    Was sold me by you

'Gainst the law of the land,
   And I grieves it is true!"
And he buried his face in his blanket and wept as
   he hid it from view.

   "But you're tried and condemned
      And skelping's your doom,"
   And he paused and he hemmed—
      But why this resume?
He was skelped 'gainst the custom of Nations, and
   cut off like a rose in its bloom.

   So I asks without guile,
      And I trusts not in vain,
   If this is the style
      That is going to obtain—
If here's Captain Jack still a-livin', and Nye with
   no skelp on his brain?

DON DIEGO OF THE SOUTH.

(Refectory—Mission San Gabriel, 1869.)

"Good," said the Padre, "believe me still,
'Don Giovanni' or what you will—
The type's eternal! We knew him here
As Don Diego del Sud. I fear
The story's no new one! Will you hear?"

One of those spirits you can't tell why
God has permitted. Therein I
Have the advantage, for *I* hold
That wolves are sent to the purest fold,
And we'd save the wolf if we'd get the lamb.
You're no believer? Good. I am.

Well, for some purpose, I grant you dim,
The Don loved women, and they loved him.
Each thought herself his *last* love! Worst,
Many believed that they were his *first!*

And, such are these creatures, since the Fall,
The very doubt had a charm for all!

You laugh! You are young—but *I*—Indeed
I have no patience. * * * * To proceed—

You saw, as you passed through the upper town
The *Eucinal* where the road goes down
To San Felipe. There, one morn
They found Diego. His mouth torn,
And as many holes through his doublet's band
As there were wronged husbands—you under-
    stand!

"Dying," so said the gossips. "Dead"—
Was what the friars who found him said,
May be. *Quien sabe?* Who else should know—
It was a hundred years ago,
There was a funeral. Small indeed—
Private. What would you?—To proceed:

Scarcely the year had flown. One night
The Commandante awoke in fright,—
Hearing below his casement's bar
The well known twang of the Don's guitar;
And rushed to the window, just to see
His wife a-swoon on the balcony.

One week later, Don Juan Ramirez
Found his own daughter, the Doña Inez,
Pale as a ghost leaning out to hear
The song of that phantom Cavalier.
Even Alcalde Pedro Blas
Saw, it was said, through his niece's glass
The shade of Diego twice repass.

What these gentlemen each confessed
Heaven and the Church only knows. At best
The case was a bad one. How to deal
With Sin as a Ghost, they couldn't but feel
Was an awful thing. 'Till a certain Fray
Humbly offered to shew the way.

And the way was this—Did I say before
That the Fray was a stranger? No, Señor?
Strange! very strange,—I should have said
That the very week that the Don lay dead
He came among us. Bread he broke
Silent; nor ever to one he spoke.
So he had vowed it! Below his brows
His face was hidden. There are such vows!

Strange! are they not? You do not use
Snuff? A bad habit!

      Well, the views

Of the Fray was this: That the penance done
By the caballeros was right; but one
Was due from the *cause*, and that, in brief,
Was Donna Dolores Gomez, chief,
And Inez, Sanchicha, Concepcion
And Carmen—Well, half the girls in town,
On his tablets, the Friar had written down.

These were to come on a certain day
And ask at the hands of the pious Fray
For absolution. That done, small fear
But the shade of Diego would disappear.

They came; each knelt in her turn and place
To the pious Fray with his hidden face
And voiceless lips, and each again
Took back her soul freed from spot or stain,
'Till the Doña Inez with eyes downcast
And a tear on their fringes knelt her last.

And then—perhaps that her voice was low
From fear or from shame—the monks said so—
But the Fray leaned forward, when, presto! all
Were thrilled by a scream, and saw her fall
Fainting beside the confessional.

And so was the ghost of Diego laid
As the Fray had said. Never more his shade

Was seen at San Gabriel's mission. Eh?
The girl interests you, I dare say?
"Nothing," said she when they brought her to—
"Only a faintness!" They spake more true
Who said 'twas a stubborn soul. But then—
Women are women, and men are men!

So to return. As I said before
Having got the wolf, by the same high law
We saved the lambs in the wolf's own jaw.
And that's my moral. The tale I fear
But poorly told? Yet it strikes me, here
Is stuff for a moral! What's your view?
You smile,—Don Pancho,—Ah!—that's like you!

"FOR THE KING."

(Northern Mexico, 1640.)

As you look from the plaza at Leon, west
You can see her house, but the view is best
From the porch of the church where she lies at rest,

Where much of her past still lives, I think,
In the scowling brows and sidelong blink
Of the worshiping throng that rise or sink

To the waxen saints that, yellow and lank,
Lean out from their niches, rank on rank,
With a bloodless Saviour on either flank;

In the gouty pillars, whose cracks begin
To show the *adobe* core within,—
A soul of earth in a whitewashed skin.

And I think that the moral of all, you'll say,
Is the sculptured legend that molds away
On a tomb in the choir: "Por el Rey."

"Por el Rey." Well, the king is gone,
Ages ago, and the Hapsburg one
Shot—but the rock of the church lives on.

"Por el Rey." What matters, indeed,
If king or president succeed
To a country haggard with sloth and greed,

As long as one granary is fat,
And yonder priest, in a shovel hat,
Peeps out from the bin like a sleek, brown rat!

What matters? Naught, if it serves to bring
The legend nearer,—no other thing,—
We'll spare the moral, "Live the King!"

Two hundred years ago, they say,
The viceroy, Marquis of Monte-Rey,
Rode, with his retinue, that way.

Grave as befitted Spain's grandee,
Grave as the substitute should be
Of His Most Catholic Majesty,

Yet from his black plume's curving grace
To his slim, black gauntlet's smaller space,
Exquisite as a piece of lace!

"FOR THE KING."

'Two hundred years ago—e'en so—
'The marquis stopped where the lime-trees blow,
While Leon's seneschal bent him low

And begged that the marquis would that night take
His humble roof for the royal sake,
And then, as the custom demanded, spake

The usual wish that his guest would hold
The house, and all that it might infold,
As his—with the bride scarce three days old.

Be sure that the marquis, in his place,
Replied to all with the measured grace
Of chosen speech and unmoved face,

Nor raised his head till his black plume swept
The hem of the lady's robe, who kept
Her place, as her husband backward stept.

And then (I know not how nor why)
A subtle flame in the lady's eye—
Unseen by the courtiers standing by—

Burned through his lace and titled wreath,
Burned through his body's jeweled sheath,
Till it touched the steel of the man beneath!

(And yet, mayhap, no more was meant
Than to point a well-worn compliment,
And the lady's beauty, her worst intent.)

Howbeit, the marquis bowed again:
"Who rules with awe well serveth Spain,
But best whose law is love made plain."

Be sure that night no pillow pressed
The seneschal, but with the rest
Watched,—as was due a royal guest,—

Watched from the wall till he saw the square
Fill with the moonlight, white and bare,—
Watched till he saw two shadows fare.

Out from his garden, where the shade
That the old church tower and belfry made,
Like a benedictory hand was laid.

Few words spoke the seneschal as he turned
To his nearest sentry: "These monks have learned
That stolen fruit is sweetly earned.

"Myself shall punish yon acolyte
Who gathers my garden grapes by night;
Meanwhile, wait thou till the morning light."

Yet not till the sun was riding high
Did the sentry meet his commander's eye,
Nor then—till the viceroy stood by.

To the lovers of grave formalities
No greeting was ever so fine, I wis,
As this host's and guest's high courtesies!

The seneschal feared, as the wind was west,
A blast from Morena had chilled his rest?
The viceroy languidly confessed

That cares of state, and—he dared to say—
Some fears that the king could not repay
The thoughtful zeal of his host, some way

Had marred his rest. Yet he trusted much
None shared his wakefulness! Though such
Indeed might be! If he dared to touch

A theme so fine—the bride, perchance,
Still slept? At least, they missed her glance
To give this greeting countenance.

Be sure that the seneschal, in turn,
Was deeply bowed with the grave concern
Of the painful news his guest should learn:

"Last night, to her father's dying bed
By a priest was the lady summonèd;
Nor know we yet how well she sped,

"But hope for the best." The grave viceroy
(Though grieved his visit had such alloy)
Must still wish the seneschal great joy

Of a bride so true to her filial trust!
Yet now as the day waxed on, they must
To horse, if they'd 'scape the noonday dust.

"Nay," said the seneschal, "at least,
To mend the news of this funeral priest,
Myself shall ride as your escort, east."

The viceroy bowed. Then turned aside
To his nearest follower: "With me ride—
You and Felipe—on either side.

"And list! Should anything me befall,
Mischance of ambush or musket-ball,
Cleave to his saddle yon seneschal!

"No more." Then gravely in accents clear
Took formal leave of his late good cheer:
Whiles the seneschal whispered a musketeer,

Carelessly stroking his pommel top,
"If from the saddle ye see me drop,
Riddle me quickly you solemn fop!"

So these, with many a compliment,
Each on his one dark thought intent,
With grave politeness onward went,

Riding high, and in sight of all,
Viceroy, escort, and seneschal,
Under the shade of the Almandral.

Holding their secret, hard and fast,
Silent and grave, they ride at last
Into the dusty traveled Past;

Even like this they passed away
Two hundred years ago to-day.
What of the lady?   Who shall say?

Do the souls of the dying ever yearn
To some favored spot for the dust's return—
For the homely peace of the family urn?

I know not.   Yet did the seneschal,
Chancing in after years to fall
Pierced by a Flemish musket-ball,

Call to his side a trusty friar
And bid him swear, as his last desire,
To bear his corse to San Pedro's choir

At Leon, where 'neath a shield azûre
Should his mortal frame find sepulture;
This much, for the pains Christ did endure.

Be sure that the friar loyally
Fulfilled his trust by land and sea,
'Till the spires of Leon silently

Rose through the green of the Almandral,
As if to beckon the seneschal
To his kindred dust 'neath the choir wall.

I wot that the saints on either side
Leaned from their niches open-eyed,
To see the doors of the church swing wide—

That the wounds of the Saviour on either flank
Bled fresh, as the mourners, rank by rank,
Went by with the coffin, clank on clank,

For why? When they raised the marble door
Of the tomb untouched for years before,
The friar swooned on the choir floor;

For there, in her laces and festal dress,
Lay the dead man's wife, her loveliness
Scarcely changed by her long duress;

As on the night she had passed away—
Only that near her a dagger lay,
With the written legend, "Por el Rey."

What was their greeting—the groom and bride,
They whom that steel and the years divide?
I know not. Here they lie side by side.

Side by side. Though the king has his way,
Even the dead at last have their day.
Make you the moral. "Por el Rey."

FRIAR PEDRO'S RIDE.

It was the morning season of the year;
  It was the morning era of the land;
The water-courses rang full loud and clear;
  Portala's cross stood where Portala's hand
Had planted it when Faith was taught by Fear;
  When Monks and Missions held the sole command
Of all that shore beside the peaceful sea
Where spring-tides beat their long-drawn reveille.

Out of the Mission of San Luis Rey,
  All in that brisk, tumultuous spring weather,
Rode Friar Pedro, in a pious way,
  With six dragoons in cuirasses of leather,
Each armed alike for either prayer or fray,
  Handcuffs and missals they had slung together;
And as an aid the gospel truth to scatter
Each swung a lasso—*alias* a "riata."

In sooth, that year the harvest had been slack,
  The crop of converts scarce worth computation;

Some souls were lost, whose owners had turned
    back
  To save their bodies frequent flagellation,
And some preferred the songs of birds, alack,
  To Latin matins and their soul's salvation,
And thought their own wild whoopings were less
    dreary
Than Father Pedro's droning *miserere*.

To bring them back to matins and to prime,
  To pious works and secular submission,
To prove to them that liberty was crime,
  This was in fact the Padre's present mission;
To get new souls perchance at the same time
  And bring them to a "sense of their condi-
    tion"—
That easy phrase which in the past and present
Means making that condition most unpleasant.

He saw the glebe land guiltless of a furrow;
  He saw the wild oats wrestle on the hill;
He saw the gopher working in his burrow;
  He saw the squirrel scampering at his will;
He saw all this and felt no doubt a thorough
  And deep conviction of God's goodness; still
He failed to see that in His glory He
Yet left the humblest of His creatures free.

He saw the flapping crow, whose frequent note
  Voiced the monotony of land and sky,

Mocking with graceless wing and rusty coat
  His priestly presence as he trotted by.
He would have cursed the bird by bell and rote,
  But other game just then was in his eye—
A savage camp, whose occupants preferred
Their heathen darkness to the living Word.

He rang his bell, and at the martial sound
  Twelve silver spurs their jingling rowels clashed;
Six horses sprang across the level ground
  As six dragoons in open order dashed;
Above their heads the lassos circled round;
  In every eye a pious fervor flashed;
They charged the camp, and in one moment more
They lassoed six and reconverted four.

The Friar saw the conflict from a knoll,
  And sang *Laus Deo*, and cheered on his men:
"Well thrown, Bautista—that's another soul!
  After him, Gomez—try it once again;
This way, Felipe! there the heathen stole;
  Bones of St. Francis!—surely that makes *ten;*
Te deum laudamus—but they're very wild;
Non nobis dominus—all right, my child."

When at that moment—as the story goes—
  A certain squaw, who had her foes eluded,
Ran past the Friar—just before his nose.
  He stared a moment, and in silence brooded,

Then in his breast a pious frenzy rose
    And every other prudent thought excluded;
He caught a lasso, and dashed in a canter
After that Occidental Atalanta.

High o'er his head he swirled the dreadful noose,
    But as the practice was quite unfamiliar,
His first cast tore Felipe's captive loose,
    And almost choked Tiburcio Camilla,
And might have interfered with that brave youth's
    Ability to gorge the tough *tortilla;*
But all things come by practice, and at last
His flying slip-knot caught the maiden fast.

Then rose above the plain a mingled yell
    Of rage and triumph—a demoniac whoop;
The Padre heard it like a passing knell,
    And would have loosened his unchristian loop;
But the tough raw-hide held the captive well,
    And held, alas, too well the captor-dupe;
For with one bound the savage fled amain,
Dragging horse, friar, down the lonely plain.

Down the *arroyo*, out across the mead,
    By heath and hollow, sped the flying maid,
Dragging behind her still the panting steed,
    And helpless friar, who in vain essayed
To cut the lasso or to check his speed.
    He felt himself beyond all human aid,

And trusted to the saints—and for that matter
To some weak spot in Felipe's *riata*.

Alas! the lasso had been duly blessed,
   And, like baptism, held the flying wretch.
A doctrine that the priest had oft expressed—
   Which, like the lasso, might be made to stretch
But would not break—so neither could divest
   Themselves of it, but like some awful *fetch*,
The holy friar had to recognize
The image of his fate in heathen guise.

He saw the glebe land guiltless of a furrow;
   He saw the wild oats wrestle on the hill;
He saw the gopher standing in his burrow;
   He saw the squirrel scampering at his will;
He saw all this, and felt no doubt how thorough
   The contrast was to his condition; still
The squaw kept onward to the sea, till night
And the cold sea fog hid them both from sight.

The morning came above the serried coast,
   Lighting the snow-peaks with its beacon fires,
Driving before it all the fleet-winged host
   Of chattering birds above the Mission spires,
Filling the land with light and joy—but most
   The savage woods with all their leafy lyres;
In pearly tints, and opal flame and fire
The morning came—but not the holy Friar.

Weeks passed away. In vain the Fathers sought
   Some trace or token that might tell his story.
Some thought him dead, or like Elijah caught
   Up to the heavens in a blaze of glory.
In this surmise, some miracles were wrought
   On his account, and souls in purgatory
Were thought to profit from his intercession—
In brief, his absence made a "deep impression."

A twelvemonth passed; the welcome spring once more
   Made green the hills beside the white-faced Mission,
Spread her bright dais by the western shore,
   And sat enthroned—a most resplendent vision.
The heathen converts thronged the chapel-door
   At morning mass; when, says the old tradition,
A frightful whoop throughout the church resounded,
And to their feet the congregation bounded.

A tramp of hoofs upon the beaten course—
   Then came a sight that made the bravest quail:
A phantom friar, on a spectre horse,
   Dragged by a creature decked with horns and tail.
By the lone Mission, with the whirlwind's force,
   They madly swept, and left a sulphurous trail—
And that was all—enough to tell the story
   And leave unblessed those souls in purgatory.

And ever after, on that fatal day
   That Friar Pedro rode abroad lassoing,
A ghostly couple came and went away
   With savage whoop and heathenish hallooing,
Which brought discredit on San Luis Rey,
   And proved the Mission's ruin and undoing;
For ere ten years had passed, the squaw and Friar
Performed to empty walls and fallen spire.

The Mission is no more; upon its walls
   The golden lizards slip, or breathless pause
Still as the sunshine brokenly that falls
   Through crannied roof and spider-webs of gauze;
No more the bell its solemn warning calls—
   A holier silence thrills and overawes;
And the sharp lights and shadows of To-Day
Outline the Mission of San Luis Rey.

MISS BLANCHE SAYS.

And you are the poet, and so, you want
    Something—what is it?—a theme, a fancy?
Something or other the muse won't grant
    In your old poetical necromancy;
        Why one half your poets—you can't deny—
Don't know the muse when you chance to meet her,
    But sit in your attics and mope and sigh
For a faineant goddess to drop from the sky,
    When flesh and blood may be standing by
Quite at your service, should you but greet her.

What if I told you my own romance?
    Women are poets, if you so take them,
One-third poet—the rest what chance
    Of man and marriage may choose to make them.
Give me ten minutes before you go,—
    Here at the window we'll sit together,
Watching the currents that ebb and flow;
    Watching the world as it drifts below

Up to the hot avenue's dusty glow:
   Isn't it pleasant—this bright June weather?

Well it was after the war broke out,
   And I was a school girl fresh from Paris;
Papa had contracts, and roamed about
   And I—did nothing—for I was an heiress.
Picked some lint, now I think; perhaps
   Knitted some stocking—a dozen nearly;
   Havelocks made for the soldiers' caps;
   Stood at fair tables and peddled traps
   Quite at a profit. The shoulder straps
Thought I was pretty. Ah, thank you, really.

Still, it was stupid. Ratatat-tat!
   Those were the sounds of that battle summer
Till the earth seemed a parchment round and flat.
   And every footfall the tap of a drummer;
And, day by day, down the avenue went
   Cavalry, Infantry, all together,
Till my pitying angel one day sent
   My fate in the shape of a regiment
That halted, just as the day was spent,
Here at our door in the bright June weather.

None of your dandy warriors they
   Men from the west, but where I know not;
Haggard and travel-stained, worn and gray
   With never a ribbon or lace or bow-knot:

And I opened the window, and leaning there,
   I felt in their presence the free winds blowing;
My neck and shoulders and arms were bare—
   I did not dream that they might think me fair,
But I had some flowers that night in my hair,
And here, on my bosom, a red rose glowing.

And I looked from the window along the line,
   Dusty and dirty and grim and solemn,
'Till an eye like a bayonet flash met mine
   And a dark face grew from the darkening column,
And a quick flame leaped to my eyes and hair
Till cheeks and shoulders burned all together,
And the next I found myself standing there
With my eyelids wet and my cheeks less fair,
And the rose from my bosom tossed high in air
Like a blood-drop falling on plume and feather.

Then I drew back quickly: there came a cheer,
   A rush of figures, a noise and tussle,
And then it was over, and high and clear,
   My red rose bloomed on his gun's black muzzle.
Then far in the darkness a sharp voice cried,
   And slowly, and steadily all together,
     Shoulder to shoulder, and side to side,
     Rising and falling, and swaying wide,
     But bearing above them the rose, my pride,
They marched away in the twilight weather.

And I leaned from my window and watched my
    rose
  Tossed on the waves of the surging column,
Warmed from above in the sunset glows,
  Borne from below by an impulse solemn.
Then I shut the window. I heard no more
  Of my soldier friend, my flower neither,
    But lived my life as I did before;
    I did not go as a nurse to the war—
    Sick folks to me are a dreadful bore—
So I didn't go to the hospital, either.

You smile, O poet, and what do you?
  You lean from your window, and watch life's
    column
Trampling and struggling through dust and dew,
  Filled with its purposes grave and solemn;
An act, a gesture, a face—who knows?—
  Touches your fancy to thrill and haunt you,
And you pluck from your bosom the verse that
    grows,
And down it flies like my red, red rose,
And you sit and dream as away it goes,
  And think that your duty is done—now don't you?

I know your answer. I'm not yet through.
  Look at this photograph—"In the Trenches:"
That dead man in the coat of blue
  Holds a withered rose in his hand. That clenches
Nothing! Except that the sun paints true,

And a woman is sometimes prophetic-minded.
And that's my romance. And, poet, you
Take it and mould it to suit your view;
And who knows but you may find it too
Come to your heart once more as mine did.

DOLLY VARDEN.

Dear Dolly! who does not recall
The trilling page that pictured all
Those charms that held our sense in thrall
    Just as the artist caught her—
As down that English lane she tripped,
In bowered chintz, hat sideways tipped,
'Trim-bodiced, bright-eyed, roguish-lipped—
    The locksmith's pretty daughter?

Sweet fragment of the Master's art!
O simple faith! O rustic heart!
O maid that hath no counterpart
    In life's dry, dog-eared pages!
Where shall we find thy like? Ah, stay!
Methinks I saw her yesterday
In chintz that flowered, as one might say,
    Perennial for ages.

Her father's modest cot was stone,
Five stories high. In style and tone
Composite, and, I frankly own,
    Within its walls revealing

Some certain novel, strange ideas:
A Gothic door with Roman piers,
And floors removed some thousand years
   From their Pompeiian ceiling.

The small *salon* where she received
Was Louis Quatorze, and relieved
By Chinese cabinets, conceived
   Grotesquely by the heathen;
The sofas were a classic sight—
The Roman bench (*sedilia* hight);
The chairs were French, in gold and white,
   And one Elizabethan.

And she, the goddess of that shrine,
Two ringed fingers placed in mine—
The stones were many carats fine,
   And of the purest water—
Then dropped a courtesy, far enough
To fairly fill her *cretonne* puff
And show the petticoat's rich stuff
   That her fond parent bought her.

Her speech was simple as her dress—
Not French the more, but English less,
She loved; yet sometimes, I confess,
   I scarce could comprehend her.
Her manners were quite far from shy:
There was a quiet in her eye

Appalling to the Hugh who'd try
    With rudeness to offend her.

"But whence," I cried, "this masquerade?
Some figure for to-night's charade—
A Watteau shepherdess or maid?"
    She smiled, and begged my pardon:
"Why, surely you must know the name—
That woman who was Shakspeare's flame,
Or Byron's—well, it's all the same:
    Why, Lord! I'm Dolly Varden!"

CALDWELL OF SPRINGFIELD.

(NEW JERSEY, 1780.)

Here's the spot. Look around you. Above on the height
Lay the Hessians encamped. By that church on the right
Stood the gaunt Jersey farmers. And here ran a wall—
You may dig anywhere and you'll turn up a ball.
Nothing more. Grasses spring, waters run, flowers blow,
Pretty much as they did ninety-three years ago.

Nothing more did I say? Stay one moment; you've heard
Of Caldwell, the parson, who once preached the word
Down at Springfield? What, No? Come—that's bad, why he had
All the Jerseys aflame! And they gave him the name

Of the "rebel high priest." He stuck in their
 gorge,
For he loved the Lord God—and he hated King
 George!

He had cause, you might say! When the Hessians
 that day
Marched up with Knyphausen they stopped on their
 way
At the "farms," where his wife, with a child in her
 arms,
Sat alone in the house. How it happened none
 knew
But God—and that one of the hireling crew
Who fired the shot! Enough!—there she lay
And Caldwell, the chaplain, her husband, away!

Did he preach—did he pray? Think of him, as you
 stand
By the old church to-day;—think of him and that
 band
Of militant ploughboys! See the smoke and the
 heat
Of that reckless advance—of that straggling re-
 treat!
Keep the ghost of that wife, foully slain in your
 view—
And what could you, what should you, what would
 you do?

Why, just what *he* did! They were left in the lurch
For the want of more wadding. He ran to the church,
Broke the door, stripped the pews, and dashed out in the road
With his arms full of hymn-books, and threw down his load
At their feet! Then above all the shouting and shots,
Rang his voice—"Put Watts into 'em—Boys, give 'em Watts!"

And they did. That is all. Grasses spring, flowers blow
Pretty much as they did ninety-three years ago.
You may dig anywhere and you'll turn up a ball—
But not always a hero like this—and that's all.

POEM

DELIVERED ON THE FOURTEENTH ANNIVERSARY OF CALIFORNIA'S ADMISSION INTO THE UNION.

September 9th, 1864.

We meet in Peace, though from our native East
The sun that sparkles on our birthday feast
Glanced as he rose in fields whose dews were red
With darker tints than those Aurora spread;
Though shorn his rays—his welcome disc concealed
In the dim smoke that veiled each battle-field,
Still striving upward, in meridian pride,
He climbed the walls that East and West divide—
Saw his bright face flashed back from golden sand,
And sapphire seas that lave the Western land.

Strange was the contrast that such scenes disclose
From his high vantage o'er eternal snows;
There War's alarm the brazen trumpet rings—
Here his love song the mailed cicala sings;

There bayonets glitter through the forest glades—
Here yellow corn-fields stack their peaceful blades;
There the deep trench where Valor finds a grave—
Here the long ditch that curbs the peaceful wave;
There the bold sapper with his lighted train—
Here the dark tunnel and its stores of gain,
Here the full harvest and the wain's advance—
There the Grim Reaper and the ambulance.

With scenes so adverse, what mysterious bond
Links our fair fortunes to the shores beyond?
Why come we here—last of a scattered fold—
To pour new metal in the broken mould?
To yield our tribute, stamped with Cæsar's face,
To Cæsar, stricken in the market place?

Ah, Love of Country is the secret tie
That joins these contrasts 'neath one arching sky;
Though brighter paths our peaceful steps explore—
We meet together at the Nation's door.
War winds her horn, and giant cliffs go down
Like the high walls that girt the sacred town,
And bares the pathway to her throbbing heart,
From clustered village and from crowded mart.

Part of God's providence it was to found
A nation's bulwark on this chosen ground—
Not Jesuit's zeal nor Pioneer's unrest
Planted these pickets in the distant West;

But He who first the nation's fate forecast
Placed here His fountains sealed for ages past,
Rock-ribbed and guarded till the coming time
Should fit the people for their work sublime;
When a new Moses with his rod of steel
Smote the tall cliffs with one wide-ringing peal,
And the old miracle in record told
To the new nation was revealed in Gold.

Judge not too idly that our toils are mean,
Though no new levies marshal on our green;
Nor deem too rashly that our gains are small,
Weighed with the prizes for which heroes fall.
See, where thick vapor wreathes the battle line;
There Mercy follows with her oil and wine;
Or when brown Labor with its peaceful charm
Stiffens the sinews of the Nation's arm.
What nerves its hands to strike a deadlier blow,
And hurl its legions on the rebel foe?
Lo! for each town new rising o'er our State
See the foe's hamlet waste and desolate,
While each new factory lifts its chimney tall,
Like a fresh mortar trained on Richmond's wall.

For this, oh! brothers, swings the fruitful vine,
Spread our broad pastures with their countless kine;
For this o'erhead the arching vault springs clear,
Sunlit and cloudless for one half the year;
For this no snow-flake, e'er so lightly pressed,
Chills the warm impulse of our mother's breast.

Quick to reply, from meadows brown and sere,
She thrills responsive to Spring's earliest tear;
Breaks into blossom, flings her loveliest rose
Ere the white crocus mounts Atlantic shows;
And the example of her liberal creed
Teaches the lesson that to-day we need.

Thus ours the lot with peaceful, generous hand
To spread our bounty o'er the suffering land;
As the deep cleft in Mariposa's wall
Hurls a vast river splintering in its fall—
Though the rapt soul who stands in awe below,
Sees but the arching of the promised bow—
Lo! the far streamlet drinks its dews unseen,
And the whole valley makes a brighter green.

AT THE HACIENDA

Know I not whom thou mayst be
  Carved upon this olive tree—
    "Manuela of La Torre,"
For, around on broken walls
Summer sun and Spring rain falls,
And in vain the low wind calls
    "Manuela of La Torre."

Of that song no words remain
  But the musical refrain:
    "Manuela of La Torre."
Yet at night, when winds are still,
Tinkles on the distant hill,
A guitar, and words that thrill
  Tell to me the old, old story—
Old when first thy charms were sung,
Old when these old walls were young,
    "Manuela of La Torre."

WHAT THE CHIMNEY SANG.

Over the chimney the night wind sang
And chanted a melody no one knew;
And the Woman stopped, as her babe she tossed,
And thought of the one she had long since lost,
And said, as her tear drops back she forced,
"I hate the wind in the chimney."

Over the chimney the night wind sang
And chanted a melody no one knew;
And the Children said as they closer drew,
"'Tis some witch cleaving the black night through,—
'Tis a fairy trumpet that just then blew,
And we fear the wind in the chimney."

Over the chimney the night wind sang
And chanted a melody no one knew;
And the Man as he sat on his hearth below,
Said to himself "It will surely snow,
And fuel is dear, and wages low,
And I'll stop the leak in the chimney."

Over the chimney the night wind sang
And chanted a melody no one knew;
But the Poet listened and smiled, for he
Was *man* and *woman* and *child*—all three,
And said "It is God's own harmony—
This wind we hear in the chimney."

THE END.

PRINTING OFFICE OF THE PUBLISHER.

Sold by all the principal booksellers on the Continent.

February  1894.

TAUCHNITZ EDITION.

Each volume 1 Mark 60 Pf. or 2 Francs.

This Collection of British Authors, Tauchnitz Edition, will contain the new works of the most admired English and American Writers, immediately on their appearance, with copyright for continental circulation.

Contents:

Collection of British Authors, vol. 1—2963   Page 2-14.
Collection of German Authors, vol. 1—51 .   „   15.
Series for the Young, vol. 1—30 . . . .   „   15.
Manuals of Conversation . . . .   „   15.
Dictionaries . . . .   „   16.

Latest Volumes:

A Gentleman of France. By *Stanley J. Weyman*, 2 vols.
Dodo. A Detail of the Day. By *E. F. Benson*, 1 vol.
The Handsome Humes. By *William Black*, 2 vols.
Two Offenders. By *Ouida*, 1 vol.
The Hoyden. By *Mrs. Hungerford*, 2 vols.
The Brownies, etc. By *Juliana Horatia Ewing*, 1 vol.
Montezuma's Daughter. By *H. Rider Haggard*, 2 vols.
Marion Darche. By *F. Marion Crawford*, 1 vol.
Barabbas. By *Marie Corelli*, 2 vols.
Of Course. By *F. C. Philips*, 1 vol.
A Lily among Thorns. By *Emma Marshall*, 1 vol.

Collection of British Authors.

Rev. W. Adams: Sacred Allegories 1 v.
Miss Aguilar: Home Influence 2 v. The Mother's Recompense 2 v.
H. Aïdé: Rita 1 v. Carr of Carrlyon 2 v. The Marstons 2 v. In that State of Life 1 v. Morals and Mysteries 1 v. Penruddocke 2 v. "A nine Days' Wonder" 1 v. Poet and Peer 2 v. Introduced to Society 1 v.
W. Harrison Ainsworth: Windsor Castle 1 v. Saint James's 1 v. Jack Sheppard (w. Portrait) 1 v. The Lancashire Witches 2 v. The Star-Chamber 2 v. The Flitch of Bacon 1 v. The Spendthrift 1 v. Mervyn Clitheroe 2 v. Ovingdean Grange 1 v. The Constable of the Tower 1 v. The Lord Mayor of London 2 v. Cardinal Pole 2 v. John Law 2 v. The Spanish Match 2 v. The Constable de Bourbon 2 v. Old Court 2 v. Myddleton Pomfret 2 v. The South-Sea Bubble 2 v. Hilary St. Ives 2 v. Talbot Harland 1 v. Tower Hill 1 v. Boscobel; or, The Royal Oak 2 v. The Good Old Times 2 v. Merry England 2 v. The Goldsmith's Wife 2 v. Preston Fight 2 v. Chetwynd Calverley 2 v. The Leaguer of Lathom 2 v. The Fall of Somerset 2 v. Beatrice Tyldesley 2 v. Beau Nash 2 v. Stanley Brereton 2 v.
Louisa M. Alcott: Little Women 2 v. Little Men 1 v. An Old-Fashioned Girl 1 v. Jo's Boys 1 v.
Thomas Bailey Aldrich: Marjorie Daw, etc. 1 v. The Stillwater Tragedy 1 v.
Mrs. Alexander: A Second Life 3 v. By Woman's Wit 1 v. Mona's Choice 2 v. A Life Interest 2 v. A Crooked Path 2 v. Blind Fate 2 v. A Woman's Heart 2 v. For His Sake 2 v. The Snare of the Fowler 2 v. Found Wanting 2 v.
Alice, Grand Duchess of Hesse (with Portrait) 2 v.
Lizzie Alldridge: By Love and Law 2 v. The World she awoke in 2 v.
"All for Greed," Author of—All for Greed 1 v. Love the Avenger 2 v.
F. Anstey: The Giant's Robe 2 v. A Fallen Idol 1 v. The Pariah 3 v. The Talking Horse, etc. 1 v. Voces Populi 1 v.
Matthew Arnold: Essays in Criticism 2 v. Essays in Criticism, 2nd Series, 1 v.
Sir E. Arnold: The Light of Asia (with Portrait) 1 v.
Miss Austen: Sense and Sensibility 1 v. Mansfield Park 1 v. Pride and Prejudice 1 v. Northanger Abbey 1 v. Emma 1 v.

Baring-Gould: Mehalah 1 v. John Herring 2 v. Court Royal 2 v.
Lady Barker: Station Life in New Zealand 1 v. Station Amusements in New Zealand 1 v. A Year's Housekeeping in South Africa 1 v. Letters to Guy, and A Distant Shore—Rodrigues 1 v.
F. Barrett: The Smuggler's Secret 1 v. Out of the Jaws of Death 2 v.
Miss Bayle's Romance, Author of—vide W. Fraser Rae.
Rev. R. H. Baynes: Lyra Anglicana, Hymns and Sacred Songs 1 v.
Beaconsfield: vide Disraeli.
A. Beaumont: Thornicroft's Model 2 v. Currer Bell (Charlotte Brontë): Jane Eyre 2 v. Shirley 2 v. Villette 2 v. The Professor 1 v.
Ellis & Acton Bell: Wuthering Heights, and Agnes Grey 2 v.
E. Bellamy: Looking Backward 1 v.
F. Lee Benedict: St. Simon's Niece 2 v.
E. F. Benson: Dodo 1 v.
Walter Besant: The Revolt of Man 1 v. Dorothy Forster 2 v. Children of Gibeon 2 v. The World went very well then 2 v. Katharine Regina 1 v. Herr Paulus 2 v. The Inner House 1 v. The Bell of St. Paul's 2 v. For Faith and Freedom 2 v. Armorel of Lyonesse 2 v. Verbena Camellia Stephanotis 1 v.
W. Besant & James Rice: The Golden Butterfly 2 v. Ready-Money Mortiboy 2 v. By Celia's Arbour 2 v.
A. Bierce: In the Midst of Life 1 v.
E. Bisland: vide Miss Broughton.
William Black: A Daughter of Heth 2 v. In Silk Attire 2 v. Adventures of a Phaeton 2 v. A Princess of Thule 2 v. Kilmeny 1 v. The Maid of Killeena, etc. 1 v. Three Feathers 2 v. Lady Silverdale's Sweetheart 1 v. Madcap Violet 2 v. Green Pastures and Piccadilly 2 v. Macleod of Dare 2 v. White Wings 2 v. Sunrise 2 v. The Beautiful Wretch 1 v. Mr. Pisistratus Brown, M.P., in the Highlands 1 v. Shandon Bells (w. Portrait) 2 v. Judith Shakespeare 2 v. The Wise Women of Inverness, etc. 1 v. White Heather 2 v. Sabina Zembra 2 v. Strange Adventures of a House Boat 2 v. In Far Lochaber 2 v. The New Prince Fortunatus 2 v. Stand Fast, Craig Royston 2 v. Donald Ross of Heimra 2 v. Magic Ink, etc. 1 v. Wolfenberg 2 v. The Handsome Humes 2 v. The Black-Box Murder 1 v.

The price of each volume is 1 Mark 60 Pfennig.

Richard Doddridge Blackmore: Alice Lorraine 2 v. Mary Anerley 3 v. Christowell 2 v. Tommy Upmore 2 v.
"Blackwood," Tales from — 1 v.— Second Series 1 v.
Isa Blagden: The Woman I loved, and the Woman who loved me, etc. 1 v.
Lady Blessington: Meredith 1 v. Strathern 2 v. Memoirs of a Femme de Chambre 1 v. Marmaduke Herbert 2 v. Country Quarters (with Portrait) 2 v.
Baroness Bloomfield: Reminiscences of Court and Diplomatic Life (with the Portrait of Her Majesty the Queen) 2 v.
Rolf Boldrewood: Robbery under Arms 2 v. Nevermore 2 v.
Miss Braddon: Lady Audley's Secret 2 v. Aurora Floyd 2 v. Eleanor's Victory 2 v. John Marchmont's Legacy 2 v. Henry Dunbar 2 v. The Doctor's Wife 2 v. Only a Clod 2 v. Sir Jasper's Tenant 2 v. The Lady's Mile 2 v. Rupert Godwin 2 v. Dead-Sea Fruit 2 v. Run to Earth 2 v. Fenton's Quest 2 v. The Lovels of Arden 2 v. Strangers and Pilgrims 2 v. Lucius Davoren 3 v. Taken at the Flood 3 v. Lost for Love 2 v. A Strange World 2 v. Hostages to Fortune 2 v. Dead Men's Shoes 2 v. Joshua Haggard's Daughter 2 v. Weavers and Weft 1 v. In Great Waters, etc. 1 v. An Open Verdict 3 v. Vixen 3 v. The Cloven Foot 3 v. Barbara 2 v. Just as I am 2 v. Asphodel 3 v. Mount Royal 2 v. The Golden Calf 2 v. Flower and Weed 1 v. Phantom Fortune 3 v. Under the Red Flag 1 v. Ishmael 3 v. Wyllard's Weird 3 v. One Thing Needful 2 v. Cut by the County 1 v. Like and Unlike 2 v. The Fatal Three 2 v. The Day will come 2 v. One Life, One Love 2 v. Gerard; or, The World, the Flesh, and the Devil 2 v. The Venetians 2 v. All along the River 2 v.
Lady Brassey: A Voyage in the "Sunbeam" 2 v. Sunshine and Storm in the East 2 v. In the Trades, the Tropics, and the Roaring Forties 2 v.
The Bread-Winners 1 v.
Bret Harte: vide Harte.
Rev. W. Brock: A Biographical Sketch of Sir H. Havelock, K. C. B. 1 v.
Shirley Brooks: The Silver Cord 3 v. Sooner or Later 3 v.
Miss Rhoda Broughton: Cometh up as a Flower 1 v. Not wisely, but too well 2 v. Red as a Rose is She 2 v. Tales for Christmas Eve 1 v. Nancy 2 v. Joan 2 v. Second Thoughts 2 v. Belinda 2 v. Doctor Cupid 2 v. Alas! 2 v. Mrs. Bligh 1 v.
Broughton & Bisland: A Widower Indeed 1 v.
John Brown: Rab and his Friends 1 v.
E. Barrett Browning: A Selection from her Poetry (w. Port.) 1 v. Aurora Leigh 1 v.
R. Browning: Poet. Works (w. Portr.) 4 v.
Edward Bulwer (Lord Lytton): Pelham (w. Portrait) 1 v. Eugene Aram 1 v. Paul Clifford 1 v. Zanoni 1 v. The Last Days of Pompeii 1 v. The Disowned 1 v. Ernest Maltravers 1 v. Alice 1 v. Eva, and the Pilgrims of the Rhine 1 v. Devereux 1 v. Godolphin and Falkland 1 v. Rienzi 1 v. Night and Morning 1 v. The Last of the Barons 2 v. Athens 2 v. The Poems and Ballads of Schiller 1 v. Lucretia 2 v. Harold 2 v. King Arthur 2 v. The New Timon, St Stephen's 1 v. The Caxtons 2 v. My Novel 4 v. What will he do with it? 4 v. Dramatic Works 2 v. A Strange Story 2 v. Caxtoniana 2 v. The Lost Tales of Miletus 1 v. Miscellaneous Prose Works 4 v. The Odes and Epodes of Horace 2 v. Kenelm Chillingly 4 v. The Coming Race 1 v. The Parisians 4 v. Pausanias, the Spartan 1 v.
Henry Lytton Bulwer (Lord Dalling): Historical Characters 2 v. The Life of Viscount Palmerston 3 v.
J. Bunyan: The Pilgrim's Progress 1 v.
"Buried Alone," 1 v.
F. Hodgson Burnett: Through one Administration 2 v. Little Lord Fauntleroy 1 v. Sara Crewe and Editha's Burglar 1 v. The Pretty Sister of José 1 v.
Miss Burney: Evelina 1 v.
R. Burns: Poetical Works (w. Port.) 1 v.
Richard F. Burton: Pilgrimage to Mecca and Medina 3 v.
Mrs. B. H. Buxton: "Jennie of 'The Prince's,'" 2 v. Won! 2 v. Great Grenfell Gardens 2 v. Nell—on and off the Stage 2 v. From the Wings 2 v.
Lord Byron: Poet. Works (w. Port.) 5 v.
Hall Caine: The Bondman 2 v.
V. Lovett Cameron: Across Africa 2 v.
Mrs. Campbell-Praed: Zéro 1 v. Affinities 1 v. The Head Station 2 v.
Rosa Nouchette Carey: Not Like other Girls 2 v. "But Men must Work" 2 v. Sir Godfrey's Grand-Daughters 2 v.
Thomas Carlyle: The French Revolution 3 v. Frederick the Great 13 v. Oliver

The price of each volume is 1 Mark 60 Pfennig.

Cromwell's Letters and Speeches 4 v. The Life of Schiller 1 v.
A. Carr: Treherne's Temptation 2 v.
Egerton Castle: Consequences 2 v. "La Bella" etc. 1 v.
Maria Louisa Charlesworth: Oliver of the Mill 1 v.
M. Cholmondeley: Diana Tempest 2 v.
"Chronicles of the Schönberg-Cotta Family," Author of—Chronicles of the Schönberg-Cotta Family 2 v. The Draytons and the Davenants 2 v. On Both Sides of the Sea 2 v. Winifred Bertram 2 v. Diary of Mrs. Kitty Trevylyan 1 v. The Victory of the Vanquished 1 v. The Cottage by the Cathedral 1 v. Against the Stream 2 v. The Bertram Family 2 v. Conquering and to Conquer 1 v. Lapsed, but not Lost 1 v.
Mrs. W. K. Clifford: Love-Letters of a Worldly Woman 1 v. Aunt Anne 2 v. The Last Touches, etc. 1 v. Mrs. Keith's Crime 1 v. A Wild Proxy 1 v.
Frances Power Cobbe: Re-Echoes 1 v.
Coleridge: The Poems 1 v.
C. R. Coleridge: An English Squire 2 v.
Charles A. Collins: A Cruise upon Wheels 2 v.
Mortimer Collins: Sweet and Twenty 2 v. A Fight with Fortune 2 v.
Wilkie Collins: After Dark 1 v. Hide and Seek 2 v. A Plot in Private Life, etc. 1 v. The Woman in White 2 v. Basil 1 v. No Name 3 v. The Dead Secret, etc. 2 v. Antonina 2 v. Armadale 3 v. The Moonstone 2 v. Man and Wife 3 v. Poor Miss Finch 2 v. Miss or Mrs.? 1 v. The New Magdalen 2 v. The Frozen Deep 1 v. The Law and the Lady 2 v. The Two Destinies 1 v. My Lady's Money, and Percy and the Prophet 1 v. The Haunted Hotel 1 v. The Fallen Leaves 2 v. Jezebel's Daughter 2 v. The Black Robe 2 v. Heart and Science 2 v. "I say No," 2 v. The Evil Genius 2 v. The Guilty River and The Ghost's Touch 1 v. The Legacy of Cain 2 v. Blind Love 2 v.
"Cometh up as a Flower," Author of—vide Broughton.
Hugh Conway: Called Back 1 v. Bound Together 2 v. Dark Days 1 v. A Family Affair 2 v. Living or Dead 2 v.
Fenimore Cooper: The Spy (with Portrait) 1 v. The Two Admirals 1 v. The Jack O'Lantern 1 v.
M. Corelli: Vendetta! 2 v. Thelma 2 v. A Romance of Two Worlds 2 v. "Ardath"

3 v. Wormwood. A Drama of Paris 2 v. The Hired Baby, etc. 1 v. Barabbas 2 v.
The County 1 v.
George L. Craik: A Manual of English Literature and Language 2 v.
Mrs. Craik (Miss Mulock): John Halifax, Gentleman 2 v. The Head of the Family 2 v. A Life for a Life 2 v. A Woman's Thoughts about Women 1 v. Agatha's Husband 1 v. Romantic Tales 1 v. Domestic Stories 1 v. Mistress and Maid 1 v. The Ogilvies 1 v. Lord Erlistoun 1 v. Christian's Mistake 1 v. Bread upon the Waters 1 v. A Noble Life 1 v. Olive 2 v. Two Marriages 1 v. Studies from Life 1 v. Poems 1 v. The Woman's Kingdom 2 v. The Unkind Word, etc. 2 v. A Brave Lady 2 v. Hannah 2 v. Fair France 1 v. My Mother and I 1 v. The Little Lame Prince 1 v. Sermons out of Church 1 v. The Laurel Bush, etc. 1 v. A Legacy 2 v. Young Mrs. Jardine 2 v. His Little Mother, etc. 1 v. Plain Speaking 1 v. Miss Tommy 1 v. King Arthur: not a Love Story 1 v.
Miss Georgiana Craik: Lost and Won 1 v. Faith Unwin's Ordeal 1 v. Leslie Tyrrell 1 v. Winifred's Wooing, etc. 1 v. Mildred 1 v. Esther Hill's Secret 2 v. Hero Trevelyan 1 v. Without Kith or Kin 2 v. Only a Butterfly, etc. 1 v. Sylvia's Choice; Theresa 2 v. Anne Warwick 1 v. Dorcas 2 v. Two Women 2 v.
G. M. Craik & M. C. Stirling: Two Tales of Married Life (Hard to Bear, by Miss Craik; A True Man, by M. C. Stirling) 2 v.
Mrs. Augustus Craven: Eliane. Translated by Lady Fullerton 2 v.
F. Marion Crawford: Mr. Isaacs 1 v. Doctor Claudius 1 v. To Leeward 1 v. A Roman Singer 1 v. An American Politician 1 v. Zoroaster 1 v. A Tale of a Lonely Parish 2 v. Saracinesca 2 v. Marzio's Crucifix 1 v. Paul Patoff 2 v. With the Immortals 1 v. Greifenstein 2 v. Sant' Ilario 2 v. A Cigarette-Maker's Romance 1 v. Khaled 1 v. The Witch of Prague 2 v. The Three Fates 2 v. Don Orsino 2 v. The Children of the King 1 v. Pietro Ghisleri 2 v. Marion Darche 1 v.
J. W. Cross: v. George Eliot's Life.
Miss Cummins: The Lamplighter 1 v. Mabel Vaughan 1 v. El Fureidîs 1 v. Haunted Hearts 1 v.
P. Cushing: The Blacksmith of Voe 2 v.
"Daily News": The War Correspondence 1877 by A. Forbes, etc. 3 v.

The price of each volume is 1 Mark 60 Pfennig.

Dark 1 v.
R. Harding Davis: Gallegher, etc. 1 v. Van Bibber and Others 1 v.
De Foe: Robinson Crusoe 1 v.
M. Deland: John Ward, Preacher 1 v.
Democracy 1 v.
Demos *vide* George Gissing.
Charles Dickens: The Pickwick Club (w. Port.) 2 v. American Notes 1 v. Oliver Twist 1 v. Nicholas Nickleby 2 v. Sketches 1 v. Martin Chuzzlewit 2 v. A Christmas Carol; The Chimes; The Cricket on the Hearth 1 v. Master Humphrey's Clock (Old Curiosity Shop; Barnaby Rudge, etc.) 3 v. Pictures from Italy 1 v. The Battle of Life; the Haunted Man 1 v. Dombey and Son 3 v. David Copperfield 3 v. Bleak House 4 v. A Child's History of England (2 v. 8° M. 2,70.) Hard Times 1 v. Little Dorrit 4 v. A Tale of two Cities 2 v. Hunted Down; The Uncommercial Traveller 1 v. Great Expectations 2 v. Christmas Stories 1 v. Our Mutual Friend 4 v. Somebody's Luggage; Mrs. Lirriper's Lodgings; Mrs. Lirriper's Legacy 1 v. Doctor Marigold's Prescriptions; Mugby Junction 1 v. No Thoroughfare; The Late Miss Hollingford 1 v. The Mystery of Edwin Drood 2 v. The Mudfog Papers, etc. 1 v. *Vide* Household Words, Novels and Tales, and J. Forster.

Charles Dickens: The Letters of Charles Dickens edited by his Sister-in-law and his eldest Daughter 4 v.

B. Disraeli (Lord Beaconsfield): Coningsby 1 v. Sybil 1 v. Contarini Fleming (w. Port.) 1 v. Alroy 1 v. Tancred 2 v. Venetia 2 v. Vivian Grey 2 v. Henrietta Temple 1 v. Lothair 2 v. Endymion 2 v.

W. Hepworth Dixon: Personal History of Lord Bacon 1 v. The Holy Land 2 v. New America 2 v. Spiritual Wives 2 v. Her Majesty's Tower 4 v. Free Russia 2 v. History of two Queens 6 v. White Conquest 2 v. Diana, Lady Lyle 2 v.

L. Dougall: Beggars All 2 v.

Ménie Muriel Dowie: A Girl in the Karpathians 1 v.

A. C. Doyle: The Sign of Four 1 v. Micah Clarke 2 v. The Captain of the Pole-Star 1 v. The White Company 2 v. A Study in Scarlet 1 v. The Great Shadow, etc. 1 v. Sherlock Holmes 2 v. The Refugees 2 v. The Firm of Girdlestone 2 v.

Professor Henry Drummond: The Greatest Thing in the World, etc. 1 v.

The Earl and the Doctor: South Sea Bubbles 1 v.
The Earl of Dufferin: Letters from High Latitudes 1 v.
Mrs. Edwardes: Archie Lovell 2 v. Steven Lawrence, Yeoman 2 v. Ought we to Visit her? 2 v. A Vagabond Heroine 1 v. Leah: A Woman of Fashion 2 v. A Blue-Stocking 1 v. Jet: Her Face or Her Fortune? 1 v. Vivian the Beauty 1 v. A Ballroom Repentance 2 v. A Girton Girl 2 v. A Playwright's Daughter, and Bertie Griffiths 1 v. Pearl-Powder 1 v.
Miss A. B. Edwards: Barbara's History 2 v. Miss Carew 2 v. Hand and Glove 1 v. Half a Million of Money 2 v. Debenham's Vow 2 v. In the Days of my Youth 2 v. Untrodden Peaks, etc. 1 v. Monsieur Maurice 1 v. Black Forest 1 v. A Poetry-Book of Elder Poets 1 v. A Thousand Miles up the Nile 2 v. A Poetry-Book of Modern Poets 1 v. Lord Brackenbury 2 v.
Miss M. Betham-Edwards: The Sylvestres 1 v. Felicia 2 v. Brother Gabriel 2 v. Forestalled; or, The Life-Quest 1 v. Exchange no Robbery, etc. 1 v. Disarmed 1 v. Doctor Jacob 1 v. Pearla 1 v. Next of Kin Wanted 1 v. The Parting of the Ways 1 v. For One and the World 1 v. The Romance of a French Parsonage 1 v. France of To-day 1 v. Two Aunts and a Nephew 1 v. A Dream of Millions 1 v. The Curb of Honour 1 v.

Barbara Elbon: Bethesda 2 v.

E. Eggleston: The Faith Doctor 2 v. George Eliot: Scenes of Clerical Life 2 v. Adam Bede 2 v. The Mill on the Floss 2 v. Silas Marner 1 v. Romola 2 v. Felix Holt 2 v. Daniel Deronda 4 v. The Lifted Veil, and Brother Jacob 1 v. Impressions of Theophrastus Such 1 v. Essays and Leaves from a Note-Book 1 v.

George Eliot's Life as related in her Letters and Journals. Edited by her Husband J. W. Cross 4 v.

Mrs. Elliot: Diary of an Idle Woman in Italy 2 v. Old Court Life in France 2 v. The Italians 2 v. Diary of an Idle Woman in Sicily 1 v. Pictures of Old Rome 1 v. Diary of an Idle Woman in Spain 2 v. The Red Cardinal 1 v. Sophia 1 v. Diary of an Idle Woman in Constantinople 1 v.

Henry Erroll: An Ugly Duckling 1 v.
Essays and Reviews 1 v.
Estelle Russell 2 v.
D'Esterre-Keeling: *vide* Keeling.

The price of each volume is 1 Mark 60 Pfennig.

Euthanasia 1 v.
J. H. Ewing: Jackanapes; The Story of a Short Life; Daddy Darwin's Dovecot 1 v. A Flat Iron for a Farthing 1 v. The Brownies, etc. 1 v.
Expiated 2 v.
F. W. Farrar: Darkness and Dawn 3 v. The Fate of Fenella, by 24 authors, 1 v.
Percy Fendall: *vide* F. C. Philips.
George Manville Fenn: The Parson o' Dumford 2 v. The Clerk of Portwick 2 v.
Fielding: Tom Jones 2 v.
Five Centuries of the English Language and Literature (vol. 500) 1 v.
George Fleming: Kismet. A Nile Novel 1 v. Andromeda 2 v.
A. Forbes: My Experiences of the War between France and Germany 2 v. Soldiering and Scribbling 1 v. See also "Daily News," War Correspondence.
R. E. Forrest: Eight Days 2 v.
Mrs. Forrester: Viva 2 v. Rhona 2 v. Roy and Viola 2 v. My Lord and My Lady 2 v. I have Lived and Loved 2 v. June 2 v. Omnia Vanitas 1 v. Although he was a Lord 2 v. Corisande 1 v. Once Again 2 v. Of the World, Worldly 1 v. Dearest 2 v.
J. Forster: Life of Charles Dickens 6 v.
Life and Times of Oliver Goldsmith 2 v.
Jessie Fothergill: The First Violin 2 v. Probation 2 v. Made or Marred, and "One of Three" 1 v. Kith and Kin 2 v. Peril 2 v. Borderland 2 v.
"Found Dead," Author of — *vide* James Payn.
Caroline Fox: Memories of Old Friends from her Journals, edited by H. N. Pym 2 v.
Frank Fairlegh 2 v.
Edward A. Freeman: The Growth of the English Constitution 1 v. Select Historical Essays 1 v. Sketches from French Travel 1 v.
James Anthony Froude: Oceana 1 v. The Spanish Story of the Armada, etc. 1 v.
Lady G. Fullerton: Ellen Middleton 1 v. Grantley Manor 2 v. Lady Bird 2 v. Too Strange not to be True 2 v. Constance Sherwood 2 v. A stormy Life 2 v. Mrs. Gerald's Niece 2 v. The Notary's Daughter 1 v. The Lilies of the Valley, and The House of Penarvan 1 v. The Countess de Bonneval 1 v. Rose Leblanc 1 v. Seven Stories 1 v. The Life of Luisa de Carvajal 1 v. A Will and a Way, etc. 2 v. Eliane 2 v. (*vide* Craven). Laurentia 1 v.
Mrs. Gaskell: Mary Barton 1 v. Ruth 2 v. North and South 1 v. Lizzie Leigh, etc. 1 v. The Life of Charlotte Brontë 2 v. Lois the Witch, etc. 1 v. Sylvia's Lovers 2 v. A Dark Night's Work 1 v. Wives and Daughters 3 v. Cranford 1 v. Cousin Phillis, and other Tales 1 v.
Dorothea Gerard: Lady Baby 2 v. Recha 1 v. Orthodox 1 v.
E. Gerard: A Secret Mission 1 v.
Agnes Giberne: The Curate's Home 1 v.
G. Gissing: Demos. A Story of English Socialism 2 v. New Grub Street 2 v.
Right Hon. W. E. Gladstone: Rome and the Newest Fashions in Religion 1 v. Bulgarian Horrors, and Russia in Turkistan 1 v. The Hellenic Factor in the Eastern Problem 1 v.
Goldsmith: The Select Works: The Vicar of Wakefield, etc. (w. Portrait) 1 v.
Edward J. Goodman: Too Curious 1 v.
J. Gordon: A Diplomat's Diary 1 v.
Major-Gen. C. G. Gordon's Journals, at Kartoum. Introduction and Notes by A. E. Hake (with eighteen Illustrations) 2 v.
Mrs. Gore: Castles in the Air 2 v. The Dean's Daughter 2 v. Progress and Prejudice 2 v. Mammon 2 v. A Life's Lessons 2 v. Two Aristocracies 2 v. Heckington 2 v.
Miss Grant: Victor Lescar 2 v. The Sun-Maid 2 v. My Heart's in the Highlands 2 v. Artiste 2 v. Prince Hugo 2 v. Cara Roma 2 v.
M. Gray: The Silence of Dean Maitland 2 v. The Reproach of Annesley 2 v.
Ethel St. Clair Grimwood: My Three Years in Manipur (with Portrait) 1 v.
W. A. Baillie Grohman: Tyrol and the Tyrolese 1 v.
Archibald Clavering Gunter: Mr. Barnes of New York 1 v.
"Guy Livingstone," Author of — Guy Livingstone 1 v. Sword and Gown 1 v. Barren Honour 1 v. Border and Bastille 1 v. Maurice Dering 2 v. Sans Merci 2 v. Breaking a Butterfly 2 v. Anteros 2 v. Hagarene 2 v.
J. Habberton: Helen's Babies & Other People's Children 1 v. The Bowsham Puzzle 1 v. One Tramp; Mrs. Mayburn's Twins 1 v.
H. Rider Haggard: King Solomon's Mines 1 v. She 2 v. Jess 2 v. Allan Quatermain 2 v. The Witch's Head 2 v. Maiwa's Revenge 1 v. Mr. Meeson's Will 1 v. Colonel Quaritch, V.C. 2 v. Cleopatra 2 v. Allan's Wife 1 v. Beatrice 2 v. Dawn 2 v. Montezuma's Daughter 2 v.

The price of each volume is 1 Mark 60 Pfennig.

H. Rider Haggard and Andrew Lang: The World's Desire 2 v.
Hake: *vide* "Gordon's Journals."
Mrs. S. C. Hall: Can Wrong be Right? 1 v. Marian 2 v.
Philip Gilbert Hamerton: Marmorne 1 v. French and English 2 v.
Thomas Hardy: The Hand of Ethelberta 2 v. Far from the Madding Crowd 2 v. The Return of the Native 2 v. The Trumpet-Major 2 v. A Laodicean 2 v. Two on a Tower 2 v. A Pair of Blue Eyes 2 v. A Group of Noble Dames 1 v. Tess of the D'Urbervilles 2 v.
Agnes Harrison: Martin's Vineyard 1 v.
Bret Harte: Prose and Poetry (Tales of the Argonauts; Spanish and American Legends; Condensed Novels; Civic and Character Sketches; Poems) 2 v. Idyls of the Foothills 1 v. Gabriel Conroy 2 v. Two Men of Sandy Bar 1 v. Thankful Blossom, and other Tales 1 v. The Story of a Mine 1 v. Drift from Two Shores 1 v. An Heiress of Red Dog, and other Sketches 1 v. The Twins of Table Mountain, etc. 1 v. Jeff Briggs's Love Story, etc. 1 v. Flip and other Stories 1 v. On the Frontier 1 v. By Shore and Sedge 1 v. Maruja 1 v. Snow-bound at Eagle's and Devil's Ford 1 v. The Crusade of the "Excelsior" 1 v. A Millionaire of Rough-and-Ready, etc. 1 v. Captain Jim's Friend, etc. 1 v. Cressy 1 v. The Heritage of Dedlow Marsh, etc. 1 v. A Waif of the Plains 1 v. A Ward of the Golden Gate 1 v. A Sappho of Green Springs, etc. 1 v. A First Family of Tasajara 1 v. Colonel Starbottle's Client, etc. 1 v. Susy 1 v. Sally Dows, etc. 1 v.
Sir H. Havelock: *vide* Rev. W. Brock.
G. Hawthorne: *vide* "Miss Molly."
Nathaniel Hawthorne: The Scarlet Letter 1 v. Transformation 2 v. Passages from the English Note-Books 2 v.
"Heir of Redclyffe," Author of—*vide* Yonge.
Sir Arthur Helps: Friends in Council 2 v. Ivan de Biron 2 v.
Mrs. Hemans: Select Poet. Works 1 v.
Admiral Hobart Pasha: Sketches from my Life 1 v.
Mrs. Cashel Hoey: A Golden Sorrow 2 v. Out of Court 2 v.
Oliver Wendell Holmes: The Autocrat of the Breakfast-Table 1 v. The Professor at the Breakfast-Table 1 v. The Poet at the Breakfast-Table 1 v. Over the Teacups 2 v.

A. Hope: Mr. Witt's Widow 1 v. A Change of Air 1 v.
Ernest William Hornung: A Bride from the Bush 1 v. Under Two Skies 1 v. Tiny Luttrell 1 v.
Household Words: conducted by Charles Dickens. 1851-56. 36 v. Novels and Tales reprinted from Household Words by Charles Dickens. 1856-59. 11 v. How to be Happy though Married 1 v.
Miss Howard: One Summer 1 v. Aunt Serena 1 v. Guenn 2 v. Tony, the Maid, etc. 1 v. The Open Door 2 v. A Fellowe and His Wife 1 v.
W. D. Howells: A Foregone Conclusion 1 v. The Lady of the Aroostook 1 v. A Modern Instance 2 v. The Undiscovered Country 1 v. Venetian Life (w. Portrait) 1 v. Italian Journeys 1 v. A Chance Acquaintance 1 v. Their Wedding Journey 1 v. A Fearful Responsibility, and Tonelli's Marriage 1 v. A Woman's Reason 2 v. Dr. Breen's Practice 1 v. The Rise of Silas Lapham 2 v.
Thomas Hughes: Tom Brown's School Days 1 v.
Mrs. Hungerford: Molly Bawn 2 v. Mrs. Geoffrey 2 v. Faith and Unfaith 2 v. Portia 2 v. Loÿs, Lord Berresford, etc. 1 v. Her First Appearance, etc. 1 v. Phyllis 2 v. Rossmoyne 2 v. Doris 2 v. A Maiden all Forlorn, etc. 1 v. A Passive Crime, etc. 1 v. Green Pleasure and Grey Grief 2 v. A Mental Struggle 2 v. Her Week's Amusement; Ugly Barrington 1 v. Lady Branksmere 2 v. Lady Valworth's Diamonds 1 v. A Modern Circe 2 v. Marvel 2 v. The Hon. Mrs. Vereker 1 v. Under-Currents 2 v. In Durance Vile, etc. 1 v. A Troublesome Girl, etc. 1 v. A Life's Remorse 2 v. A Born Coquette 2 v. The Duchess 1 v. Lady Verner's Flight 1 v. A Conquering Heroine and "When in Doubt" 1 v. Nora Creina 2 v. A Mad Prank, etc. 1 v. The Hoyden 2 v.
Jean Ingelow: Off the Skelligs 3 v. Poems 2 v. Fated to be Free 2 v. Sarah de Berenger 2 v. Don John 2 v.
The Hon. Lady Inglis: The Siege of Lucknow 1 v.
John H. Ingram: *vide* E. A. Poe.
Washington Irving: The Sketch Book (with Portrait) 1 v. The Life of Mahomet 1 v. Successors of Mahomet 1 v. Oliver Goldsmith 1 v. Chronicles of Wolfert's Roost 1 v. Life of Washington 5 v.

The price of each volume is 1 Mark 60 Pfennig.

Helen Jackson (H. H.): Ramona 2 v.
Charles T. C. James: Holy Wedlock 1 v.
G. P. R. James: Morley Ernstein (with Portrait) 1 v. Forest Days 1 v. The False Heir 1 v. Arabella Stuart 1 v. Rose d'Albret 1 v. Arrah Neil 1 v. Agincourt 1 v. The Smuggler 1 v. The Step-Mother 2 v. Beauchamp 1 v. Heidelberg 1 v. The Gipsy 1 v. The Castle of Ehrenstein 1 v. Darnley 1 v. Russell 2 v. The Convict 2 v. Sir Theodore Broughton 2 v.
Henry James: The American 2 v. The Europeans 1 v. Daisy Miller, etc. 1 v. Roderick Hudson 2 v. The Madonna of the Future, etc. 1 v. Eugene Pickering, etc. 1 v. Confidence 1 v. Washington Square, etc. 2 v. The Portrait of a Lady 3 v. Foreign Parts 1 v. French Poets and Novelists 1 v. The Siege of London, etc. 1 v. Portraits of Places 1 v. A Little Tour in France 1 v.
J. Cordy Jeaffreson: A Book about Doctors 2 v. A Woman in Spite of Herself 2 v. The Real Lord Byron 3 v.
Mrs. Jenkin: "Who Breaks—Pays" 1 v. Skirmishing 1 v. Once and Again 2 v. Two French Marriages 2 v. Within an Ace 1 v. Jupiter's Daughters 1 v.
Edward Jenkins: Ginx's Baby, etc. 2 v.
"Jennie of 'the Prince's,'" Author of —vide B. H. Buxton.
Jerome K. Jerome: The Idle Thoughts of an Idle Fellow 1 v. Diary of a Pilgrimage 1 v.
Douglas Jerrold: History of St. Giles and St. James 2 v. Men of Character 2 v.
"John Halifax," Author of—vide Mrs. Craik.
"Johnny Ludlow," Author of—vide Mrs. Henry Wood.
Johnson: The Lives of the English Poets 2 v.
Emily Jolly: Colonel Dacre 2 v.
"Joshua Davidson," Author of—vide E. Lynn Linton.
Miss Kavanagh: Nathalie 2 v. Daisy Burns 2 v. Grace Lee 2 v. Rachel Gray 1 v. Adèle 3 v. The Two Sicilies 2 v. Seven Years, etc. 2 v. French Women of Letters 1 v. English Women of Letters 1 v. Queen Mab 2 v. Beatrice 2 v. Sybil's Second Love 2 v. Dora 2 v. Silvia 2 v. Bessie 2 v. John Dorrien 3 v. Two Lilies 2 v. Forget-me-nots 2 v.
A. Keary: Oldbury 2 v. Castle Daly 2 v.
Elsa D'Esterre-Keeling: Three Sisters 1 v. A Laughing Philosopher 1 v. The Professor's Wooing 1 v. In Thoughtland and in Dreamland 1 v. Orchardcroft 1 v.
Kempis: vide Thomas a Kempis.
R. B. Kimball: Saint Leger 1 v. Romance of Student Life abroad 1 v. Undercurrents 1 v. Was he Successful? 1 v. To-Day in New-York 1 v.
A. W. Kinglake: Eothen, a Narrative from the East 1 v. The Invasion of the Crimea 14 v.
Charles Kingsley: Yeast 1 v. Westward ho! 2 v. Two Years ago 2 v. Hypatia 2 v. Alton Locke 1 v. Hereward the Wake 2 v. At Last 2 v.
Charles Kingsley: His Letters and Memories of his Life, ed. by his Wife 2 v.
H. Kingsley: Ravenshoe 2 v. Austin Elliot 1 v. The Recollections of Geoffry Hamlyn 2 v. The Hillyars and the Burtons 2 v. Leighton Court 1 v. Valentin 1 v. Oakshott Castle 1 v. Reginald Hetherege 2 v. The Grange Garden 2 v.
Rudyard Kipling: Plain Tales from the Hills 1 v.
May Laffan: Flitters, Tatters, and the Counsellor, etc. 1 v.
Charles Lamb: The Essays of Elia and Eliana 1 v.
A. Lang: vide H. R. Haggard.
Mary Langdon: Ida May 1 v.
"The Last of the Cavaliers," Author of—The Last of the Cavaliers 2 v. The Gain of a Loss 2 v.
The Hon. Emily Lawless: Hurrish 1 v.
Leaves from the Journal of our Life in the Highlands from 1848 to 1861 1 v. More Leaves from the Journal of a Life in the Highlands from 1862 to 1882 1 v.
Holme Lee: vide Miss Parr.
S. Le Fanu: Uncle Silas 2 v. Guy Deverell 2 v.
Mark Lemon: Wait for the End 2 v. Loved at Last 2 v. Falkner Lyle 2 v. Leyton Hall, etc. 2 v. Golden Fetters 2 v.
Charles Lever: The O'Donoghue 1 v. The Knight of Gwynne 3 v. Arthur O'Leary 2 v. The Confessions of Harry Lorrequer 2 v. Charles O'Malley 3 v. Tom Burke of "Ours" 3 v. Jack Hinton 2 v. The Daltons 4 v. The Dodd Family Abroad 3 v. The Martins of Cro' Martin 3 v. The Fortunes of Glencore 2 v. Roland Cashel 3 v. Davenport Dunn 3 v. Confessions of Con Cregan 2 v. One of Them 2 v. Maurice Tiernay 2 v. Sir Jasper

The price of each volume is 1 Mark 60 Pfennig.

Carew 2 v. Barrington 2 v. A Day's Ride: A Life's Romance 2 v. Luttrell of Arran 2 v. Tony Butler 2 v. Sir Brook Fossbrooke 2 v. The Bramleighs of Bishop's Folly 2 v. A Rent in a Cloud 1 v. That Boy of Norcott's 1 v. St. Patrick's Eve; Paul Gosslett's Confessions 1 v. Lord Kilgobbin 2 v.

G. H. Lewes: Ranthorpe 1 v. Physiology of Common Life 2 v. On Actors and the Art of Acting 1 v.

E. Lynn Linton: Joshua Davidson 1 v. Patricia Kemball 2 v. The Atonement of Leam Dundas 2 v. The World well Lost 2 v. Under which Lord? 2 v. With a Silken Thread, etc. 1 v. Todhunters' at Loanin' Head, etc. 1 v. "My Love!" 2 v. The Girl of the Period, etc. 1 v. Ione 2 v.

L. W. M. Lockhart: Mine is Thine 2 v.

Lord Augustus Loftus (w. Portr.) 2 v.

Longfellow: The Poetical Works (with Portrait) 3 v. The Divine Comedy of Dante Alighieri 3 v. The New-England Tragedies 1 v. The Divine Tragedy 1 v. Flower-de-Luce, and Three Books of Song 1 v. The Masque of Pandora 1 v.

Margaret Lonsdale: Sister Dora (with a Portrait of Sister Dora) 1 v.

A Lost Battle 2 v.

Sir J. Lubbock: The Pleasures of Life 1 v. The Beauties of Nature (w. Illust.) 1 v.

Lutfullah: Autobiography of Lutfullah, by Eastwick 1 v.

Edna Lyall: We Two 2 v. Donovan 2 v. In the Golden Days 2 v. Knight-Errant 2 v. Won by Waiting 2 v.

Lord Lytton: *vide* Bulwer.

Robert Lord Lytton (Owen Meredith): Poems 2 v. Fables in Song 2 v.

Maarten Maartens: The Sin of Joost Avelingh 1 v. An Old Maid's Love 2 v. God's Fool 2 v.

Lord Macaulay: The History of England (w. Port.) 10 v. Critical and Historical Essays 5 v. Lays of Ancient Rome 1 v. Speeches 2 v. Biographical Essays 1 v. William Pitt, Atterbury 1 v. (See also Trevelyan).

Justin McCarthy: The Waterdale Neighbours 2 v. Dear Lady Disdain 2 v. Miss Misanthrope 2 v. A History of our own Times 5 v. Donna Quixote 2 v. A short History of our own Times 2 v. A History of the Four Georges vols. 1 & 2.

George Mac Donald: Alec Forbes of Howglen 2 v. Annals of a Quiet Neighbourhood 2 v. David Elginbrod 2 v. The Vicar's Daughter 2 v. Malcolm 2 v. St. George and St. Michael 2 v. The Marquis of Lossie 2 v. Sir Gibbie 2 v. Mary Marston 2 v. The Gifts of the Child Christ, etc. 1 v. The Princess and Curdie 1 v.

Mrs. Mackarness: Sunbeam Stories 1 v. A Peerless Wife 2 v. A Mingled Yarn 2 v.

Eric Mackay: Love Letters of a Violinist 1 v.

Chas. McKnight: Old Fort Duquesne 2 v.

Norman Macleod: The old Lieutenant and his Son 1 v.

Mrs. Macquoid: Patty 2 v. Miriam's Marriage 2 v. Pictures across the Channel 2 v. Too Soon 1 v. My Story 2 v. Diane 2 v. Beside the River 2 v. A Faithful Lover 2 v.

"Mademoiselle Mori," Author of— Mademoiselle Mori 2 v. Denise 1 v. Madame Fontenoy 1 v. On the Edge of the Storm 1 v. The Atelier du Lys 2 v. In the Olden Time 2 v.

Lord Mahon: *vide* Stanhope.

E. S. Maine: Scarcliff Rocks 2 v.

L. Malet: Colonel Enderby's Wife 2 v.

Lord Malmesbury: Memoirs of an Ex-Minister 3 v.

Mary E. Mann: A Winter's Tale 1 v.

R. Blachford Mansfield: The Log of the Water Lily 1 v.

Marmone: *v.* Philip G. Hamerton.

Capt. Marryat: Jacob Faithful (w. Port.) 1 v. Percival Keene 1 v. Peter Simple 1 v. Japhet, in Search of a Father 1 v. Monsieur Violet 1 v. The Settlers 1 v. The Mission 1 v. The Privateer's-Man 1 v. The Children of the New-Forest 1 v. Valerie 1 v. Mr. Midshipman Easy 1 v. The King's Own 1 v.

Florence Marryat: (Mrs. Francis Lean): Love's Conflict 2 v. For Ever and Ever 2 v. The Confessions of Gerald Estcourt 2 v. Nelly Brooke 2 v. Véronique 2 v. Petronel 2 v. Her Lord and Master 2 v. The Prey of the Gods 1 v. Life of Captain Marryat 1 v. Mad Dumaresq 2 v. No Intentions 2 v. Fighting the Air 2 v. A Star and a Heart 1 v. The Poison of Asps, etc. 1 v. A Lucky Disappointment, etc. 1 v. "My own Child" 2 v. Her Father's Name 2 v. A Harvest of Wild Oats 2 v. A Little Stepson 1 v. Written in Fire 2 v. Her World against a Lie 2 v. A Broken Blossom 2 v. The Root of all Evil 2 v. The Fair-haired Alda 2 v. With Cupid's Eyes

The price of each volume is 1 Mark 60 Pfennig.

2 v. My Sister the Actress 2 v. Phyllida 2 v. How They Loved Him 2 v. Facing the Footlights (w. Portrait) 2 v. A Moment of Madness, etc. 1 v. The Ghost of Charlotte Cray, etc. 1 v. Peeress and Player 2 v. Under the Lilies and Roses 2 v. The Heart of Jane Warner 2 v. The Heir Presumptive 2 v. The Master Passion 1 v. Spiders of Society 2 v. Driven to Bay 2 v. A Daughter of the Tropics 2 v. Gentleman and Courtier 2 v. On Circumstantial Evidence 2 v. Mount Eden. A Romance 2 v. Blindfold 2 v. A Scarlet Sin 1 v.

Mrs. Marsh: Ravenscliffe 2 v. Emilia Wyndham 2 v. Castle Avon 2 v. Aubrey 2 v. The Heiress of Haughton 2 v. Evelyn Marston 2 v. The Rose of Ashurst 2 v.

Emma Marshall: Mrs. Mainwaring's Journal 1 v. Benvenuta 1 v. Lady Alice 1 v. Dayspring 1 v. Life's Aftermath 1 v. In the East Country 1 v. No. XIII; or, The Story of the Lost Vestal 1 v. In Four Reigns 1 v. On the Banks of the Ouse 1 v. In the City of Flowers 1 v. Alma 1 v. Under Salisbury Spire 1 v. The End Crowns All 1 v. Winchester Meads 1 v. Eventide Light 1 v. Winifrede's Journal 1 v. Bristol Bells 1 v. In the Service of Rachel Lady Russell 1 v. A Lily among Thorns 1 v.

Helen Mathers (Mrs. Henry Reeves): "Cherry Ripe!" 2 v. "Land o' the Leal" 1 v. My Lady Green Sleeves 2 v. As he comes up the Stair, etc. 1 v. Sam's Sweetheart 2 v. Eyre's Acquittal 2 v. Found Out 1 v. Murder or Manslaughter? 1 v. The Fashion of this World (80 Pf.) Blind Justice, etc. 1 v. What the Glass Told and A Study of a Woman 1 v.

Colonel Maurice: The Balance of Military Power in Europe 1 v.

"Mehalah," Author of—vide Baring-Gould.

Whyte-Melville: Kate Coventry 1 v. Holmby House 2 v. Digby Grand 1 v. Good for Nothing 2 v. The Queen's Maries 2 v. The Gladiators 2 v. The Brookes of Bridlemere 2 v. Cerise 2 v. The Interpreter 2 v. The White Rose 2 v. M. or N. 1 v. Contraband; or A Losing Hazard 1 v. Sarchedon 2 v. Uncle John 2 v. Katerfelto 1 v. Sister Louise 1 v. Rosine 1 v. Roy's Wife 2 v. Black but Comely 2 v. Riding Recollections 1 v.

George Meredith: The Ordeal of Richard Feverel 2 v. Beauchamp's Career 2 v. The Tragic Comedians 1 v.

Owen Meredith: v. R. Lord Lytton.

Henry Seton Merriman: Young Mistley 1 v. Prisoners and Captives 2 v. From One Generation to Another 1 v.

Milton: The Poetical Works 1 v.

"Miss Molly," Author of—Geraldine Hawthorne 1 v.

"Molly Bawn," Author of—vide Mrs. Hungerford.

Miss Montgomery: Misunderstood 1 v. Thrown Together 2 v. Thwarted 1 v. Wild Mike 1 v. Seaforth 2 v. The Blue Veil 1 v. Transformed 1 v. The Fisherman's Daughter; to which is added: A Very Simple Story 1 v.

Frank Frankfort Moore: "I forbid the Banns" 2 v.

Moore: Poet. Works (w. Portr.) 5 v.

Lady Morgan's Memoirs 3 v.

Henry Morley: Of English Literature in the Reign of Victoria. With Facsimiles of the Signatures of Authors in the Tauchnitz Edition (v. 2000).

William Morris: Poems. Edited with a Memoir by Francis Hueffer 1 v.

D. Christie Murray: Rainbow Gold 2 v.

E. C. Grenville: Murray: The Member for Paris 2 v. Young Brown 2 v. The Boudoir Cabal 3 v. French Pictures in English Chalk (1st Series) 2 v. The Russians of To-day 1 v. French Pictures in English Chalk (2nd Series) 2 v. Strange Tales 1 v. That Artful Vicar 2 v. Six Months in the Ranks 1 v. People I have met 1 v.

"My Little Lady," Author of—vide E. Frances Poynter.

The New Testament [v. 1000].

Mrs. Newby: Common Sense 2 v.

Dr. J. H. Newman: Callista 1 v.

"Nina Balatka," Author of—vide Anthony Trollope.

"No Church," Author of—No Church 2 v. Owen:—a Waif 2 v.

Lady Augusta Noel: From Generation to Generation 1 v. Hithersea Mere 2 v.

W. E. Norris: My Friend Jim 1 v. A Bachelor's Blunder 2 v. Major and Minor 2 v. The Rogue 2 v. Miss Shafto 2 v. Mrs. Fenton 1 v. Misadventure 2 v.

Hon. Mrs. Norton: Stuart of Dunleath 2 v. Lost and Saved 2 v. Old Sir Douglas 2 v. Not Easily Jealous 2 v.

Novels & Tales v. Household Words.

Laurence Oliphant: Altiora Peto 2 v. Masollam 2 v.

The price of each volume is 1 Mark 60 Pfennig.

Mrs. Oliphant: The Last of the Mortimers 2 v. Margaret Maitland 1 v. Agnes 2 v. Madonna Mary 2 v. The Minister's Wife 2 v. The Rector and the Doctor's Family 1 v. Salem Chapel 2 v. The Perpetual Curate 2 v. Miss Marjoribanks 2 v. Ombra 2 v. Memoir of Count de Montalembert 2 v. May 2 v. Innocent 2 v. For Love and Life 2 v. A Rose in June 1 v. The Story of Valentine and his Brother 2 v. Whiteladies 2 v. The Curate in Charge 1 v. Phœbe, Junior 2 v. Mrs. Arthur 2 v. Carità 2 v. Young Musgrave 2 v. The Primrose Path 2 v. Within the Precincts 3 v. The greatest Heiress in England 2 v. He that will not when he may 2 v. Harry Joscelyn 2 v. In Trust 2 v. It was a Lover and his Lass 3 v. The Ladies Lindores 3 v. Hester 3 v. The Wizard's Son 3 v. A Country Gentleman and his Family 2 v. Neighbours on the Green 1 v. The Duke's Daughter 1 v. The Fugitives 1 v. Kirsteen 2 v. Isle of Laurence Oliphant 1 v. The Little Pilgrim in the Unseen 1 v. The Heir Presumptive and the Heir Apparent 2 v. The Sorceress 2 v.

Ossian: Poems 1 v.

Ouida: Idalia 1 v. Tricotrin 2 v. Puck 2 v. Chandos 2 v. Strathmore 2 v. Under two Flags 2 v. Folle-Farine 2 v. A Leaf in the Storm, and other Stories 1 v. Cecil Castlemaine's Gage, etc. 1 v. Madame la Marquise, etc. 1 v. Pascarèl 2 v. Held in Bondage 2 v. Two little Wooden Shoes 1 v. Signa (w. Portr.) 3 v. In a Winter City 1 v. Ariadnê 2 v. Friendship 2 v. Moths 3 v. Pipistrello 1 v. A Village Commune 2 v. In Maremma 3 v. Bimbi 1 v. Wanda 3 v. Frescoes, etc. 1 v. Princess Napraxine 3 v. Othmar 3 v. A Rainy June (60 Pf.). Don Gesualdo (60 Pf.). A House Party 1 v. Guilderoy 1 v. Syrlin 3 v. Ruffino, etc. 1 v. Santa Barbara, etc. 1 v. Two Offenders 1 v.

The Outcasts: vide Roy Tellet.

Miss Parr (Holme Lee): Basil Godfrey's Caprice 2 v. For Richer, for Poorer 2 v. The Beautiful Miss Barrington 2 v. Her Title of Honour 1 v. Echoes of a Famous Year 1 v. Katherine's Trial 1 v. Bessie Fairfax 2 v. Ben Milner's Wooing 1 v. Straightforward 2 v. Mrs. Denys of Cote 2 v. A Poor Squire 1 v.

Mrs. Parr: Dorothy Fox 1 v. The Prescotts of Pamphillon 2 v. The Gosau Smithy, etc. 1 v. Robin 2 v. Loyalty George 2 v.

"Paul Ferroll," Author of—Paul Ferroll 1 v. Year after Year 1 v. Why Paul Ferroll killed his Wife 1 v.

James Payn: Found Dead 1 v. Gwendoline's Harvest 1 v. Like Father, like Son 2 v. Not Wooed, but Won 2 v. Cecil's Tryst 1 v. A Woman's Vengeance 2 v. Murphy's Master 1 v. In the Heart of a Hill, etc. 1 v. At Her Mercy 2 v. The Best of Husbands 2 v. Walter's Word 2 v. Halves 2 v. Fallen Fortunes 2 v. What He cost Her 2 v. By Proxy 2 v. Less Black than we're Painted 2 v. Under one Roof 2 v. High Spirits 1 v. High Spirits (2nd Series) 1 v. A Confidential Agent 2 v. From Exile 2 v. A Grape from a Thorn 2 v. Some Private Views 1 v. For Cash Only 2 v. Kit: A Memory 2 v. The Canon's Ward (with Port.) 2 v. Some Literary Recollections 1 v. The Talk of the Town 1 v. The Luck of the Darrells 2 v. The Heir of the Ages 2 v. Holiday Tasks 1 v. Glow-Worm Tales (1st Series) 1 v. Glow-Worm Tales (2nd Series) 1 v. A Prince of the Blood 2 v. The Mystery of Mirbridge 2 v. The Burnt Million 2 v. The Word and the Will 2 v. Sunny Stories 1 v. A Modern Dick Whittington 2 v. A Stumble on the Threshold 2 v. A Trying Patient, etc. 1 v.

Miss Fr. M. Peard: One Year 2 v. The Rose-Garden 1 v. Unawares 1 v. Thorpe Regis 1 v. A Winter Story 1 v. A Madrigal, and other Stories 1 v. Cartouche 1 v. Mother Molly 1 v. Schloss and Town 2 v. Contradictions 2 v. Near Neighbours 1 v. Alicia Tennant 1 v. Madame's Grand-Daughter 1 v.

A Penitent Soul 1 v.

Bishop Percy: Reliques of Ancient English Poetry 3 v.

F. C. Philips: As in a Looking Glass 1 v. The Dean and his Daughter 1 v. Adventures of Lucy Smith 1 v. A Lucky Young Woman 1 v. Jack and Three Jills 1 v. Little Mrs. Murray 1 v. Young Mr. Ainslie's Courtship 1 v. Social Vicissitudes 1 v. Extenuating Circumstances, and A French Marriage 1 v. More Social Vicissitudes 1 v. Constance 2 v. That Wicked Mad'moiselle, etc. 1 v. A Doctor in Difficulties 1 v. Black and White 1 v. "One Never Knows" 2 v. Of Course 1 v.

The price of each volume is 1 Mark 60 Pfennig.

Collection of British Authors Tauchnitz Edition.

F. C. Philips & P. Fendall: A Daughter's Sacrifice 1 v. Margaret Byng 1 v.
F. C. Philips and C. J. Wills: The Fatal Phryne 1 v. The Scudamores 1 v. A Maiden Fair to See 1 v. Sybil Ross's Marriage 1 v.
Edgar Allan Poe: Poems and Essays, edited with a new Memoir by J. H. Ingram 1 v. Tales, edited by J. H. Ingram 1 v.
Pope: Select Poet. Works (w. Port.) 1 v.
E. Frances Poynter: My Little Lady 2 v. Ersilia 2 v. Among the Hills 1 v. Madame de Presnel 1 v.
Praed: *vide* Campbell-Praed.
Mrs. E. Prentiss: Stepping Heavenward 1 v.
The Prince Consort's Speeches and Addresses (with Portrait) 1 v.
Richard Pryce: Miss Maxwell's Affections 1 v. The Quiet Mrs. Fleming 1 v. Time and the Woman 1 v.
Horace N. Pym: *vide* Caroline Fox.
Q.: Noughts and Crosses 1 v. I Saw Three Ships 1 v. Dead Man's Rock 1 v.
W. F. Rae: Westward by Rail 1 v. Miss Bayle's Romance 2 v. The Business of Travel 1 v.
The Rajah's Heir 2 v.
Charles Reade: "It is never too late to mend" 2 v. "Love me little, love me long" 1 v. The Cloister and the Hearth 2 v. Hard Cash 3 v. Put Yourself in his Place 2 v. A Terrible Temptation 2 v. Peg Woffington 1 v. Christie Johnstone 1 v. A Simpleton 2 v. The Wandering Heir 1 v. A Woman-Hater 2 v. Readiana 1 v. Singleheart and Doubleface 1 v. "Recommended to Mercy," Author of—Recommended to Mercy 2 v. Zoe's "Brand" 2 v.
James Rice: *vide* Walter Besant.
A. Bate Richards: So very Human 3 v.
Richardson: Clarissa Harlowe 4 v.
Mrs. Riddell (F. G. Trafford): George Geith of Fen Court 2 v. Maxwell Drewitt 2 v. The Race for Wealth 2 v. Far above Rubies 2 v. The Earl's Promise 2 v. Mortomley's Estate 2 v.
Rev. F. W. Robertson: Sermons 4 v.
Charles H. Ross: The Pretty Widow 1 v. A London Romance 2 v.
Dante Gabriel Rossetti: Poems 1 v. Ballads and Sonnets 1 v.
Roy Tellet: The Outcasts 1 v. A Draughtof Lethe 1 v. Pastor & Prelate 2 v.
J. Ruffini: Lavinia 2 v. Doctor Antonio 1 v. Lorenzo Benoni 1 v. Vincenzo 2 v. A Quiet Nook in the Jura 1 v. The Paragreens on a Visit to Paris 1 v. Carlino, etc. 1 v.
W. Clark Russell: A Sailor's Sweetheart 2 v. The "Lady Maud" 2 v. A Sea Queen 2 v.
G. A. Sala: The Seven Sons of Mammon 2 v.
John Saunders: Israel Mort, Overman 2 v. The Shipowner's Daughter 2 v. A Noble Wife 2 v.
Katherine Saunders: Joan Merryweather, etc. 1 v. Gideon's Rock, etc. 1 v. The High Mills 2 v. Sebastian 1 v.
Col. R. H. Savage: My Official Wife 1 v. The Little Lady of Lagunitas (w. Port.) 2 v. Prince Schamyl's Wooing 1 v. The Masked Venus 2 v. Delilah of Harlem 2 v.
Sir Walter Scott: Waverley (w. Port.) 1 v. The Antiquary 1 v. Ivanhoe 1 v. Kenilworth 1 v. Quentin Durward 1 v. Old Mortality 1 v. Guy Mannering 1 v. Rob Roy 1 v. The Pirate 1 v. The Fortunes of Nigel 1 v. The Black Dwarf; A Legend of Montrose 1 v. The Bride of Lammermoor 1 v. The Heart of Mid-Lothian 2 v. The Monastery 1 v. The Abbot 1 v. Peveril of the Peak 2 v. The Poetical Works 2 v. Woodstock 1 v. The Fair Maid of Perth 1 v. Anne of Geierstein 1 v.
Prof. Seeley: Life and Times of Stein (with a Portrait of Stein) 4 v. The Expansion of England 1 v.
Miss Sewell: Amy Herbert 2 v. Ursula 2 v. A Glimpse of the World 2 v. The Journal of a Home Life 2 v. After Life 2 v. The Experience of Life 2 v.
Shakespeare: Plays and Poems (with Portrait) *(Second Edition)* compl. 7 v.
Shakespeare's Plays may also be had in 37 numbers, at ℳ 0,30. each number.
Doubtful Plays 1 v.
Shelley: A Selection from his Poems 1 v.
Nathan Sheppard: Shut up in Paris *(Second Edition, enlarged)* 1 v.
Sheridan: The Dramatic Works 1 v.
J. H. Shorthouse: John Inglesant 2 v. Blanche, Lady Falaise 1 v.
Smollett: Roderick Random 1 v. Humphry Clinker 1 v. Peregrine Pickle 2 v. Society in London. By a Foreign Resident 1 v.
Somerville & Martin Ross: Naboth's Vineyard 1 v.
The Spanish Brothers 2 v.
Earl Stanhope (Lord Mahon): The

The price of each volume is 1 Mark 60 Pfennig.

History of England 7 v. The Reign of Queen Anne 2 v.
Sterne: Tristram Shandy 1 v. A Sentimental Journey (with Portrait) 1 v.
Robert Louis Stevenson: Treasure Island 1 v. Dr. Jekyll and Mr. Hyde, etc. 1 v. Kidnapped 1 v. The Black Arrow 1 v. The Master of Ballantrae 1 v. The Merry Men, etc. 1 v. Across the Plains 1 v. Island Nights' Entertainments 1 v. Catriona. A Sequel to "Kidnapped," 1 v.
"Still Waters," Author of — Still Waters 1 v. Dorothy 1 v. De Cressy 1 v. Uncle Ralph 1 v. Maiden Sisters 1 v. Martha Brown 1 v. Vanessa 1 v.
M. C. Stirling: Two Tales of Married Life 2 v. Vol. II. A True Man, Vol. I. *vide* G. M. Craik.
Frank R. Stockton: The House of Martha 1 v.
"The Story of Elizabeth," Author of — *vide* Miss Thackeray.
Mrs. H. Beecher Stowe: Uncle Tom's Cabin (with Portrait) 2 v. A Key to Uncle Tom's Cabin 2 v. Dred 2 v. The Minister's Wooing 1 v. Oldtown Folks 2 v.
"Sunbeam Stories," Author of — *vide* Mrs. Mackarness.
Swift: Gulliver's Travels 1 v.
John Addington Symonds: Sketches in Italy 1 v. New Italian Sketches 1 v.
Tasma: Uncle Piper of Piper's Hill 2 v.
Baroness Tautphoeus: Cyrilla 2 v. The Initials 2 v. Quits 2 v. At Odds 2 v.
Colonel Meadows Taylor: Tara: A Mahratta Tale 3 v.
H. Templeton: Diary and Notes 1 v.
Alfred (Lord) Tennyson: The Poetical Works of, 8 v. Queen Mary 1 v. Harold 1 v. Becket; The Cup; The Falcon 1 v. Locksley Hall, etc. 1 v.
W. M. Thackeray: Vanity Fair 3 v. Pendennis 3 v. Miscellanies 8 v. Henry Esmond 2 v. The English Humourists 1 v. The Newcomes 4 v. The Virginians 4 v. The Four Georges; Lovel the Widower 1 v. The Adventures of Philip 2 v. Denis Duval 1 v. Roundabout Papers 2 v. Catherine 1 v. The Irish Sketch Book 1 v. The Paris Sketch Book (w. Portrait) 2 v.
Miss Thackeray: The Story of Elizabeth 1 v. The Village on the Cliff 1 v. Old Kensington 2 v. Bluebeard's Keys, etc. 1 v. Five Old Friends 1 v. Miss Angel 1 v. Out of the World, etc. 1 v. Fulham Lawn, etc. 2 v. From an Island 1 v. Da Capo, etc. 1 v. Madame de Sévigné, etc. 1 v. A Book of Sibyls 1 v. Mrs. Dymond 2 v.
Thomas a Kempis: The Imitation of Christ 1 v.
A. Thomas: Denis Donne 2 v. On Guard 2 v. Walter Goring 2 v. Played Out 2 v. Called to Account 2 v. Only Herself 2 v. A Narrow Escape 2 v.
Thomson: The Poetical Works (with Portrait) 1 v.
Thoth 1 v.
Tim 1 v.
F. G. Trafford: *vide* Mrs. Riddell.
George Otto Trevelyan: The Life and Letters of Lord Macaulay (w. Portrait) 4 v. Selections from the Writings of Lord Macaulay 2 v.
Trois-Etoiles: *vide* Murray.
Anthony Trollope: Doctor Thorne 2 v. The Bertrams 2 v. The Warden 1 v. Barchester Towers 2 v. Castle Richmond 2 v. The West Indies 1 v. Framley Parsonage 2 v. North America 3 v. Orley Farm 3 v. Rachel Ray 2 v. The Small House at Allington 3 v. Can you forgive her? 3 v. The Belton Estate 2 v. Nina Balatka 1 v. The Last Chronicle of Barset 3 v. The Claverings 2 v. Phineas Finn 3 v. He knew he was right 3 v. The Vicar of Bullhampton 2 v. Sir Harry Hotspur of Humblethwaite 1 v. Ralph the Heir 2 v. The Golden Lion of Granpere 1 v. Australia and New Zealand 3 v. Lady Anna 2 v. Harry Heathcote of Gangoil 1 v. The Way we live now 4 v. The Prime Minister 4 v. The American Senator 3 v. South Africa 2 v. Is He Popenjoy? 3 v. An Eye for an Eye 1 v. John Caldigate 3 v. Cousin Henry 1 v. The Duke's Children 3 v. Dr. Wortle's School 1 v. Ayala's Angel 3 v. The Fixed Period 1 v. Marion Fay 2 v. Kept in the Dark 1 v. Frau Frohmann, etc. 1 v. Alice Dugdale, etc. 1 v. La Mère Bauche, etc. 1 v. The Mistletoe Bough, etc. 1 v. An Autobiography 1 v. An Old Man's Love 1 v.
T. Adolphus Trollope: The Garstangs of Garstang Grange 3 v. A Siren 2 v.
Mark Twain (Samuel L. Clemens): The Adventures of Tom Sawyer 1 v. The Innocents Abroad; or, the New Pilgrims' Progress 2 v. A Tramp Abroad 2 v. "Roughing it" 1 v. The Innocents at Home 1 v. The Prince and the Pauper 2 v. The Stolen White Elephant, etc. 1 v.

The price of each volume is 1 Mark 60 Pfennig.

Life on the Mississippi 2 v. Sketches (w. Portrait) 1 v. The Adventures of Huckleberry Finn 2 v. Selections from American Humour 1 v. A Yankee at the Court of King Arthur 2 v. The American Claimant 1 v. The Million Pound Bank-Note, etc. 1 v.
The Two Cosmos 1 v.
"Véra," Author of—Véra 1 v. The Hôtel du Petit St. Jean 1 v. Blue Roses 2 v. Within Sound of the Sea 2 v. The Maritime Alps and their Seaboard 2 v. Ninette 1 v.
Victoria R. I.: *vide* Leaves.
Virginia 1 v.
L. B. Walford: Mr. Smith 2 v. Pauline 2 v. Cousins 2 v. Troublesome Daughters 2 v.
D. Mackenzie Wallace: Russia 3 v.
Lew. Wallace: Ben-Hur 2 v.
Eliot Warburton: The Crescent and the Cross 2 v. Darien 2 v.
Mrs. Humphry Ward: Robert Elsmere 3 v. The History of David Grieve 3 v. Miss Bretherton 1 v.
S. Warren: Passages from the Diary of a late Physician 2 v. Ten Thousand a-Year 3 v. Now and Then 1 v. The Lily and the Bee 1 v.
"The Waterdale Neighbours," Author of—*vide* Justin M°Carthy.
Hugh Westbury: Acte 2 v.
Miss Wetherell: The wide, wide World 1 v. Queechy 2 v. The Hills of the Shatemuc 2 v. Say and Seal 2 v. The Old Helmet 2 v.
Stanley J. Weyman: The House of the Wolf 1 v. The Story of Francis Cludde 2 v. A Gentleman of France 2 v.
A Whim and its Consequences 1 v.
Walter White: Holidays in Tyrol 1 v.
Beatrice Whitby: The Awakening of Mary Fenwick 2 v. In the Suntime of her Youth 2 v.
Richard Whiteing: The Island; or, An Adventure of a Person of Quality 1 v.
S. Whitman: Imperial Germany 1 v. The Realm of the Habsburgs 1 v.
"Who Breaks—Pays," Author of—*vide* Mrs. Jenkin.
K. D. Wiggin: Timothy's Quest 1 v. A Cathedral Courtship, etc. 1 v.
C. J. Wills: *vide* F. C. Philips.
J. S. Winter: Regimental Legends 1 v.
H. F. Wood: The Passenger from Scotland Yard 1 v.
Mrs. Henry Wood: East Lynne 3 v. The Channings 2 v. Mrs. Halliburton's Troubles 2 v. Verner's Pride 3 v. The Shadow of Ashlydyat 3 v. Trevlyn Hold 2 v. Lord Oakburn's Daughters 2 v. Oswald Cray 2 v. Mildred Arkell 2 v. St. Martin's Eve 2 v. Elster's Folly 2 v. Lady Adelaide's Oath 2 v. Orville College 1 v. A Life's Secret 1 v. The Red Court Farm 2 v. Anne Hereford 2 v. Roland Yorke 2 v. George Canterbury's Will 2 v. Bessy Rane 2 v. Dene Hollow 2 v. The foggy Night at Offord, etc. 1 v. Within the Maze 2 v. The Master of Greylands 2 v. Johnny Ludlow *(First Series)* 2 v. Told in the Twilight 2 v. Adam Grainger 1 v. Edina 2 v. Pomeroy Abbey 2 v. Lost in the Post, etc. By J. Ludlow 1 v. A Tale of Sin, etc. By J. Ludlow 1 v. Anne, etc. By J. Ludlow 1 v. Court Netherleigh 2 v. The Mystery of Jessy Page, etc. By J. Ludlow 1 v. Helen Whitney's Wedding, etc. By J. Ludlow 1 v. The Story of Dorothy Grape, etc. By J. Ludlow 1 v.
Margaret L. Woods: A Village Tragedy 1 v.
Wordsworth: The Poetical Works 2 v.
Lascelles Wraxall: Wild Oats 1 v.
Edm. Yates: Land at Last 2 v. Broken to Harness 2 v. The Forlorn Hope 2 v. Black Sheep 2 v. The Rock Ahead 2 v. Wrecked in Port 2 v. Dr. Wainwright's Patient 2 v. Nobody's Fortune 2 v. Castaway 2 v. A Waiting Race 2 v. The yellow Flag 2 v. The impending Sword 2 v. Two, by Tricks 1 v. A silent Witness 2 v. Recollections and Experiences 2 v.
Miss Yonge: The Heir of Redclyffe 2 v. Heartsease 2 v. The Daisy Chain 2 v. Dynevor Terrace 2 v. Hopes and Fears 2 v. The young Step-Mother 2 v. The Trial 2 v. The clever Woman 2 v. The Dove in the Eagle's Nest 2 v. The Danvers Papers, etc. 1 v. The Chaplet of Pearls 2 v. The two Guardians 1 v. The caged Lion 2 v. The Pillars of the House 5 v. Lady Hester 1 v. My young Alcides 2 v. The three Brides 2 v. Womankind 2 v. Magnum Bonum 2 v. Love and Life 1 v. Unknown to History 2 v. Stray Pearls (w. Port.) 2 v. The Armourer's Prentices 2 v. The two Sides of the Shield 2 v. Nuttie's Father 2 v. Beechcroft at Rockstone 2 v. A reputed Changeling 2 v. Two penniless Princesses 1 v. That Stick 1 v. Grisly Grisell 1 v.
"Young Mistley," Author of—*vide* Henry Seton Merriman.

The price of each volume is 1 Mark 60 Pfennig.

Collection of German Authors.

Berthold Auerbach: On the Heights, (Second Edition) 3 v. Brigitta 1 v. Spinoza 2 v.

Georg Ebers: An Egyptian Princess 2 v. Uarda 2 v. Homo Sum 2 v. The Sisters (Die Schwestern) 2 v. Joshua 2 v. Per Aspera 2 v.

Fouqué: Undine, Sintram, etc. 1 v.

Ferdinand Freiligrath: Poems (Second Edition) 1 v.

Wilhelm Görlach: Prince Bismarck (with Portrait) 1 v.

Goethe: Faust 1 v. Wilhelm Meister's Apprenticeship 2 v.

Karl Gutzkow: Through Night to Light 1 v.

F. W. Hackländer: Behind the Counter [Handel und Wandel] 1 v.

Wilhelm Hauff: Three Tales 1 v.

Paul Heyse: L'Arrabiata, etc. 1 v. The Dead Lake, etc. 1 v. Barbarossa, etc. 1 v.

Wilhelmine von Hillern: The Vulture Maiden (die Geier-Wally) 1 v. The Hour will come 2 v.

Salomon Kohn: Gabriel 1 v.

G. E. Lessing: Nathan the Wise and Emilia Galotti 1 v.

Fanny Lewald: Stella 2 v.

E. Marlitt: The Princess of the Moor (das Haideprinzesschen) 2 v.

Maria Nathusius: Joachim v. Kamern, and Diary of a poor young Lady 1 v.

Fritz Reuter: In the Year '13 1 v. An old Story of my farming Days [Ut mine Stromtid] 3 v.

Jean Paul Friedrich Richter: Flower, Fruit and Thorn Pieces 2 v.

J. Victor Scheffel: Ekkehard. A Tale of the tenth Century 2 v.

George Taylor: Klytia 2 v.

H. Zschokke: The Princess of Brunswick-Wolfenbüttel, etc. 1 v.

Series for the Young.

Lady Barker: Stories about 1 v.

Louisa Charlesworth: Ministering Children 1 v.

Mrs. Craik (Miss Mulock): Our Year 1 v. Three Tales for Boys 1 v. Three Tales for Girls 1 v.

Miss G. M. Craik: Cousin Trix 1 v.

Maria Edgeworth: Moral Tales 1 v. Popular Tales 2 v.

Bridget and Julia Kavanagh: The Pearl Fountain 1 v.

Charles and Mary Lamb: Tales from Shakspeare 1 v.

Captain Marryat: Masterman Ready 1 v.

Emma Marshall: Rex and Regina 1 v.

Florence Montgomery: The Town Crier; to which is added: The Children with the Indian-Rubber Ball 1 v.

Ruth and her Friends. A Story for Girls 1 v.

Mrs. Henry Wood: William Allair 1 v.

Miss Yonge: Kenneth; or, the Rear-Guard of the Grand Army 1 v. The Little Duke. Ben Sylvester's Word 1 v. The Stokesley Secret 1 v. Countess Kate 1 v. A Book of Golden Deeds 2 v. Friarswood Post-Office 1 v. Henrietta's Wish 1 v. Kings of England 1 v. The Lances of Lynwood; the Pigeon Pie 1 v. P's and Q's 1 v. Aunt Charlotte's Stories of English History 1 v. Dye-Words 1 v. Lads and Lasses of Langley; Sowing and Sewing 1 v.

The price of each volume is 1 Mark 60 Pfennig.

Neues Handbuch der Englischen Conversationssprache von *A. Schlessing*. bound ℳ 2,25.

A new Manual of the German Language of Conversation by *A. Schlessing*. bound ℳ 2,25.

Tauchnitz Dictionaries.

Nuevo Diccionario Español-Alemán y Alemán-Español. Por D. *Luis Tolhausen*. Second Edition. In two Volumes. Royal 8vo. Sewed ℳ 15,00. Cloth ℳ 17,50. Half-morocco ℳ 20,50.

Dictionary of the English and German languages. By *W. James*. Thirty-third Edition. Re-written by C. Stoffel. English-German and German-English in one Volume. Crown 8vo. Sewed ℳ 4,50. Bound ℳ 5,00.

A complete Dictionary of the English and French languages for general use. By *W. James* and *A. Molé*. Fourteenth Stereotype Edition. Crown 8vo. Sewed ℳ 6,00.

A complete Dictionary of the English and Italian languages for general use. By *W. James* and *Gius. Grassi*. Eleventh Stereotype Edition. Crown 8vo. Sewed ℳ 5,00.

A New Pocket Dictionary of the English and German languages. By *J. E. Wessely*. Twenty-first Stereotype Edition. 16mo. Sewed ℳ 1,50. Bound ℳ 2,25.

A New Pocket Dictionary of the English and French languages. By *J. E. Wessely*. Twentieth Stereotype Edition. 16mo. Sewed ℳ 1,50. Bound ℳ 2,25.

A New Pocket Dictionary of the English and Italian languages. By *J. E. Wessely*. Fifteenth Stereotype Edition. 16mo. Sewed ℳ 1,50. Bound ℳ 2,25.

A New Pocket Dictionary of the English and Spanish languages. By *J. E. Wessely* and *A. Gironés*. Eighteenth Stereotype Edition. 16mo. Sewed ℳ 1,50. Bound ℳ 2,25.

A New Pocket Dictionary of the French and German languages. By *J. E. Wessely*. Fifth Stereotype Edition. 16mo. Sewed ℳ 1,50. Bound ℳ 2,25.

A New Pocket Dictionary of the Italian and German languages. By *G. Locella*. Fourth Stereotype Edition. 16mo. Sewed ℳ 1,50. Bound ℳ 2,25.

A New Pocket Dictionary of the Latin and English languages. Ninth Stereotype Edition. 16mo. Sewed ℳ 1,50. Bound ℳ 2,25.

A New Pocket Dictionary of the French and Spanish languages. By *L. Tolhausen*. Second Stereotype Edition. 16mo. Sewed ℳ 1,50. Bound ℳ 2,25.

Technological Dictionary in the French, English and German languages by *A.* and *L. Tolhausen*. Complete in three Parts. Third Edition. Crown 8vo. Sewed ℳ 26,50.

A Hebrew and Chaldee Lexicon to the Old Testament. By Dr. *Julius Fürst*. Fifth Edition. Translated from the German by *Samuel Davidson*. Royal 8vo. Sewed ℳ 19,00.

No orders of private purchasers are executed by the publisher.

BERNHARD TAUCHNITZ, LEIPZIG.

March 1892.
Tauchnitz Edition.

Latest Volumes:

2811. Colonel Starbottle's Client, etc. By Bret Harte.
2809/10. The Awakening of Mary Fenwick. By Beatrice Whitby.
2808. The Talking Horse, etc. By F. Anstey.
2805-7. The History of David Grieve. By Mrs. Humphry Ward.
2804. Winifrede's Journal. By Emma Marshall.
2803. Love-Letters of a Worldly Woman. By Mrs. Clifford.
2802. The Business of Travel. By W. Fraser Rae.
2800/1. Tess of the D'Urbervilles. By Thomas Hardy.
2799. The Quiet Mrs. Fleming. By Richard Pryce.
2797/98. The Faith Doctor. By Edward Eggleston.
2796. My three Years in Manipur. By Ethel St. Clair Grimwood (with portrait).
2794/95. The Story of Francis Cludde. By Stanley J. Weyman.
2793. Over the Teacups. By Oliver Wendell Holmes.
2792. A First Family of Tasajara. By Bret Harte.
2791. Tim.
2790. The Romance of a French Parsonage. By M. Betham-Edwards.
2789. A Widower Indeed. By Broughton and Bisland.
2787/88. The White Company. By A. Conan Doyle.
2785/86. Beggars All. By L. Dougall.
2784. Blanche, Lady Falaise. By J. H. Shorthouse.
2782/83. Gerard; or, The World, the Flesh, and the Devil. By M. E. Braddon.
2781. Santa Barbara, etc. By Ouida.
2780. Sketches from French Travel. By Edward A. Freeman.
2777-79. Darkness and Dawn. By F. W. Farrar.

A complete Catalogue of the Tauchnitz Edition is attached to this work.

Bernhard Tauchnitz, Leipzig;
And sold by all booksellers.

Cornell University Library
PS 1829.I18

Idyls of the foothills.in prose and vers

3 1924 021 980 077

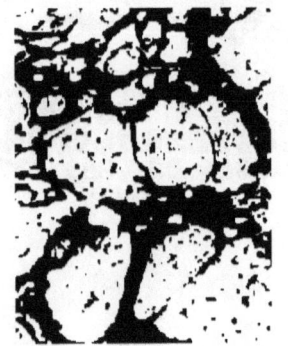

www.ingramcontent.com/pod-product-compliance
Lightning Source LLC
Chambersburg PA
CBHW032048230426
43672CB00009B/1520